THE PRE-NICENE CHURCH

THE PRE-NICENE CHURCH

*Papers read at the Summer School of
Catholic Studies, held at Cambridge,
July 28th to August 6th, 1934*

With a Preface by

FATHER C. LATTEY, S.J.

LONDON

BURNS OATES & WASHBOURNE LTD

PUBLISHERS TO THE HOLY SEE

NIHIL OBSTAT:

INNOCENTIUS APAP, S.Th.M., O.P.,
Censor deputatus.

IMPRIMATUR:

✠ JOSEPH BUTT,
Vic. Gen.

WESTMONASTERII,
die 5a Julii, 1935.

MADE AND PRINTED IN GREAT BRITAIN
FOR
BURNS OATES & WASHBOURNE LTD.
1935

PREFACE

I WAS turning over the table of contents of the Summer School book on *St. Thomas Aquinas*, for what should have been the pleasant purpose of making sure of the list of contributors among whom the annual royalty was to be divided, when I could not help being struck by the number of those who have departed this life since the lectures were delivered, a little more than a decade ago. Out of the nine lecturers, only three are alive to-day. Bishop Burton's genial presence was always most welcome at the School, to which he delivered more than one scholarly address out of his treasure of new things and old. Few things could have become him better than to speak, as he did, of "the liturgical poetry of St. Thomas." Father Bede Jarrett, now another great loss to the Catholic body, was likewise lecturing, and was to lecture again later ; but upon this occasion his helpful interest in the School showed in the clearest light his large and generous mind, for the Dominican Fathers were themselves about to celebrate the sixth centenary of the canonization of St. Thomas elsewhere.

Another brilliant lecturer was Mr. Edward Bullough, and his subject too was at once most congenial to himself and the best fitted to enable him to make a valuable contribution to our knowledge and literature: "Dante, the Poet of St. Thomas." More, indeed, was to be hoped from his pen upon this subject; but perhaps, even as it is, his inspiration will be found not to be wholly exhausted or lost. This was the only lecture that he gave for the School, in which, however, he took a considerable interest, and his position on the Summer School Committee, and also as a Fellow of Gonville and Caius College, enabled him to be of considerable service in various ways. Of all that he did outside the School this is not the place to speak. An excellent memoir of him by Mr. Evennett appeared in the *Dublin Review* for January, 1935, followed by a no less admirable one of Mr. Francis Urquhart in his Oxford days by Father Ronald Knox. The contrast between the two men was striking. Bullough had all the forceful zeal of the convert, and was as ardent a champion of Cambridge as of the Church. Urquhart had been a Catholic from childhood, having in fact been at Beaumont in the same class with Dr. Edmund Gardner, Mr. Baldwin Young and my own eldest brother (who died of fever many years ago in India, a surgeon-captain in the Army Medical Service); afterwards he joined for a while the lay students of philosophy at Stonyhurst, where he began a lifelong friendship with Archbishop Goodier. Urquhart would have been the last to press upon anybody the claims either of the Church or Oxford, but quietly and unobtrusively offered (may we not say?) the best of both to whoever was wise enough to value the gift and the giver. Twice upon my own request he read very helpful papers upon the teaching of Church History to the Conference of Higher Studies. It was interesting to see how these two men, so unlike in most respects, were at one in urging that the key to European history was to be found in Rome, that England must be looked upon as being at the circumference, not at the centre of the civilized world: that such a standpoint must be adopted, not merely in order to understand European history, but in order to understand English history itself. Even here there was a difference, for Urquhart rather looked in towards Rome from the circumference, while Bullough to a large extent rather looked outward from Italy, where was much of his heart's affection, and whence he took his wife, who all too soon has been called upon to offer her husband to God, having already offered Him her children in religion. Mr. Evennett has written of Bullough that "his election to the Chair of Italian in 1933 came to him as an unexpected and pleasurable honour. . . . The Professorship seemed to justify his doctrine, and he gave full expression to it in his Inaugural Lecture." This last was published under the title of "Italian Perspectives," and in a peculiar way may be said to represent his gospel, so far as history is concerned.

Two other names at least should be added to the above. Abbot Chapman delivered several brilliant and valuable lectures at the Summer School, and at the time when we were first discussing plans for the last School, it was taken for granted that he would be a tower of strength, for it was above all others (I think) his strong subject. In any case his work deserves a word of recognition in this book; it was his rare gift to combine wide and accurate reading with an insight almost amounting to intuition of the main lines of argument and of the chief conclusions warranted by the evidence. To me his *John the Presbyter* has always seemed his most brilliant work. He always took a great interest in the higher studies. When upon a visit to Heythrop, he fell in almost eagerly with my suggestion that the Conference of Higher Studies might perhaps be held at Downside, and he carried the arrangement through in spite of great and unexpected obstacles that would fully have justified him in abandoning or postponing the project. At that same time he spoke much of his plans for the *Downside Review* which (I think I may safely say) he did much to raise to its present high level.

A final mention is due to Père de la Taille, a rival to Cardinal Billot for the position of the greatest theologian of our own times. Having been to school at Ramsgate, he was conversant with our tongue, and lectured at the Summer School upon the Incarnation and upon the Holy Eucharist. His lecture upon the last subject is the clearest and most forcible presentation of his doctrine of the Mass ; it is to be found in the lecture-book of that year, *Catholic Faith in the Holy Eucharist*, now in its third edition, a veritable mine for those who wish to speak of all or any aspects of the Eucharist at similar schools or congresses. His discourse was possibly the most brilliant ever heard at the School ; his doctrine, although, taken as a whole, it has not met with entire assent even in his own order, will yet be found in all probability to have affected Eucharistic teaching considerably in the long run.

All these have died more or less recently, and nearly all before their time: may they rest in peace! All in their measure have helped to raise the standard of our higher studies, and that not least by the assistance which they have given to Conference or Summer School. The younger generation has not failed to respond to their inspiration. Writing at a time when conference after conference has been so successful as to raise the whole standard of achievement, and when we are preparing to hold a Summer School which offers an exceptionally strong list both of lectures and lecturers, I cannot but feel it right to acknowledge how much we owe to the mighty men of valour who have passed away, yet being dead still speak in those who have taken up their task,

et quasi cursores vitai lampada tradunt.

The future is full of promise. The Holy Father has once more shown his lively interest in the Summer School upon the occasion of the presentation of the remaining volumes; Cardinal Pacelli's letter is printed at the end of this volume. This is in fact only another manifestation of the Holy Father's practical zeal for Catholic studies, which he has also shown in other ways, for example, by his encouraging a high standard of work in the seminaries by offering them upon fixed conditions the power to confer degrees.

The present volume will be found not unworthy of its predecessors. Like many of its predecessors (and not least the volume upon the *English Martyrs*, which was never more seasonable) it appears to me to be an admirably compact and all-round presentation of its subject. The various questions that arise have been dealt with carefully, and the book should prove a valuable introduction to the whole subject of the Pre-Nicene Church, as well as a summary presentation of the Catholic position in the face of modern theories. The first general council was held at Nicaea in A.D. 325, and may conveniently be taken as the end of this early period and the beginning of a very different age, that of the fathers and councils and Christian emperors and fully developed christological heresies. It has seemed best to adopt the word "Pre-Nicene" for our period, because "Ante-Nicene" is so easily confused with "Anti-Nicene"!

Upon considering carefully the bearing of the lectures upon the epoch under consideration, I have found only one issue which might be said to call for fuller treatment; and yet not to call imperatively, for its importance is not limited to that portion of Church History which is here presented, though it is greater here than elsewhere. I refer to the question of development. For one that has no historical sense it is easy to argue that St. Peter and his immediate successors did not send forth encyclicals to the universal Church, or that such a doctrine as the Immaculate Conception is not to be traced in the Pre-Nicene documents. There are many considerations which must be borne in mind upon the other side. We know hardly anything of the everyday instruction given to Catholics even by the apostles, to say nothing of the century or two that followed them. The writers of any period can seldom be taken to be representative; and this is especially true of the ordinary life of the Catholic Church. The writers of the Pre-Nicene Church, in particular, are quite unrepresentative. A writer is at any time an abnormal phenomenon, but the Christian writer, and especially the early Christian writer, is especially untypical, and indeed makes little or no attempt to set forth any summary of ecclesiastical life and practice. We gather much useful information from an Origen or a Tertullian, but the gaps which they leave in our information are enormous. To give a really satisfactory account of the history of doctrines we should need far more and also widely different evidence.

By far the greatest development of all comes with

the rise of Aristotelian scholasticism. Speaking very roughly, as one must in these few words, one may say that the aim of the fathers had been to meet practical needs; but now speculation is rife for its own sake. Every avenue of thought is explored that can have any bearing on faith or doctrine; nor is revelation itself alone explored, but it is compounded with the truths discovered or systematized by the new philosophy in the light of pure reason, and philosophy itself is developed to the utmost in all directions. At the same time the Christian ideal of conduct is itself brought into clearer relief by saints of great historical significance, and in orders founded by them. Thus greater system is brought into Christian thought, which, however, comes thereupon to lose by degrees the force and fervour of the first stirring, perhaps in part for lack of digging deeper into learning of a more scholarly and historical and scientific type, such as Roger Bacon urged upon it. In actual history it was the reaction to the shock of Protestantism and of modern rationalism that once more produced a marked intellectual progress, such as we may hope will be safeguarded by the new papal scheme of ecclesiastical studies.

These few remarks, however, are by no means intended, needless to say, to exhaust the subject of the development of doctrine; on the contrary, the development of doctrine itself offers a study much in need of development, which indeed it is a comfort to be able to prophesy. With the advance of a more historical study of theology the question of development looms ever larger, and receives more attention; it is a promising sign, for example, that it will come up for discussion at the next Conference of Higher Studies. In this preface it must be enough to forestall possible objections by pointing to this recognition of the principle of development as the proper method of approach to such a subject of study as the Pre-Nicene Church : by pointing also to the great classic which may not unjustly be called the foundation of modern studies in this department, Cardinal Newman's *Essay on the Development of Christian Doctrine*. The more the importance of the subject is understood, the more clearly also will be seen the intellectual grandeur of the author.

C. L.

CONTENTS

THE PRE-NICENE CHURCH

THE WITNESS OF THE GOSPELS

By the Very Rev. John M. T. Barton, D.D., Lic.S.Script.
Professor of Holy Scripture, St. Edmund's College,
Ware, Consultor of the Pontifical Biblical Commission.

I. PRELIMINARY

In one of Mr. Belloc's earlier volumes of essays[1] there
is a study that no reader, least of all a Catholic reader,
is likely to forget. It describes an early morning visit
to the Cathedral of Notre Dame; the author's impression of the vast interior "paved and floored with
human beings"; the majesty of the procession that
was taking place within it; the sight, at the end of the
cortège, of the aged Cardinal-Archbishop, vested ponti-
fically with mitre and bearing a crozier "that was
studded with gems . . . and that seemed to be made
of gold; the same hands had twisted the metal of it
as had hammered the hinges of the cathedral doors."
"Certainly," continues Mr. Belloc, "there here appeared one of the resurrections of Europe. . . . The
pagan altar of Tiberius, the legend of Dionysius, the
whole circle of the wars came into this one pageant,
and the old man in his office and his blessing was

[1] *Hills and the Sea*, 14th ed., pp. 196–204.

I

understood by all the crowd before him to transmit the centuries." A similar vision of the Church's great age and uninterrupted continuity was granted to an older contemporary of Mr. Belloc, a non-Catholic and later the revered head of a great Oxford College, during an audience with Pope Leo XIII. "It need not be said," he wrote, "that I gazed at him reverently but with all my eyes, the last and living representative of the long, historic, sacred line stretching back through the centuries, through a thousand vicissitudes to the apostolic age, to the beginnings of the Church, to the era of the Acts and the Epistles, to the days which immediately followed on and remembered the sojourn of Our Lord Himself on earth."[1]

Yet this, the unbroken succession of those who carry on the apostolic office, is only a part, though a great part, of the Church's claims and prerogatives. She is not merely, like some work of human policy and human industry, an old-established society which can point to many centuries of continuous progress. She is this, but she is far more. She claims to be a divine foundation, a foundation which, as surely as the visible universe and the living races of mankind but in a manner far more marvellous and wholly supernatural, is a divine creation. And, implicit in this claim there is the assertion that, if we turn to the life and teaching of her founder, Christ, we shall find, in the written records of His life, not one or two passages only having reference to her but a whole series. We shall find that it is not simply *a* dogma of the faith, but one of the central dogmas that Our Lord founded, a visible external society which was to carry on His work, to

[1] *Herbert Warren of Magdalen, President and Friend*, 1853–1930, by Laurie Magnus, London, 1932, p. 77.

speak in His name, to represent Him in all ages till the end of time; that in her own appointed sphere this society enjoys her Divine Founder's gift of infallible teaching; that she has various qualities—perpetuity, universality, indefectibility—that are her guaranteed possession.

II. THE TERM "KINGDOM OF GOD" IN THE GOSPELS

We shall not, it is true, find many allusions to the Christian society under the actual term ἐκκλησία, or Church, in the pages of the gospels, though it is of frequent occurrence in the apostolic writings. In the gospels themselves ἐκκλησία only comes three times— once in the great commission to St. Peter (*Matt.* xvi, 18) and twice in that later passage in *St. Matthew* (xviii, 17) where Our Lord insists upon the duty of telling the Church when other means of fraternal correction have failed. If we seek to discover the principal references to the Church in the gospel records, we must turn to that doctrine which is everywhere present in Our Lord's teaching by parables, and indeed throughout His whole revelation—the doctrine of the Kingdom of heaven, or, as it is also called, of the Kingdom of God.

These two expressions "Kingdom of God" and "Kingdom of heaven" are strictly synonymous and we need not delay over the misguided attempts that have been made to establish some distinction, however subtle, between them. The ordinary reader of the gospels who has not the time for prolonged study, may be recommended to compare *Matthew* v, 3 ("Blessed are the poor in spirit for theirs is the Kingdom of heaven") with the parallel verse in *St. Luke* vi, 20

("Blessed are ye poor, for yours is the Kingdom of God"), which comparison, in spite of slight stylistic variants, proves clearly that the terms under discussion are in essential meaning equivalent. Actually, as any concordance will show, the term "Kingdom of heaven" (in Greek ἡ βασιλεία τῶν οὐρανῶν, in Aramaic *malkhūthā diŝmayyā*, in Hebrew *malkhūth ŝāmayīm*) is peculiar to St. Matthew's gospel, where it is found 33 times. In all the other writings of the New Testament (with a doubtful exception in *John* iii, 5, where a variant reading gives "Kingdom of heaven") the phrase used is "the Kingdom of God" (in Greek ἡ βασιλεία τοῦ Θεοῦ). It occurs 63 times in the New Testament, that is 4 times in *St. Matthew* (in *Matt.* xix, 24, there is an alternative "Kingdom of heaven"), 14 times in *St. Mark*, 32 times in *St. Luke*, twice in *St. John's* gospel, 6 times in *Acts*, 4 times in *St. Paul* and once in the *Apocalypse*. The substitution by St. Matthew of "heaven" for "God" may be explained in terms of the tendency among the post-exilic Jews to make use of various alternatives for the Holy Name of Yahweh. So we read in 2 *Maccabees* vii, 9, "the King of the world"; in *Tobias* xiii, 11, "the King of heaven"; in *Henoch* lxiii, 4, "The Lord of kings"; and in 2 *Maccabees* iii, 24, "the Sovereign of spirits." St. Matthew, who, according to tradition, wrote for Palestinian Jews whose everyday languages were Aramaic and, in some cases at least, Mishnaic Hebrew, almost always made the change over that was very common and wrote "the Kingdom of heaven."[1]

[1] On the equivalence of the terms, see G. Dalman, *The Words of Jesus*, Eng. trans., Edinburgh, 1902, pp. 93 ff. and 218 ff. The various substitutes for the name of Yahweh are somewhat more fully explained in my pamphlet on "The Religion of Post-Exilic Judaism," No. 19 in the C.T.S. *Studies in Comparative Religion*, pp. 17–18.

When we leave the etymology and incidence of the phrase "Kingdom of God" and turn to the doctrine as it is discernible in the New Testament, we are at once forced to realize that, among non-Catholic scholars, there is no real or even apparent unanimity regarding Our Lord's teaching on this matter. It would, in fact, be no exaggeration to say that, next to the question of Our Lord's own person, there is no problem of New Testament exegesis that has been so constantly in dispute outside the unity of the Faith as the problem of Christ's doctrine concerning the Kingdom.[1]

III. ERRONEOUS CONCEPTIONS OF THE KINGDOM OF GOD

In discussing the various systems that have been devised to explain this doctrine—a doctrine manifestly of the very first importance—it is necessary for our purpose to make a selection, since the number of erroneous conceptions is so great. It would not be relevant to the present issue to discuss at any length the so-called "Christ Myth" school, which seeks to deny the very existence of Jesus of Nazareth. It has had very little success in this or any other country; the majority of scholars have resolutely refused to take it seriously; even M. Loisy, radical sceptic as he has now become, in what promises to be his last book on the subject of Christian origins, feels obliged to declare

[1] There is a well-known debate, subsidiary in character to the main problem, whether βασιλεία should be translated "Kingdom" or "Reign." "No doubt can be entertained," writes Dalman, "that both in the Old Testament and in Jewish literature *malkhūth*, when applied to God, means always the 'kingly rule,' never the kingdom, as if it were meant to suggest the territory governed by Him." (*Words of Jesus*, p. 94.) But it appears equally certain that Our Lord did not invariably use the term in its primary, active sense and that, on His lips, it, at times, had its passive and local sense of "Kingdom."

from the start that: "The author of this book humbly
avows that he has not yet discovered that Jesus did
not exist. The clamorous conjectures by which certain
persons have endeavoured, in recent years, to explain
Christianity without him whom Christianity regards
as its founder seem to him [i.e. the author] to be
likewise ever unstable. . . . Such hypotheses have
the common defect of being constructed in the air
and of not explaining the origin of Christianity."[1]

Nor would it be really useful to attempt to isolate
a doctrine concerning the Kingdom of God in the
works of Professors Bultmann, Bertram and the other
exponents of the *formgeschichtliche Methode* or method
of form criticism, which has enjoyed not a little success,
mostly in Germany, during the past fifteen years.
Since the central tenets of that school are that the
gospel tradition originally consisted of fragments in
free circulation and that such fragments were largely
the creation of the primitive community, it would
evidently be impossible to avoid a lengthy preliminary
discussion on the veracity and integrity of the New
Testament books. I must rest content with a reference
to one or two works in which the Method is discussed
and criticized.[2]

[1] *La Naissance du Christianisme*, Nourry, Paris, 1933, pp. 5–6.
On the book as a whole see Fr. Guy Brinkworth, S.J., "M.
Loisy goes on hoping" in the *Clergy Review*, Vol. VII, pp. 468–79.
On the Christ Myth school, see my remarks in the Summer School
volume on *The Atonement*, Heffer, Cambridge, 1928, pp. 87–90.
[2] One may recommend with some reservations (see *The Clergy
Review*, Vol. V, pp. 316–17) Dr. Vincent Taylor's *The Formation of
the Gospel Tradition*, London, 1933. For a Catholic estimate, see
Père F.-M. Braun, O.P., *Où en est le Problème de Jésus*, Gabalda,
Paris, 1932, pp. 215–65. I am greatly indebted to Père Braun, my
friend and former fellow-student, for the criticism that follows;
we owe a common debt of gratitude to our eminent former master,
Père M.-J. Lagrange, O.P., for his work translated into English
under the title: *The Meaning of Christianity according to Luther and
his followers in Germany;* Longmans, London, 1920.

The leading hypotheses of those who reject the one true and traditional conception of the Kingdom of God may be reduced to three main systems. First, there are those who, like Reimarus in the eighteenth century and Dr. Robert Eisler in our own day, have striven to prove that Our Lord taught a political Messianism and conceived of the Kingdom as a purely political one to be gained by force of arms. Secondly, there are those who, like Ritschl, von Harnack and all the members of the old German Liberal School, maintained that Jesus inaugurated a merely internal Kingdom, present in the souls of men. Finally, there are the supporters of the eschatological school, who proclaim that Jesus was mainly, or even exclusively, concerned with the advent of a future Messianic Kingdom which He believed to be imminent. We may set out the main lines of each system together with certain criticisms, premising the remark that the final and Catholic solution is, in itself, the best of all answers to such erroneous or imperfect hypotheses as those we are about to consider.

(a) *Jesus preached a purely political Kingdom.*

The school that represents Christ as having preached a political Kingdom has, as its chief members, Hermann Samuel Reimarus (1694–1768), Eduard von Hartmann (*Das Christentum des Neuen Testaments*, Sachsa, 1905), and Dr. Robert Eisler in his enormous work translated into English under the title of *The Messiah Jesus and John the Baptist.*[1] It will be sufficient to

[1] English version by Alexander H. Knappe, Methuen, London 1931, pp. 666. For Reimarus and von Hartmann, see Dr. Albert Schweitzer, *The Quest of the Historical Jesus*, a translation of the *Geschichte der Leben-Jesu-Forschung* (Tübingen, 1913) in its first edition entitled *Von Reimarus zu Wrede*, 1906. The English edition is published by Black, London, 1911. See especially pp. 13–26 and pp. 318–21. For Dr. Eisler, see Père Braun, op. cit., pp. 82–110.

discuss the latest statement of the case, which was prepared and developed for some years in the form of papers read to various learned societies. On the appearance of this work in its definite English form, there was a certain measure of journalistic excitement, mainly on account of the professedly authentic description of Our Lord's appearance, which was printed by Dr. Eisler. Since then little has been heard of the *magnum opus*, and its author appears to have turned his attention to currency problems, in which we may wish him greater success and better judgement.

In Eisler's conception the Gospel history is one episode out of many in the revolutionary movement that was preparing in Palestine for many years with a view to casting off the Roman overlordship. While Herod the Great was alive, there was some degree of order in the country; when he died a revolt broke out. John the Baptist was the apostle of the revolutionary party and preached about the coming liberator who was shortly to appear.

While John was preaching and conferring a symbolic baptism, Jesus came to him. His appearance—elderly, very short, bent, with a long nose and eyebrows meeting about the nose—is described, in the light of the documents just mentioned, on pp. 411–30 of the English edition. He came to approve of the revolutionary movement and to join John's party; ultimately He was persuaded that He was the Messiah. His initial policy, like Gandhi's, was one of civil disobedience without bloodshed. He named twelve overseers of the twelve tribes and seventy-two disciples to conquer other parts of the world; He organized a general exodus into the desert; finally He was moved to attempt an attack upon the city. The disciples camped on the Mount of Olives and, later, Jesus made an entry into the Holy City; His followers seized the Temple and the Tower of Siloe without resistance on the part of the Roman soldiery. Pilate was then at Cæsarea; he returned and put down the revolt with great brutality. Jesus was captured on the Mount of Olives, tried by summary court-martial and executed between two brigands who had assisted Him to lead the revolt. Barabbas, the son of a Jerusalem priest, was taken inadvertently, but was able to prove non-complicity. Three days later, the twin brother of Jesus was seen by some of the disciples and women; they imagined that it was Jesus risen from the dead. Thus was born the faith that inspired the early Church to martyrdom and a world-wide apostolate.

It will be seen at once that this vulgar travesty (it is nothing less) of the Gospel history would involve not simply a re-interpretation, but a complete re-writing of our existing sources. And where is the evidence that any such re-writing is necessary or desirable? I do not feel inclined to modify in any sense the judgement I passed on the book when it first appeared in its English translation. "In place of the witness of the New Testament writers and of Christian tradition to the life and teaching of Jesus, we are asked to accept as a controlling authority a possibly authentic Slavonic version of Josephus's *Jewish War* which derives from very late and, on Dr. Eisler's now showing, much interpolated manuscripts. Eisler professes to be able to determine the exact nature of the interpolations and to separate what Josephus could have written from what he could not have written. Then, on this insecure foundation, he proceeds to draw conclusions often quite unwarranted by the manuscripts themselves. As a study in futuribles or as a romance the book might be of some interest. As history it is quite impossible. Dr. Eisler's quaintest conceit is shown in the assumption that Josephus and his latest interpreter are more likely to be impartial regarding Christian origins than were the earliest Christian witnesses. This is, of course, the old rationalist fable—that the only impartial witnesses regarding an institution are those who have reason cordially to detest it! We may well say with our greatest Catholic authority on the Gospels: "Nous ne sommes pas si crédules." (Lagrange in *Revue biblique*, 1930, p. 45.) Let us leave it at that.[1]

The system just outlined is, in effect, an almost pure perversion of the Gospel record. Like all error it contains an element of truth, but this only means that it contains a few genuine facts (e.g. the names John, Jesus, Barabbas, Pilate) already recorded in the authentic sources. As a system there is nothing to be said for it, since, as Père Braun has not unfairly remarked of it, it is the product of Dr. Eisler's "undisciplined imagination and of unpardonable liberties in regard of the texts."[2]

We may now examine two further hypotheses which, as they are usually expressed, are, at best, imperfect and one-sided presentations of Our Lord's teaching. We do not deny that they enshrine a substantial measure of truth; we say, however, that, in so far as they are exclusive, and lay claim to be

[1] *The Clergy Review*, Vol. I, pp. 534–5. Good, non-technical reviews of Eisler may be found in *The Morning Post* for March 3, 1931 (E. B. Osborn) and in *The Sunday Times*, March 8, 1931 (E. Shillito).
[2] Op. cit., p. 108.

completely representative of Christ's teaching, they are certainly and gravely at fault.

(b) *Jesus preached a purely inward Kingdom.*

The first of the two is the version of Christ's doctrine of the Kingdom which is found concisely stated in the late Prof. Adolf von Harnack's *Das Wesen des Christentums*, translated into English as *What is Christianity?*[1] It would take us too long to consider von Harnack's determination of the sources available for such an enquiry, his rejection of St. John's Gospel and his concentration of attention upon the *Zweiquellen-hypothese* or theory of two sources (St. Mark and the document known as Q.). As regards the teaching of Jesus, he decides that it may be grouped under three heads, i.e. (1) the Kingdom of God and its coming; (2) God the Father and the infinite value of the human soul; (3) the higher righteousness and the commandment of love (p. 52). Apropos of the first, which is our immediate concern, he admits that there is some apparent ambiguity in the Gospel presentation of the Kingdom, since it might appear to have both a future and a present aspect. Yet, he says, to seize the essential feature of Christ's teaching, one must realize that the Kingdom, in its most original and striking phase, is an inward one. "The Kingdom of God comes by coming to the individual, by entering into his soul and laying hold of it. True, the Kingdom of God is the rule of God; but it is the rule of the holy God in the hearts of individuals; it is God Himself in His power" (p. 57). Later in the book, he declares that "the Kingdom has a triple meaning." It is supernatural; it is "a purely religious blessing, the inner link with the living God"; thirdly, it is a dominating

[1] Williams and Norgate, London, 3rd revised edition, 1912.

experience in man's life (p. 64). "This is Jesus'
message of the Kingdom. Everything else that He
proclaimed can be brought into connection with this;
His whole 'doctrine' can be conceived as a message
of the Kingdom."

Now we do not quarrel with von Harnack for insisting
upon the inward aspect of the Kingdom, except in so
far as he is exclusive, in so far as he maintains that this
inward aspect is the only one worth considering. In
recent years, it is true, this liberal interpretation has been
more and more neglected by scholars, and the reason for
this is not far to seek. It has been succinctly expressed
by the Anglican writer, Dr. Maurice Jones, in his able
book *The New Testament in the Twentieth Century*.[1] The
Liberals' "treatment of the Gospel documents lays
them open to the charge of retaining only so much
of the material that has come down to them as fits
in with their construction of the facts and their own
conception of the historical possibilities." This is a
weakness and a fatal one. An examination of the
evidence will prove that such a system can only be
maintained by disregarding ordinary critical standards,
the objective treatment of documentary record and
the principles of sane exegesis.

(c) *Jesus preached an exclusively future Kingdom.*

Finally, in this rapid survey of erroneous conceptions, we come to the eschatological interpretation of
the Kingdom, the system which pleads for an exclusively
future Kingdom and a preoccupation, on the part of
Christ and His disciples, with a coming world-renewal.
This hypothesis owes much of its success to the three
great names that are associated with it—those of

[1] Macmillan, London, 2nd ed. (1924), p. 21. A third edition
appeared in the summer of the present year (1934.)

Johann Weiss, Alfred Loisy and Albert Schweitzer,[1] and not a little, it may be, to the failure of the liberal Christology of Harnack and his associates in its attempt, to use a phrase of Archdeacon Rawlinson, to "domesticate Jesus."[2] It is impossible, however, to deny that the eschatological theory itself has been much blown upon in recent years and that it no longer commands a great deal of attention. Yet it contributes, however unintentionally, an important element to the true solution and so merits some examination.

It starts with the assertion that the Jews, at the time of Christ's birth, were in expectation of a coming Kingdom, of a new heaven and a new earth, of a complete renewal of all things. Jesus the carpenter of Nazareth shared this opinion; John the Baptist preached its near approach. Jesus also came to believe that He was the Messiah, the Son of Man in Daniel's prophetic vision (*Dan.* vii, 13–14). During His lifetime He was not, in His own thought, the Son in His final definitive stage, but only in a phase of human pre-existence. All was soon to be changed and then He would be manifested to men in His glory. So, in answer to the high priest's question: "Art thou the Christ, the Son of the blessed God?" He replied:"I am. And you shall see the Son of Man sitting at the right hand of the Power and coming with the clouds of heaven." (*Mark* xiv, 61–62). When precisely was this Kingdom to come? At first, according to the

[1] Weiss in *Die Predigt Jesu vom Reiche Gottes*, 1892, 2nd enlarged edition, 1900; Loisy in *L'Evangile et l'Eglise* (Eng. trans., *The Gospel and the Church*, Isbister, London, 1903), 5th edition, with a new preface, 1929; Schweitzer in *The Quest of the Historical Jesus*, already mentioned.

[2] See *The New Testament Doctrine of the Christ*, Longmans, London, 1926, p. 8.

eschatologists, Jesus believed that it would take place in His lifetime, before the Twelve had finished their preaching in the towns and villages of Palestine (*Matt.* x, 23). Later, He realized that a period of penance must precede the coming of the Kingdom and that He must offer His life before being taken up into the glory of the second advent. Yet the end was not far off. "This generation shall not pass away before all these things shall come to pass." (*Mark* xiii, 30.)

Even after His death, belief in Jesus and in His pretensions did not disappear; the disciples' faith was too strong. Not long after the crucifixion, some enthusiasts came to believe in His resurrection. There were numbers of legendary saviour-gods at the time (Attis, Mithra, Osiris . . .) and stories concerning them were interwoven with the Christian story and led to a belief in Christ as redeemer, saving mankind in virtue of His death and resurrection. As regards the Church, Loisy has expressed his standpoint in one sentence: "Jesus foretold the Kingdom and it was the Church that came";[1] that is, Jesus foretold a future, eschatological Kingdom and there came a visible, hierarchical Church.

A full examination of this system cannot be attempted here.[2] It will be enough for us to notice that, while we do not challenge the existence of a marked eschatological element in the Gospels, the system just described is not only one-sided and incomplete as a

---

[1] *The Gospel and the Church*, p. 166; in the latest French edition, p. 153. Compare also in his latest work *La Naissance du Christianisme*, p. 93: "Mais Jésus ne voulait pas fonder une religion, et il n'a pas songé à celle-là."

[2] See Lagrange, *The Meaning of Christianity*, pp. 267–307; Braun, *Où en est le Problème de Jésus*, pp. 111–56; Maurice Jones, *The New Testament in the Twentieth Century*, pp. 87–119.

statement of Our Lord's teaching on the Kingdom; it contains manifest errors.

First, it is not true to say that, in Our Lord's time, the *general* Jewish expectation was focused upon a coming world catastrophe. This feature represents only a small element in the Jewish Messianic hope and one that is chiefly to be observed in the apocalyptic writings.[1] It is only really prominent in the *Assumption of Moses*, a pseudepigraphic work that may be assigned to the first decade before Christ; in this, and other such works, it is noteworthy that the term "Kingdom of God" or its equivalent "Kingdom of heaven" is not found. A quite opposite tendency is manifested in such a work as the *Book of Jubilees* (end of second century B.C.), which represents the reign of God as coming not catastrophically but slowly and progressively by the gradual recognition of God and obedience to His laws. Prof. Simpson in his erudite study just mentioned thinks it is very doubtful whether those who expected the former type of Kingdom were numerous.

Again, as von Harnack has shown, we frequently find in Christ's sayings a reference to a Reign of God which was actually in existence at the time of His life on earth and which, in one of its aspects, was an inward gift. (*Luke* xvii, 20–21.)

Further, the eschatologists are reduced to claiming that the teaching of Jesus on right conduct was merely an *Interimsethik*, a system devised for a short period under abnormal conditions. Against this we

[1] On Messianic expectation, see Père M.-J. Lagrange, O.P., *Le Judaisme avant Jésus Christ*, Gabalda, Paris, 1931, pp. 363–87; Prof. D. C. Simpson, "Judaism the Religion in which Christ was educated," in *The History of Christianity in the Light of Modern Knowledge*, Blackie, London, 1929, pp. 164–5.

may remark, first, that Christ's teaching is by no means exhausted by its eschatological element; secondly that the theory misrepresents the moral teaching of the Gospels. The Gospel virtues are not merely helps to securing a safe entrance into the heavenly Kingdom; they have an essential and absolute value in themselves. Read, for example, the parable of the sheep and the goats, where "the reward comes as a complete surprise and . . . the Parable of the Pounds and the Talents where the recompense is for duty done for duty's sake."[1]

Yet, as we have said, the theory is not wholly without value. In a striking passage in his recent reflections on Loisy's *Mémoires pour servir à l'histoire religieuse de notre temps*, Père Lagrange has suggested that even the apparently negative criticism of recent years, which has so much influenced the Protestant world of scholarship, has not been entirely without profit to Catholic exegesis. He does not, of course, conceive this in the sense that Catholic scholars are reduced to the role of treasure-seekers among the ruins of great intellectual systems, but in the sense that "if any one of the doctrines put forward has anything in it to allure, we shall attempt to show that this [factor] was already contained in the ecclesiastical *magisterium*."[2] So the mainly destructive school that concentrates upon the comparative study of the history of religions (in German *die religionsgeschichtliche Schule*) has laid stress upon the earliest believers' faith in the mystical reality of the sacraments, in grace, and in justification. The school of form criticism has been radical enough, but it has

[1] Dr. Maurice Jones, op. cit., p. 109.
[2] *M. Loisy et le Modernisme*, Editions du Cerf, Juvisy, 1932, pp. 243 ff.

at least recognized that the worship of Jesus our Lord goes back to the very origins of Christianity. Even the "Christ Myth" school has been of some negative service, since its frantic and abortive efforts to disprove the historicity of Christ have proved how solidly grounded is that fundamental truth. In like manner, M. Loisy's eschatological system has underlined in unmistakable fashion the importance of Our Lord's references to the Kingdom in its future aspect. As Père Lagrange has expressed it:

"It is indeed quite certain that Jesus announced the immediate coming of the Reign of God upon earth. What He did not say was that it would be accompanied by the end of the world. He left undetermined the date of His second coming, the nature of which is not very precise and which could take place in stages (*peut être successive*) in expectation of a supreme manifestation. The fact which clearly proves that the end of the world was not determined within a short space of time is that He laid down a programme for the world's betterment. The Kingdom of God is come, it is the Church, and He prepared pastors for it when He trained His disciples for their mission."[1]

IV. THE CATHOLIC DOCTRINE OF THE KINGDOM OF GOD

So let us leave the partial and incomplete hypotheses which, at best, only account for some of the Gospel data, in order to examine the Catholic doctrine of the Kingdom, which is consistent, which accounts for all the data, and which does not twist and adapt the evidence but accepts it at its true value. Since we

[1] Op. cit., p. 244.

cannot, in so short a time, proceed analytically, it
is well to begin with a definition—that almost classic
one of Père Jean-Baptiste Frey, C.S.Sp., the distinguished Secretary of the Pontifical Biblical Commission. It is given in his article "Royaume de Dieu" in
Vigouroux's *Dictionnaire de la Bible*, t. V, coll. 1237–1257.
The Kingdom of God in the Gospels is defined as:

> "The actualization of the eternal sovereignty of
> God *in souls* by their free submission to the law of
> God their Creator and Saviour; *in the world* by the
> establishment and progressive development of the
> society of the faithful (the Church); *in the next world*
> by the definitive union of the elect with God (eternal
> life) and their incorporation into the Church
> Triumphant" (col. 1257).[1]

Clear as this definition is, it may be reduced to even
fewer terms. The Kingdom of God in the Gospels is,
in its various phases, the life of grace in the soul,
the visible society of the Church, and the eternal life
of the saints in heaven. So it has *both* a present *and* a
future aspect, and, from another standpoint is *both*
internal and individual *and* external and social. The
earthly period is initial, imperfect and perfectible,
preparatory to the future, perfect consummation in
heaven.

Briefly, therefore, we may outline the proof by parts
of the definition already given. First, A. *The Kingdom
of God in Our Lord's teaching is both present and future.*

[1] The pages that follow owe a great deal to Père Frey's luminous
and satisfying treatment; to Père J.-M. Vosté, O.P., for his chapter
"De parabolarum doctrina seu de Regno Dei" in his *Parabolae
selectae Domini nostri Jesu Christi*, ed. 2a (1933), vol. i, pp. 86–118;
and to Père A. Medebielle of the Sacred Heart Congregation of
Betharram, for his article "Eglise" in Pirot's *Supplément au Dictionnaire de la Bible*, t. ii, coll. 487–691.

As regards its *present* phase we know that by the
Baptist, Jesus Himself and the disciples, the Kingdom
is preached as already present. "The Kingdom of
God is come nigh unto you" (*Luke* x, 9) is according
to Our Lord's instructions to be the watchword and
standard greeting of the seventy-two disciples. Again,
apropos of casting out demons: "If I by the finger of
God cast out devils, doubtless the Kingdom of God
is come upon you." (*Luke* xi, 20.) So the more Satan
and his demons are expelled, by so much the more is
the Kingdom of God established among men. When
the Pharisees asked Christ: "When should the Kingdom of God come?" Our Lord answered: "The Kingdom of God is within (*or, perhaps better* among) you,"
that is, it is already in your midst, it is even now
being manifested in its members (*Luke* xvii, 21).[1] It is
sufficient to seek it with a right intention as the
disciples have done. "Fear not, little flock, for it
hath pleased your Father to give you a kingdom."
(*Luke* xii, 31–32.)

The present, earthly period is one of inception;
it is something to be perfected. Hence Christ's
followers must pray: "Thy kingdom come!" or "Thy
reign come!" (in Aramaic *tētē malkūtāk*); again, "Thy
will be done" (*tehē ṣibyōnāk*), i.e. that the will of God
on earth may be more perfectly fulfilled. (*Matt.* vi,

---

[1] Whether ἐντὸς ὑμῶν should be translated "within you" or
"among you" is in the present writer's judgement a singularly barren
subject of dispute. Our Lord, as may be proved from many other
passages, is certainly not speaking in an exclusive sense, even if the
sense really is "within you"; on the other hand, we believe and
profess that the Reign of God, in addition to its other aspects, is
something internal, spiritual, and beyond observation by the senses.
See Lagrange, *Evangile selon S. Luc*, in loc.; Dr. Frederick Field, *Notes
on the Translation of the New Testament*, Cambridge, 1899, p. 71
in loc.

c

9–10.) For parables expressive of the growth, development and perfectibility of the present Kingdom, we may turn to those of the Sower (*Matt.* xiii, 3–23) of the Mustard Seed (*Matt.* xiii, 31–32) and of the Seed growing secretly (*Mark* iv, 26–29).

Yet this earthly Kingdom is not to endure for ever. The *future* final consummation of the Kingdom of God is in heaven. One may recall the words of the good thief: "Lord, remember me when thou shalt come into thy Kingdom!" (*Luke* xxiii, 42), and the reward specified in the parable of the Talents: "Well done, good and faithful servant, enter thou into the joy of thy Lord!" (*Matt.* xxv, 21.) The possession of this future Kingdom is promised to the poor in spirit and to those who suffer persecution for the sake of justice. (*Matt.* v, 3 and 10.) And to it Our Lord refers in declaring: "Not everyone that saith to me, Lord, lord, shall enter into the Kingdom of heaven, but he that doth the will of my Father who is in heaven." (*Matt.* vii, 21.) It is a reward promised to children and to the childlike (*Matt.* xviii, 2–3; xix, 14), and for all those who pass through this life and obtain it, it will be inaugurated by death and the judgement to come. (*Matt.* xxiv, 30; xxv, 31–46.) The Son of Man will come at an unexpected time and his "day" is likened to a thief in the night. (*Matt.* xxiv, 42–44; 1 *Thess.* v, 2.) Then will He gather up from His Kingdom "all the scandals and the doers of iniquity." (*Matt.* xiii, 41.) He will separate good from bad as men separate sheep from goats, wheat from cockle, and wholesome fish from worthless. (*Matt.* xiii, 24–30, 36–43, 47–50; xxv, 32 ff.)

This condition of things has all the marks of a perfect Kingdom. It is eternal life for the individual; the

communion of saints for the society. In that day,
says Our Lord: "The just shall shine as the sun in the
Kingdom of their Father" (*Matt.* xiii, 43), and it is
to them that the Messianic King speaks at the great
assize: "Come, ye blessed of my Father, inherit the
Kingdom prepared for you from the foundation of
the world." (*Matt.* xxv, 34.) It is clear that these
different periods or stages do not constitute different
kingdoms, but different aspects of the same Kingdom.
As an illustration of the occasional duplication or even
triplication of aspects of the Kingdom in one and the
same passage of the Gospels, Père Frey calls attention
to the *logion* preserved in precisely identical words in
Mark x, 15, and *Luke* xviii, 17. "Amen I say to you,
whosoever shall not receive the Kingdom of God as a
little child shall not enter into it." So, as Frey says,
the kingdom is a reign which one should receive as well
as a kingdom to be entered from that time onwards in
order to have access to the heavenly Kingdom.[1] One
and the same kingdom is inaugurated on earth, grows
and is perfected in the society and in the souls of its
members, and is finally consummated in heaven.

(b) *The Kingdom is* both *internal and individual* and *external and social.*

It seems unnecessary to delay over the proof of the
first part, which has been emphasized almost to weari-
ness by von Harnack. It is admitted that the Jews
were in very general expectation (we cannot put it higher
than that) of a glorious political kingdom that was to
bring with it material prosperity and every sort of
worldly pleasure. But, in contrast with this expectation, the Kingdom of Jesus is spiritual and moral.
This is clear from its origin, its purpose, the conditions

[1] Frey, op. cit., col. 1246.

of entrance to it, and the means of attaining to it. Its *origin and foundation* are the recognition of the divine Fatherhood and the Sonship of Jesus. "This is eternal life that they may know thee the only true God and Jesus Christ whom thou hast sent." (*John* xvii, 3.) Its *purpose* is the salvation of souls, the remission of sins and the victory of virtue over vice in the hearts and lives of all. The *conditions of entry* are clearly laid down by Our Lord. "Amen, I say to you, unless you be converted and become as little children, you shall not enter into the Kingdom of heaven." (*Matt.* xviii, 3.) The religion of Jesus is indeed a religion of spirit and truth (*John* iv, 23–24), for Our Lord insists upon the insufficiency of purely external religion and the need for a worship that is at once spiritual and sincere. Many *means of attaining* to this Kingdom are offered to men. It is a divine gift, freely bestowed and freely accepted, and he who has accepted it must strive to retain his right to it. Hence it is said (*Matt.* xi, 13): "The Kingdom of heaven suffereth violence and the violent take possession of it," that is, it is constantly being taken, as it were by storm, by ardent and enthusiastic souls.[1]

Secondly, the Kingdom is *external and social*. First, it is *universal*. The conditions of entry are independent of class or country. All true believers become the sons of the Father and the children of His Kingdom. Hence the fatherhood of God is preached by Jesus as a truth that, given due appreciation and receptivity, should lead to a universal bestowal of salvation and adopted sonship. It is no restriction on the univer-

---

[1] This supposes the interpretation of this verse that is discussed in the present writer's adaptation of Buzy's *Life of St. John the Baptist*, Burns, Oates and Washbourne, London, 1933, pp. 201–2.

sality of the Kingdom that He proclaims (*Matt.* xv, 24): "I am not sent but to the lost sheep of the house of Israel," since this qualification is plainly only a temporary one and implies no more than that Christ's first appeal was made to His own people. As an example of what may be regarded as a mission to the gentiles, we read in *Mark* vii, 31, of His journey from the coast of Tyre when He "came by Sidon towards the Sea of Galilee through the midst of the district of Decapolis," thus passing through a land that was in great part pagan. In *Matthew* viii, 11–12, He speaks of the salvation of the gentiles, when "many shall come from east and west (see *Mal.* i, 11) and shall feast with Abraham and Isaac and Jacob in the Kingdom of heaven, but the children of the Kingdom shall be cast forth into outer darkness." After His resurrection He commands His disciples to preach the Gospel to all nations, baptizing all in the name of the Triune Godhead. (*Matt.* xxviii, 19; *Mark* xvi, 15.)

Naturally, a kingdom or the exercise of kingly power over men supposes a congregation of subjects. It would, therefore, be indeed extraordinary, if Christ, when speaking of the Kingdom of God, had never mentioned any society with external qualities. And, in fact, so many texts could be adduced in favour of the externality of the Kingdom under this aspect that limits of space compel a selection. The arguments drawn from the Synoptists have been reduced by Père Medebielle in his recent study to three categories.[1] First, there are the texts which prove that Our Lord claimed to bring the salvation promised by the prophets (*Luke* iv, 16–22; cp. *Isa.* lxi, 1–9) which was to consist in the manifestation of God to mankind

[1] See the article "Eglise" already cited, col. 518.

in a public and unmistakable manner. Now it is true that the Kingdom in its Christian realization was a spiritual one, but, so far as was consistent with its spiritual character, it presented all the traits of the new Jerusalem foretold by the prophets. In two of the great eighth-century prophets, the Judæans Isaias (ii, 1-4) and Micheas (iv, 1-5), there is an oracle that speaks of the new Jerusalem, built upon the summit of the mountains as a meeting-point of all nations, to which all men will flock to be instructed in the law of the Lord. And Our Lord, in fulfilment of prophecy, tells His disciples that they are the city set upon a hill that cannot be hidden. (*Matt.* v, 14.) Again, there is the promise that Jerusalem will be a city of light (*Isa.* lx, 1-3) and that the Messiah will be a light to the gentiles to bear salvation unto the end of the earth (*Isa.* xlix, 6), which was realized in those passages of the Gospel where first Our Lord Himself (*John* i, 4-9; Luke ii, 32) and then His disciples (*Matt.* v, 14-16) are proclaimed to be the light of the world. Lastly, Ezechiel (xvii, 22-24) compares the Messianic Kingdom to a mighty cedar, planted upon a mountain-top, bearing goodly fruit and giving shelter to all the fowl of the air. And this again is fulfilled in Our Lord's imagery of the Kingdom as a grain of mustard that became a great tree. (*Matt.* xiii, 31-32.)

Further, there are many passages in the Gospels that refer, at least by implication, to the public, external, social character of the Kingdom. Not only is the society of Christians to be as a city set on a hill, as a light shining before men (*Matt.* v, 14-16); it is to be known to all because of its proclamation by its members (*Matt.* x, 33) who will be persecuted and put to death by reason of their public recognition as such

(*Matt.* x, 17–22); those who receive them as Christ's, receive Christ Himself. (*Matt.* x, 40.)

Finally, there is the witness of the parables which abounds. We have already referred to the parable of the mustard, which, in addition to its chief lesson regarding the continuous progress and growth of the Christian society, points to the close connection between the members and their union with the trunk. As the good grain is collected in the granary (*Matt.* xiii, 30) so will be the members of the society; as there is a definite union of a society at the last judgement, so it is to be inferred that this external bond, this union, will be present during the earthly phase, since as we have seen, there is so perfect a continuity between the various aspects of the Kingdom. Further, the parables of the cockle (*Matt.* xiii, 24–30; 37–43) and of the net (*Matt.* xiii, 47–50) prove that there are both good and bad in the Kingdom, as, elsewhere, we learn that there are greater and lesser. (*Matt.* v, 19; xi, 11.)

Yet, in the Synoptic Gospels, there is no text that speaks more strongly for the identification of the Kingdom (in one of its aspects) with the Church than the promise to Peter in *Matthew* xvi, 18–19. It is true that we do not know with certainty which of the three Aramaic words for "Church" ('*idtā, keništā, qehālā*) was used by Our Lord; on the whole, the term *qehālā* seems to be the one most favoured. It is likewise true that so excellent a scholar as the late Mgr Pierre Batiffol was of the opinion that the Church on earth and the Kingdom of heaven in these verses were not equated and that the Kingdom here is that of the future.[1] But it is, it may be said with all due deference,

[1] *L'Eglise naissante et le Catholicisme*, 2nd edition, 1909, p. 107.

far more probable that the Kingdom in this passage *is* the Church, though admittedly the Church on earth does not exhaust all the senses of Our Lord's use of the term "Kingdom of God." In proof of this, one may refer to the parallelism that has been observed between the two clauses ("And upon this rock . . ." and "I will give to thee the keys . . .") in which the second takes up and, as it were, reintroduces the first. This may be remarked in the late Prof. C. F. Burney's re-translation of the Greek into Aramaic, where the clauses are rendered:

we 'al hādēn kēphā́	*ebn'ḗ likništī́*
And upón this róck	I will build my Chúrch
'ēhab lā́k mahptehayyā́	*demalkū́tā dišmayyā́*
I will gíve thee the kéys	of the Kíngdom of heáven[1]

"Yet," writes Père Medebielle, "the substitution of the term 'Kingdom' for that of 'Church' introduces an appreciable nuance; it recalls the grandeur and holiness of that Church which, already constituting as she does the Kingdom of heaven upon earth, leads her children towards heaven and assures them of the possession of it in advance, in such a way that all the measures undertaken by her chief in virtue of his title as Vicar of Christ concern man's ultimate destiny and will have their echo in eternity."[2]

Unhappily, there is no space here for a discussion of some of the Church's attributes—perpetuity, indefectibility and holiness. Even apart from their Scripture proofs, it may be claimed that these are all deducible from the fact that the Church is the Kingdom of God

---

[1] *The Poetry of Our Lord*, Oxford, 1925, p. 117.
[2] Op. and loc. cit.

upon earth, and has all the qualities that one would expect in such a Kingdom. One further note must, however, be added concerning the Johannine usage. In St. John's Gospel, the term "Kingdom of God" rarely occurs (only in iii, 3 and 5), but instead there is a corresponding and (in one respect) a synonymous term that is found seventeen times in the Gospel and six times in the First Epistle—that of "everlasting life." Those who possess that life are the sons of God (i, 12), united as members of the same visible society, separated from the world (xv, 19) and bound together by bonds of mutual charity (xiii, 35). The visible character of the society appears even more plainly in the allegory of the vine and its branches (xv, 1–10) which recalls the parable of the mustard seed in the Synoptists; it is prominent, likewise, in the allegory of the good shepherd (x, 1–18). It is through Jesus that His sheep enter into the sheepfold (x, 9), and He has yet other sheep which are not from this fold; them also must He bring and they shall hear His voice and there shall be one flock, one shepherd (x, 16).

The thought of the life of grace, of our present membership of the Church on earth, and of the glorious future that awaits us seems to be caught up and summarized in a single verse of St. John's First Epistle (iii, 2): "Beloved, now we are children of God and it hath not yet been made manifest what we shall be. We know that if He shall be manifested, we shall be like to Him, because we shall see Him even as He is."

THE APOSTOLIC AGE

By the Rev. C. LATTEY, S.J., M.A.
Professor of Fundamental Theology at Heythrop College.

A. INTRODUCTION: DOGMA, MINISTRY, ORGANIZATION

IF there were question, not of a single lecture, but of a whole Summer School upon the Apostolic Age, it would still be a problem what to select and what to omit in dealing with so vast a subject, full of the gravest issues. One might insist upon the teaching or dogmatic side of the Church; St. Paul, for instance, is steeped in dogma, he proposes (or rather, pre-supposes) one article of faith after another, he insists upon justification by faith, certainly a dogmatic faith, since (for example) it embraced the resurrection and the Godhead of Christ (*Rom.* x, 9), and he protests more than once that his doctrine is the same as that of the other Apostles (e.g., *Gal.* ii; I *Cor.* xv, 11; *Ephes.* iv, 5). No doubt in the Apostolic Age the Catholic Faith had not attained to that development which we behold to-day; but it was very far from being an age in which the Christian could believe what he liked.

Some of the so-called Christians of to-day almost pride themselves upon doubting or denying the resurrection and the Godhead of Christ; but St. Paul wrote what is now a long chapter of his First Epistle to the *Corinthians* to confute the doubters and deniers of his own time, and made the Godhead of Christ the foundation of his whole doctrine.

The power of ministry or order in the Church, which we may briefly describe as that of sacrifice and sacrament, offers another large field for discussion. It would chiefly turn upon St. Paul's First Epistle to the *Corinthians*, wherein we find so much that takes us by surprise: the common evening meal, followed by the Holy Eucharist, at both of which those present reclined on couches: the absence of vestments or ceremonies: the reception by all of the mixed cup and ordinary bread, followed by a literal kiss of peace: the exercise thereafter of the *charismata*, such as prophesying and speaking with tongues.

Liturgical development began even in the Apostolic Age, and must have been rapid towards the end of the first century and beginning of the second. St. Paul himself separated the Holy Eucharist from the taking of the evening meal. (1 *Cor.* xi, 21, 34.) His appeal is for greater reverence, pushed home by an appeal to the real presence, which he obviously supposes to be already a familiar doctrine to his hearers; and we may remind ourselves that it is no less clearly taught in the later Gospel of *St. John*.

In 1929 we took for our Summer School subject "Six Sacraments," having already dealt with the Holy Eucharist separately. My own lectures were on Baptism, the beginnings of which I discussed at some little length, and therefore gladly refrain from treating now. I think it necessary, however, to call attention to Baptism no less than to the Holy Eucharist, because the early evidence for both these two sacraments is overwhelming, and unless it be accepted the discussion of other sacraments is futile. The mentality of the modern critic is so entirely alien from that of the New Testament that it is difficult for him to interpret it in a reasonable spirit. Here, as so often elsewhere, it is faith that safeguards reason.

Upon the whole I have thought it best to lay the heaviest emphasis upon the Church's power to govern, rather than upon her other two powers of teaching and ministry; that is, upon her right of independent organization, for it is this which makes the Church as such, constituting her a supreme society, subject to none within her own sphere. Once we have the Church existing in theory and in fact, we may take a brief survey of her expansion within the period allotted to me, and conclude with one or two fairly obvious reflections.

B. ORGANIZATION

When Our Lord called His first apostles to follow Him, this need not of itself have implied a complete break with the existing system of government. The Old Testament prophets before Him had claimed a revelation and a mission directly from God, independent yet not subversive of other jurisdiction. Our Lord Himself recognized the authority even of the scribes and pharisees (*Matt.* xxiii, 1–3), which was not directly based upon divine institution; there can be no doubt that He likewise recognized that of the priests. Nevertheless it was evident from much that He said, not merely that He was founding a body which was to last, but that the Old Testament system which He found existing was to perish, He was therefore truly superseding the Old Testament, and this He showed more and more clearly in the course of His ministry.

In this, as in some other matters, the full significance of His words had not been grasped. The question whether Christian Jews and whether gentile converts were obliged to observe the Mosaic Law was one that in the abstract perhaps might have been kept distinct from that of the complete independence of the new Christian community, but in the concrete such independence could only have been maintained with the greatest difficulty, if at all. In practice the observance of the Mosaic Law would have entailed attendance in the Temple and the synagogues, and submission to the officials there in charge. The baptism of Cornelius and his household (*Acts* x) settled the question for ever, and to it St. Peter appealed later at the Council of Jerusalem (*Acts* xv, 7–11); to be a Christian it was sufficient to have faith and to be baptized, without circumcision or any such Jewish practices. In actual history the brunt of the struggle fell upon St. Paul, the apostle of the gentiles, who was constantly resisting attempts by converted and unconverted Jews to enforce judaizing observances upon his gentile converts. The struggle was so severe that in order to avoid unnecessary trouble he himself remained faithful to all the Jewish observances, and made no attempt to dissuade other Jewish Christians from doing the like; but he made it clear that there was no obligation of this kind even for Jewish Christians. Paul himself had realized quickly enough the significance of the new Christian community, and had fought to maintain intact what he believed to be still the only religion founded by Almighty God; he disputed with Stephen, and helped to bring about his death, but in his death Stephen conquered. Stephen was the first of all Christian martyrs, but he was also the first to die for the freedom of the Church, and by the shedding of his blood merited from God a still greater successor in the person of his persecutor.

It is difficult for us to realize that it was first of all necessary to vindicate the independence of the Church from Judaism and the whole system of the Old Testament; we should have to abstract altogether from the New Testament, and from ecclesiastical literature and history from the beginning down to our own time, and to steep ourselves in those of the Old Testament and of the Jews instead. But surely no effort should be needed in order to understand that Our Lord did not subject His Church to the State: that He did not Himself appoint a Pilate to govern the Christian Jews, or expect St. Peter and St. Paul to bow in matters spiritual to a Nero? In actual fact the Roman emperors were claiming, not merely to be the high priests, but the very gods of a State religion, against which St. John thunders in the Apocalypse. The beast which the whole earth worships (*Apoc.* xiii, 4) is the Roman emperor, and the second beast, which "maketh the earth and all the dwellers therein to adore the first beast" (*Apoc.* xiii, 12), appears to be the world-wide imperial priesthood; the two signify for ever the encroachments of the civil Government and of its politicians upon the spiritual sphere, encroachments which the totalitarian state of to-day does not suffer us to forget.

The Church, then, was not to be a mere continuation of the Old Testament, nor yet (needless to say) a mere department of the State. It may be said to have been founded when Christ, acting purely upon His own divine authority, called His first two disciples (Andrew and presumably John) to follow him. (*John* i, 39.) From this pair, who upon that first morning came to listen to His teaching, there is unbroken continuity down to ourselves. Others were called, some at once, some a little later. From being mere learners they became teachers, with certain inchoate powers of government and ministry; during the early Judæan ministry they were baptizing (*John* iv, 2), and just before the Sermon on the Mount Christ's chief followers were constituted a definite body with the title of apostles, "in order that they might be with Him, and that He might send them out to preach." (*Mark* iii, 14.) The preaching evidently involved authority to teach, and they evidently exercised also a certain control over Christ's followers, especially when "with Him." At the Last Supper they become the priests of the New Law; after the resurrection they are given power to forgive sins. Even before the descent of the Holy Ghost we have an assembly of Christ's followers, from among whom by St. Peter's direction the college of the twelve apostles is made up, Matthias taking the place of Judas. There is no true break in the continuity.

St. Paul, chosen later to the apostolate by a special vision, more than once asserts his rights in vigorous terms, but he claims to be nothing more and nothing less than one of this body of apostles. " Am I not an apostle," he cries (1 *Cor.* ix, 1); and he usually begins his epistles by calling himself an apostle. He asserts his authority strongly, especially in his Galatian and his two Corinthian epistles. He does not appear to have succeeded entirely in bringing the Corinthians to order, for before the end of the first century we find them again being rebuked for their unruliness by the Roman Church, in the epistle of Pope Clement. Nevertheless it is monstrous to say with Auguste Sabatier[1] that in these Corinthian epistles "while insisting upon his apostolic authority, Paul neither understood nor exercised it as any other than a moral authority, wholly of persuasion." On the contrary, it is evident again and again that in what concerns his apostolic office he claims true authority and rule. "What will you?" he writes. "Shall I come to you with a rod, or in love and the spirit of meekness?" (1 *Cor.* iv, 21). The veriest schoolboy will tell us that the way of the rod is not the way of mere persuasion— and in St. Paul's time the schoolboy appears to have suffered from it far more than to-day.

St. Paul also may suffice, in a short paper like this, to illustrate the catholicity and unity of the Church; it was to be a single organization, with a mission to the whole world. This universal right and duty to evangelize all mankind can easily be recognized in *Galatians* ii, 9; James and Peter and John are to work among the Jews, Paul among the gentiles. The gospel was evidently being preached to the Jews, and elsewhere also St. Paul often claims a mission to all the gentiles, for example in *Romans* i, 14: "to Greeks and barbarians, to learned and ignorant I am a debtor." Indeed, the grace of the apostolate which he has received is unto the winning of all nations to obedience of faith (*Rom.* i, 5). But nothing could have been farther from the Apostle's mind than to suppose that each of the local or provincial churches was to gang

---

[1] *The Religions of Authority and the Religion of the Spirit:* English translation, p. 70.

its own gait, as they say, without any organic connection with the rest; such an idea would have been fundamentally opposed to his doctrine that the Church was the one body of Christ. I say advisedly "body," not "mystical body"; for the word "mystical" in this connection, though its use goes well back into the Middle Ages, has been used in our own day to confuse the whole issue of the visible Church, and worse than this, we even read in some High Church writings of "the mystical Church." But to St. Paul the Church was a single organization, or better still, a single organism; she was alive with the life of her divine Founder and Spouse, communicated to her through His Divine Spirit. Thus she was one body and one soul (*Ephes.* iv, 4,) like any human being, a doctrine clearly expounded in the Ephesian epistle, which so clearly sets forth the Apostle's central doctrine of the Christian's unity with Christ; and indeed, the almost classical edition of that epistle by Dr. Armitage Robinson, the late Dean of Wells, leaves but little to be desired from the Catholic point of view either in regard of this matter or of any other. But the Apostle also sets forth the Church as the body of Christ, elsewhere, chiefly in 1 *Corinthians* xii and *Romans* xii; and that he is not referring merely to internal unity is clear from the fact that his whole anxiety is about harmony in the exercise of external functions. Nor again can it be seriously contended that he is speaking only of the unity of a local church. His reference to the apostles, for instance, as holding the first place in *the* church (with the definite article) in 1 *Corinthians* xii, 28, excludes this.

That St. Paul believed and taught that the Church was one body, one in itself and the only one of its

D

kind, is beyond all question. We must not confuse this
issue with the ulterior issue of the precise bond of unity.
He does not say much about the primacy of St. Peter,
though he does confirm it. He laid before Peter,
James and John the gospel which he was preaching
among the Gentiles, lest he might be running or had
run in vain (*Gal.* ii, 2): they were to work among the
Jews, as he among the Gentiles (ii, 9): but he thinks
it enough to say in explanation that the apostolate
of the Jews was Peter's, as that of the gentiles was
his own (ii, 8). Thus Peter and Paul divide the world
between them, but Paul must agree with Peter, not
Peter with Paul. After this Paul mentions that he
rebuked Peter for his timidity in judaizing (ii, 11–14),
and he lets us see that he did not think it a small
thing to rebuke Peter; but this does not in any way
cancel his previous deference to Peter. It was precisely
because everything turned on Peter that Paul felt
bound to remonstrate; for one in Peter's position to
judaize was to "*compel* the gentiles to judaize" also
(ii, 14).

Once more in the last instance we must appeal to
St. Paul's solidarity with his fellow-apostles. The well-
known Petrine passage in *St. Matthew's* gospel (xvi,
18–19) shows clearly enough what was the view taken
of Peter in the mother-church at Jerusalem; and the
promise there made of primacy in the Church was
fulfilled in the last chapter of the Gospel of *St. John*
(xxi, 15–18). No doubt this chapter is a later addition,
but by St. John himself, and it shows the mind of the
apostolic age. That all too ingenious critic, the late
Prof. Bacon of Yale University, is surely letting the
cat out of the bag when he makes this last chapter of
St. John a Roman forgery of the middle of the second

century;[1] evidently Prof. Bacon would have regarded it as not unreasonable to suppose that Peter lived in his successors. But there is no reason to suppose in the writers or redactors of the four Gospels such diabolical cunning that we have had to wait for the arrival of Prof. Bacon upon the scene to have their guiles unravelled. It is far more reasonable to suppose that Christ intended His Church to have a visible head; any other hypothesis plays ducks and drakes with the evidence.

We may now pass on to consider no less briefly the origin of monarchical episcopacy, that is to say, of the diocesan bishop. The apostles do not seem to have made it their business to set up bishops at once over every new community of Christians. The Catholic thesis is that the bishops were and are the successors of the apostles, not their contemporaries; the college of apostles was gradually replaced by the college of bishops. The Apostles had a universal jurisdiction, in virtue of which they could establish local bishops wherever they saw fit, once the need for them began to be felt. In actual fact the creation of the orders, all of them a partial sharing in the apostolic powers, appears to have proceeded from below. It is a reasonably certain view that at the beginning of *Acts* vi we have the first institution of deacons. Presumably there was a first institution of priests a few years later; they seem to be implied in *Acts* xi, 30; and in *Acts* xiv, 23, we find Paul and Barnabas appointing them in every city. St. Paul appears regularly to have set up in his churches colleges of priests, whom he controlled by his own visits and letters, and by the visits of such companions and delegates as Timothy and Titus.

[1] *The Fourth Gospel in Research and Debate*, Yale, 1918, p. 224.

There is only one reasonably certain example in the New Testament itself of what appears to be monarchical episcopacy; St. James, the brother of the Lord and an apostle, appears to have fixed his see at Jerusalem, where, for example, St. Paul finds him in *Acts* xxi, 18.[1] But the evidence outside the New Testament for the apostolic origin of monarchical episcopacy is overwhelming. Irenæus, Hegesippus, Tertullian and others had no doubt that there were churches whose episcopal succession went back to the apostles; they lay emphasis upon this fact as a guarantee, not of valid orders (which they took for granted) but of true doctrine. St. Ignatius of Antioch, writing somewhere between A.D. 98 and 117, is a still earlier and very important witness. He writes to St. Polycarp as Bishop of Smyrna, to which see, according to St. Irenæus, the apostles had appointed him. Three other bishops come to see him, and he speaks of himself as bishop of Syria; he speaks also of bishops settled in the farthest parts of the world. More than all this: he lays such tremendous emphasis upon the office of the diocesan bishop that it is inconceivable that he should be foisting upon these important churches some new idea of his own. Evidently they knew that he had full warrant for what he said; and the warrant could only be apostolic tradition.

St. Ignatius, however, belongs to another lecture, and I must not dilate upon him. But I cannot feel much doubt that it is to St. John the Evangelist that we must look for the origin of the episcopacy in all these

---

[1] In what follows I am drawing largely on the very valuable appendix to Vol. III, of the Westminster Version, dealing with "the Ministry in the Apostolic Church," by my colleague Father Keogh. I have also made use in this paper of other parts of the Westminster Version, e.g., of my own notes on the Acts of the Apostles.

important churches. It is perhaps significant that, as Polycrates, bishop of Ephesus, tells us before the end of the second century (or at all events, this is what he seems to mean), St. John was of a priestly family among the Jews, and used to wear the golden plate which the high priest used to bear in the front of his mitre or turban (Eusebius, *Church History*, V, 24, 3). In any case St. Ignatius himself is steeped in Johannine thought, a fact which at that early date may well imply personal contact; and the angels of the churches in the opening chapters of the Apocalypse are best understood to be bishops. In 1 *Corinthians* xi, 10, the " angels " are probably the ministers generally. Finally, we have the plain statement from St. Jerome about St. John, that he founded and ruled all the churches of Asia (*De Viris Illustribus*, chap. 9). By Asia would be meant the Roman province of Asia, very roughly the western half of Asia Minor; and since it must have been evident to St. Jerome that St. Paul founded some, if not most of these churches (*cf. Acts* xix, 10, 26), we may interpret him to mean that St. John established diocesan bishops in the cities where hithero there had only been colleges of priests.

I close with St. Peter at Rome. That he established his see there is a fact which only the most prejudiced can bring themselves to deny, and I cannot spare the time required for the proof. Mr. Blenkin, an Anglican minister, in his edition of St. Peter's first epistle in the *Cambridge Greek Testament for Schools and Colleges*, writes (p. xvi) that "St. Peter's work and martyrdom in Rome are attested by evidence so early, so widespread and so unanimous that even the most determined opponent of papal claims could not dispute it with any success." He cites Clement of Rome,

Ignatius, Papias, Dionysius of Corinth, Irenæus, Clement of Alexandria, Tertullian, Gaius the Roman presbyter, and Origen. "Babylon," whence the epistle is written (1 *Pet.* v, 13), also stands for Rome in the Apocalypse (*Apoc.* xvii), and in two works of the Jewish apocalyptic literature, the Syriac *Apocalypse of Baruch* (xi, 1) and the Sibylline Oracles (V, 159). And if St. Peter was at Rome at all, it is still more futile to deny that he established his see there; the old die-hards saw clearly enough that he must not be allowed to set foot in the place. The decay of Protestantism has released much history.

C.   CONCLUSION: GEOGRAPHICAL SURVEY

Having thus endeavoured to understand what the Church had grown to be, so to speak, from within, we may conclude with a rapid sketch of her external growth. This can best be done upon a geographical basis, and we may name the chief stages after four cities: Jerusalem, Antioch, Corinth, Rome.

Jerusalem, of course, was the centre of Judaism, where the apostles and their Jewish disciples joined in the national worship; the number even of the Jewish priests who became Christians was at one time large (*Acts* vi, 7). At an early stage persecution tended to break up the mother-church at Jerusalem; but it was the destruction of the city in A.D. 70 that finally wrecked its postion in the Catholic Church at large. After that the Jewish church as such was of less and less account, being regarded in fact with some suspicion; it is as a gentile church that Jerusalem gradually develops a new importance, marked towards the end of the period under consideration in this School by the visit of the Empress Helen and the building of basilicas.

Jerusalem, then, from being the mother-church soon becomes a mere backwater, and the Jewish Christians lose all importance in the Church. "Hadst thou but known!" It might have been far otherwise, with Jerusalem for Rome, and Palestine for the sacred states of the Church. But already in the Acts we behold the rapid development of Antioch, soon to be the queen of the Christian as of the pagan East, the chief of the Greek-speaking churches. Egypt and Alexandria were too isolated, in ecclesiastical as in political history, to wield much influence upon the world at large ; desert and sea were a protection, but made communication difficult both ways. Rome herself no doubt began in large measure as a Greek-speaking church, but in any case the study of the origins, both of the liturgy and of the Biblical text, seems to point to a considerable debt to Antioch. The progress of St. Ignatius of Antioch through Asia Minor to his martyrdom sufficiently attests the leading position of his Church, but in that region the aggressive policy of the upstart patriarchate of Constantinople was to hinder the natural development of the ecclesiastical hierarchy. For our present purposes it must be remembered that all through the Pre-Nicene period Asia Minor is by far the most Christian country, so far as we may call such a vast and heterogeneous region a country at all ; and at the end of the period it is there alone that Christianity may even be called the dominating religion. This was largely the work of St. Paul, but St. Peter had also worked in the north, and there must have been other workers of varying importance.

The Churches of Asia Minor, Syria and Egypt may

be called the hellenistic or semi-Oriental Churches; to a large extent Greek is their liturgical language, but (once more, to a large extent) not their only language, and the amount of Greek or Macedonian blood in their veins was for the most part very small. They had a varying but usually rather thin veneer of Greek culture, and it is necessary to a proper understanding of their history to allow for their Oriental descent and character. In the hinterland of these hellenistic churches lay others less subject to Greek influence, the Armenian, Syrian and Coptic Churches; but these come into such importance as is theirs later on, and we must pass them over here.

Next we come to the Greek churches proper, to the Aegean, the chief seat of St. Paul's activity; if I take Corinth as the typical city here, it is partly because it is in Greece proper, and partly because for our purposes Ephesus looks east rather than west, having been from the first a base of operations for the evangelization of Asia Minor. Greece made progress at about the same brisk rate as the Latin churches of southern and eastern Spain and Carthaginian Africa; but the Greek churches have no very striking history, partly perhaps because of the Greek city-spirit of isolation and independence. Paul found the Corinthians difficult; and (as has already been remarked) his rebukes are caught up with startling promptness by the Roman Church before the end of the first century.

From the Jewish, the hellenistic, the hellenic churches, we thus pass to Rome. She enters dramatically upon the scene with St. Paul's tremendous epistle, wherein he begins by thanking God that the faith of the Roman Christians is proclaimed throughout the world; less than ten years afterwards, indeed, not merely their steadfast faith but their large numbers were to become manifest in the persecution of Nero. Like St. Ignatius of Antioch after him, the Apostle hails with reverence the church in the midst of which he is to lay down his life for Christ, and he unfolds to them his teaching in the most dogmatic and difficult of his epistles—merely to refresh their memories, as he deprecatingly remarks towards the end of the epistle (xv, 15).

Italy as a whole acquired the faith but slowly, so slowly that it must remain a question whether Carthage or Spain or Gaul owed their actual beginnings to Italy or Rome. In France the Gospel seems rather to have come from Asia Minor by way of the Greek colonies of the south, such as Marseilles, and was a long time in spreading, but the very first beginnings may well go back to the Apostolic Age. From the outset, Rome was the acknowledged mistress of the Latin west, which formed her patriarchate, and gave her a position of great strength in dealing with the eastern churches. She was long bilingual, and from her central position dealt with the west in Latin, and with the east in Greek. But in the Apostolic Age she is on the outer fringe of the Christian world, with Western Christianity not yet risen in its might beneath her fostering care. The epistle of Clement, however, written perhaps before the death of the last apostle, shows the Roman Church already conscious of authority even over Corinth, the great Apostolic Church of Greece. At the beginning of his paper upon "the patristic period" at the Summer School on the Papacy (1923), the late Abbot Chapman (whose loss the Summer School must deplore most of all in dealing with such a subject as the Pre-Nicene Church) emphatically repudiated as unhistorical the assumption of a very gradual development of the papal power in the Early Church, and his lecture (still to be read in the Summer School volume for that year) went far to justify his protest. By the end of the Apostolic Age the position of Rome in the Catholic Church was already clear in all essentials.

I have not spoken of the pagan background to all this growth of the Church; something is to be said of it in other lectures, and in any case there is no time to speak of what is peculiar to the Apostolic Age. I dismiss it, therefore with only one remark, that the same Paganism is all about us to-day. We see various forms of Christianity, but they have largely lost their meaning, as had the old pagan religions, and to a large extent, once more as of old, they have been replaced by a false emotionalism ; this collapse of belief, as of old, has led to the collapse of morals. Once more the Church offers the only remedy, which is her Divine Lord Himself, to a sick and despairing world. In large measure the Apostolic Age is the age in which we live. "Save yourself from this perverse generation" (*Acts* ii, 40).

FROM ST. IGNATIUS OF ANTIOCH TO THE CONVERSION OF CONSTANTINE

By the Rev. PHILIP HUGHES, Lic.Sc.Hist.

WE can arrange the facts of this history in three groups. There are certain details of the relations between the Church and Paganism organized politically, i.e. the Roman Empire to which almost all the members of the Church were subject. There are details of the Church's first relations with Paganism organized intellectually. There are details, finally, of domestic controversy between the Christians themselves either in matters of belief or in what concerns the practice of religious life. Nowhere in what has come down to us of early Christian literature is there any work which purports to be a detailed, studied account of the new religion, a scientific, systematic exposition of its beliefs and practices. It is from writings composed for special circumstances, and whose information is conditioned by the circumstances that called them forth, that we must gather all that is to be gathered about such matters as the organization of the Church, the hierarchy of bishops and their interrelations, the relations between the bishops and the Bishop of Rome, the sacramental practice, the Christian daily life, the detail of development and of the new religion's geographical expansion. These topics are treated of in the other papers collected in this volume. Special papers also deal with the conflict with the Roman Empire and with intellectual Paganism. The purpose of this paper is then merely to sketch the background of the general history of the Church.

That general history, so far as it is known to us, is principally the history of controversies among Christians. The controversies in the second century are chiefly such as were bound to arise once the new religion came to be known and discussed in the religious world outside the Church. In the third century, with which the second half of the paper is concerned, the controversies have this in common, that they bring into the foreground the authority of the Roman See. That century is also the moment of the first attempt to present a reasoned explanation of the Christian answer to the riddle of life—the achievement of the school of Alexandria. But with this topic, too, a special paper deals.

Part I

1. THE CHURCH AND ITS FIRST CONTACTS WITH PAGAN RELIGIOUS THOUGHT

CHRISTIANITY shows itself from the beginning an organized religion with a fixed traditional doctrine and with, for its teachers, a hierarchy whose authority derives from Christ and is guaranteed by the ordination-link that unites those who exercise it with the Apostles. It is a religion revealed first to Palestinian Jews, but meant for all mankind. At the time it was revealed, religious speculation played a great part in the intellectual life of the Romano-Hellenistic world.

How did the new religion fare in its first contacts with that world?

Three features of contemporary religious life must be borne in mind. *First* the violent hostility to the new religion on the part of those who had an interest in the old classical Paganism, and notably on the part of the populace and the civil authority. *Secondly* the tendency called Syncretism, whose effect was to assimilate all cults, regarding them as no more than so many modifications, more or less diversified, of the same stock of religious ideas and personifications. *Finally* there is a more respectable force than either of these with which the Gospel had to reckon—the leaders and disciples of the philosophico-religious disciplines, e.g. the New Stoicism, Neo-Platonism and Neo-Pythagoreanism. It is from these sects that the Church gathers its first convert "intellectuals," and it it is to their quondam philosophical associates that these converts address in turn the first reasoned statements of Christian belief, the Gospel presented as the culmination of all Philosophy. These are the writers we know as the Apologists; they offer a rational explanation of the Church, and on their reasoned proof of the new religion's social value base a plea for toleration. Thus the Apologists are in contact with popular and official Paganism. Their understanding of the Syncretist movement, and their emancipated sympathy for those still striving whence they themselves are so lately emancipated, lead the Apologists to this third contact. They use methods familiar to the day's Syncretism, and Syncretist terminology to explain the traditional faith—a method of propaganda whose dangers are as obvious as are the hopes of those who employ it. Whence a new problem for the Church, a problem complicated by the appearance of Syncretism in the Church itself. The problem is the greater because these new defenders (and therefore teachers) of the new religion are not the new religion's official teachers—the bishops. No matter what their gifts, their piety, their experience, they are no more than private individuals. Syncretism tending to disfigure the Gospel, in its friendly desire to incorporate it in a hundred ready-made human philosophies, Catholic thinkers striving to convert Paganism by a reasoned exposition of the Gospel which shall reveal in it to the pagan all that is best in Paganism's promise —this is for the Church a new and terrible crisis.

The crisis is resolved safely because of the kind of thing the Church is, and the kind of thing she is essentially is clearly shown once more in the writings not of a philosopher, not of an Apologist, but of a man of action and a bishop, St. Irenæus. The Church acts according to its nature, and, its life being healthy, rejects the poisoning Gnosticism.

II. GNOSTICISM

The means through which the Syncretist spirit influenced the Church was Gnosticism. Gnosticism was first of all a tendency outside the Church, and it was already flourishing when the Gospel religion first reached the Romano-Hellenistic Paganism. To the Gnostics the Gospel was just so much new material to incorporate with their own doctrines—and these doctrines were an amazing mixture of decadent Paganism, a Neo-Pythagoreanism that was little more than magic, rites and initiations, teachings of re-incarnation and divine genealogies borrowed and

adapted from all the ancient religion of the East—
Chaldea, Persia, Syria, Egypt, even of India. These
elements were combined in a variety of systems. All
offered to the disciple a deeper insight into divine
things—KNOWLEDGE, whence the name, Gnostics, by
which we know all those whom the movement captured.

From the moment when the Church first reached the
world of Hellenism, this powerful and omnipresent
movement strove to absorb and transform its faith into
a simple religious philosophy, while on the other hand
religious thought within the Church—working in the
spirit of this movement, using its methods and accepting
its hypotheses as facts—endeavoured by means of it
to find a deeper meaning in Christianity than that
furnished in the Church's official teaching, and
threatened to transform Christianity into a mystery-
cult of dreams and initiations. Instead of the common
ordinary faith the new thinkers offered knowledge.
From the point of view of its Christian adherents, then,
Gnosticism is "historically an attempt on the part
of Christian intellectuals—some of them thinkers of
unusual power—to usurp a right of speculating, of
systematising and dogmatising in the strictest sense
of the word after the manner of the Pagan schools of
philosophy."

The systems of Gnosticism are so numerous that it is
not possible here to do more than note some of the
characteristic doctrines of what was in reality Paganism
masquerading as Christianity, and to see how Gnosis
explaining Christianity explains it away. Gnosticism
is an attempt to explain where Faith never offers an
explanation, e.g. the mysteries of the Trinity, the
Incarnation, the Redemption. Behind the bizarre
façade of Gnostic theogonies and rites is a vigorous

discussion of the most fundamental of all ideas, the nature and origin of evil, of man, of God. In the Gnostic propaganda the Christian sacred books are used—the New Testament as well as the Old—and the allegorical interpretation of them, pushed beyond the limits of reason, is a favourite arm. Finally, Gnosticism was not a merely intellectual discussion, but a religious system with ritual, and observances, regulations and officials.

A summary of the system best known to us—that of Valentine—will best convey what Gnosticism had in it to interest thinkers and at the same time to captivate the popular mind. At the summit of all being is God the Father and his companion Sigé (Silence). God is one, unique, known only to Himself, remote, inaccessible, and between God and the world there is a whole universe of "demi-gods." From the Father and Sigé proceed Intellect and Truth, and from these Word and Life, and from these again Man and the Church— in all the eight superior eons. This process of generation among the eons continues until the Pleroma is complete—the perfect society of divine beings, thirty in all. So far all is abstraction, idea. Physical reality originates through a breach of the harmony of the ideal Pleroma, "a kind of original sin. . . ." The lowest of the thirty eons, Wisdom, conceives a desire to know the Father—an inordinate desire, necessarily, since the Father is knowable only to Intellect, His own firstborn. This inordinate desire of Wisdom is a new being, imperfect necessarily and therefore cast out from the Pleroma. Its name is Hachamoth. To prevent any recurrence of such disorder Intellect and Truth produce a sixteenth pair of eons, Christ and the Holy Ghost, to teach the rest the limits of their nature. Then, in an act of Thanksgiving, all the thirty-two eons unite their powers and produce the thirty-third eon, Jesus, the Saviour. The thirty-third eon and the eon Christ are now dispatched by the Pleroma to Hachamoth—the imperfect desire of Wisdom. From the eon Christ it receives a beginning of form and the elements of consciousness—whence a sense of its own inferiority. The thirty-third eon separates the passions from it. The separated passions are inanimate matter (hyliké), Hachamoth, freed from them, is animate matter (psychiké). Hachamoth's vision of the Saviour results in a third substance, the spiritual (pneumatiké). So originate the elements of the world that is to be. Hachamoth, from the psychike, produces the Creator, Demiurge, and he gives form to the rest of creation.

Demiurge is ignorant of his own origin and believes himself supreme. He is the maker of man, material and animated, the god of the Jews and the Old Testament, a bad god and to be resisted. (Whence the common Gnostic teaching of a fundamental opposition between the Old Testament and the New.) Men are of three types, according to the element predominating in them. There are material men (*Hylikoi*), who cannot be saved, spiritual men (*Pneumatikoi*), who have no need of salvation (the Gnostics), and animate men (*Psychikoi*), who need salvation and can profit by it. For these last there is the plan of Redemption.

The Redeemer is spiritual, He is animate. He has the appearance of the material and, a fourth element in Him, He is the eon Jesus. This eon descended into Him at His baptism and remained until the trial before Pilate when it returned to the Pleroma, taking with it the spiritual element. The actor in the Passion was

E

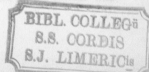

no more than the animate element with its appearance of matter. The Passion is not the source of redemption. Salvation, the redemption of the spiritual in man from the influence of the psychic, is due to the knowledge brought by the thirty-third eon—knowledge of the secret traditions and mysteries, knowledge of the Gospel, which can indeed only be truly understood through this esoteric knowledge. The possession of this knowledge is the key to life, and knowledge is the highest of virtues. Matter is the source of evil in man, and since the Gnostic is wholly spiritual his actions cannot but be good. Spirit and flesh are independent, and the spirit is not responsible for the flesh. Whence a morality at times ascetic, at times licentious. The ritual is elaborate and fantastic, a combination drawn from all manner of sources, and through this sensually attractive ritual comes salvation. The Gnostic's justification for his substitution of the Gnosis as the guide to the Gospel is an alleged secret revelation of Our Lord to the Apostles, published in the Gnostic Scriptures (Gospels of Thomas, Philip, Judas, etc.), and open now to the initiate alone. The movement produced a voluminous literature—practically all of which has perished. It is chiefly from the orthodox writers who opposed Gnosticism that our information about it derives.

III. THE APOLOGISTS

What had the Church to offer the Pagan intellectual?

Celsus, the most learned of Pagan opponents, sneered at Christianity, as a religion that began with publicans and fishermen, and he was not alone in his scorn. Nor were there wanting Christian writers ready, in their consciousness of all the Gospel held for humanity, even eager, to dismiss as so much no longer needed rubbish the legacy of the world's pre-Christian thought. Tertullian's gibe at "poor little Aristotle" is a case in point. On the other hand, a more sympathetic spirit, informed from the very beginning the generality of Christian writers, its pattern St. Paul advising the Philippians (*Phil.* iv, 8) to make their own, the true, the just, the virtuous and praise-worthy wherever they found it. To seek out and gather carefully whatever truth there was in Pagan thought and aspiration, to make the most of it that it might serve as a bridge to bring the Pagan mind to Christ, to present Christianity as the logical conclusion of all that is best in Paganism—this was the aim of the writers we call the *Apologists*. They are converts explaining Catholicism to those they have left behind, explaining it in the idiom of those they have left behind, and explaining it as the unknown towards which all men of good will unconsciously tend. (cf. St. Paul at Athens. *Acts* xvii, 20.)

It is necessary to keep in mind this aim of presenting the Gospel religion in a favourable light, and it is well to remember a second object which inspired much of their writing, viz. the hope of securing toleration from the State by proving beyond all doubt that Christians were, as such, loyal and valuable subjects. From the nature of the case there is in their work a preference for stressing points where Christianity confirmed Philosophy, for the discussion of natural virtues and the truths about God which can be known naturally (e.g. the unity and unicity of God, the immortality of the soul, the future life as a sanction of morality). The existence of mysteries the Apologists explain from the analogy of the Pagan mysteries.

The most famous of the Apologists are Aristides (fl. 136–61), Tatian, a Syrian (fl. 165), Athenagoras (fl. 176–8), Theophilus of Antioch (fl. 169–82), and above all, St. Justin Martyr (d. 165), and Tertullian (160–?). If we study St. Justin's work it will give us an idea of the philosophical apologetic at its best, while Tertullian may stand for that wider controversy, which is addressed to the Pagan world at large, and also (for Tertullian is much more than an Apologist) for the beginnings of Latin theological writing.

St. Justin was born about the year 100 in Palestine and, converted at Ephesus *c.* 138, opened a school of Christian Philosophy at Rome (138–161). He was a trained philosopher who passed from one school of thought to another in search of truth, Stoic, Aristotelian, Neo-Pythagorean, Platonist. He died a martyr under Marcus Aurelius, 165. His surviving works are his two *Apologies*, and the *Dialogue with Trypho the Jew*.

What is Christianity as St. Justin explains it to Pagan philosophy?

It is, first of all, itself a philosophy, and the points in which it resembles the Pagan philosophies are more striking than those in which they differ. The differences are shades of meaning rather than real oppositions. Faith only teaches more securely what Plato and the Stoics already affirm—more securely and more completely. The origin of this resemblance is twofold. The philosophers learnt these truths from the Old Testament, and in the second place the divine Logos, whose incarnation was the beginning of Christianity, manifested Himself before His incarnation to the

Pagan sages as well as to the Jews. This revelation to the philosophers was, by comparison, incomplete, but, none the less, sufficient to make possible their discovery of certain truths. All who lived with the Logos, before the Incarnation, whether Jews or Pagans, were really Christians, Socrates and Abraham alike. Now that the Logos has appeared incarnate the fullness of revelation has come, to correct the errors resulting from the former incompleteness. The logical philosopher, then, embraces Christianity.

There is much more, of course, in St. Justin than the development of the argumentation thus roughly summarised. What it all achieved is hard to say. We cannot see that the demonstration of the Apologists lessened the persecution, nor do we know how far it influenced the élite. It is perhaps true that we can exaggerate the effect they had on their time. It remains to consider their witness to the Church of their day, and their effect on the thought of the Church itself.

For with the Apologists, Catholic Theology is born— the development of the content of revelation by human reasoning under the guidance of the *magisterium* of Authority. Also, with this beginning of human speculation on revealed data there begins no less surely the trouble caused by the thinker who claims for his thought superiority over the revealed tradition. In these early, first, philosophical discussions on the implications of revealed doctrine lie the seeds of all the heresies. The discussions which, later, fill the fourth and fifth centuries can never be understood if their origins in the second century are ignored. Whence the need of a reference here to some points of the Apologists' primitive theology.

Inevitably the Apologists attempted an explanation, or rather a reasoned description, of the mystery we know as that of the Trinity. God was one, Jesus Christ was God, and yet Jesus Christ, the Divine Logos incarnate, was not God the Father. The difficulty did not challenge in vain. Again there was the absorbing question as to the relation of the Father and the Logos before the Incarnation, and the question of the meaning of the eternal generation of the Logos. In their discussions on these questions the Apologists were pioneers. The machinery of tested, technical language which guides the theologian of to-day in his exposition of these truths was not yet made. Whence, inevitably, an uncertain groping in the language of these early writers, confusion at times and an obscurity that left room for contrary interpretations of their teaching—and that bred an uneasiness with regard to all this "theologizing" on the part of Authority whose function it was to preserve at all costs the traditional faith and for whom the need to explain that faith's coherence philosophically was, by comparison, of secondary importance.

Here in résumé is the exposition of St. Justin's theory of the Logos.

The Father is God, the Son or Logos is God, the Holy Ghost is God. God is one. The Father is the Creator and has created through the Logos (*John* 1, 3) through whom also He has perfected His revelation (*ib.*, 1, 18) and redeemed us. The Logos is truly God, existing before the creation, not created, not made, but begotten of the Father—hence the Logos is the Son and hence His distinction from the Father. The distinction is real and does not imply any division of the indivisible divine substance, any separation of Logos from Father. Two difficulties result from the theorizing—one concerns the moment of the generation of the Logos, the other, arising from the first, concerns this "subordination" to the Father.

The Logos is represented as always, from eternity, existing in the Father—but not as a *distinct* Person. As a *distinct* Person He exists only from the moment of His generation, and that was the moment of God's willing to create. This is the theory known as that of the *temporal generation of the Logos* (the name is none too correct).

Since the Logos is, *in function*, the minister of the Father's will, He is subordinate to the Father—a subordination, note, not *of nature*, for the Logos is equally God, God is one. The "subordinationism" of St. Justin derives simply from the ministerial role of the Logos in the work of creation—it neither implies nor necessitates any inferiority.

Jesus Christ, the Redeemer, a real man (i.e. possessed of a real body and a real human soul) is also God, for He is the Logos incarnate. He is one person. He died on our behalf, to ransom us from the death which sin had caused. His death is the principal and decisive cause of our Redemption. As He restored what Adam ruined, so Mary, the Virgin, bringing Him forth and obedient to the angel is the complement to Eve whose disobedience brought forth sin and death.

IV. ST. IRENÆUS

St. Irenæus is not an Apologist, nor a philosopher, and for the philosopher's attempts to explain rationally the "how" and the "why" of mysteries he has little beyond contempt; "*quasi ipsi obstetricaverint*," he says

of the theorists busy with discussion on the generation
of the Logos. He is before all a man of action, the
Catholic bishop of a missionary diocese on the frontier
protecting his flock from Gnosticism. His earliest
associations—he was an Easterner by birth—were with
the Church at Lyons. The cosmopolitan character of
this city, the large Eastern (Asiatic, Phrygian) element
in its population (due to its commercial importance),
are reflected in the life of its Church. The persecution of
the year 177 struck it heavily. There were arrests,
the usual tortures and interrogations, a number of
apostasies, martyrdoms too. A report of the whole
was sent to Rome and the bearer of the report was
Irenæus. He succeeded as bishop to the martyr of
the persecution—Pothinas, and ruled until his death,
possibly a martyr, in 202. Of his surviving works the
best known and most important is the one generally
called, by the title of its Latin version, *Adversus Hereses*.
The Greek title better describes its character: *A
refutation and criticism of what is falsely called Knowledge*.
The method of his book is as important as its matter—
in its consequences perhaps even more important,
for it has been a model for all subsequent controversialists and it throws a flood of light on the nature
and character of primitive Christianity, showing it
once more to be essentially a *catechism*, a taught
tradition. It is this methodology which differentiates
St. Irenæus immediately from the Apologists.

As to his method—man can never fully know God,
because man is finite. It is not surprising then that the
nature of the Logos, the manner of His divine generation,
escapes us (*Generationem eius quis ennarabit ? Is*. liii, 8.)
Who shall declare his generation? Yet although *perfect*
knowledge is not for us, certain fundamental things we

can know, even heavenly things, even things about the Logos. These we know simply because God has himself taught us. Where? In the divine scriptures. These are sometimes obscure; their meaning needs to be interpreted, and for a sure interpretation we must go to the Church, to the Churches which had for their founders the Apostles and in which the succession of bishops since the Apostles is unbroken, and especially to the Church of Rome.

This general principle of St. Irenæus goes far beyond the needs of the moment. It appeals beyond the details of Gnostic objections and proofs. It establishes the verdict against the Gnostics on the very nature of the Church's version of religious truth, i.e. that it is a preserved tradition, and therefore the very fact of Gnosticism being no more than a system of principles and reasoning rules out all possibility of its being the Truth of God.

The doctrinal content of St. Irenæus is a repetition of the tradition. God is one, unique and this God is Himself the Creator; the God of the Old Testament and of the New. In this one God there are three terms (the technical word "person" is not yet forged): the Father, the Son (St. Irenæus prefers "Son" to "Logos" —characteristically), the Holy Spirit. The Logos existed before the Incarnation, for He is God. As to the mode of His divine generation St. Irenæus, unlike the Gnostics, unlike the Apologists, offers no theory. It is a mystery known only to the Father and to the Son. The Gnostic schemes are mere fantasies. Evil in the world finds its explanation in the free-will of man and in the teaching of the fall of the first man. From the effects of the fall we have been saved. In this matter of redemption revelation has been progressive. The final revelation was the work of the Redeemer Himself—Jesus Christ, who is the same as and not different from the Logos, is in fact the Logos incarnate. Once again St. Irenæus is content to register the traditional faith that Our Lord is God and Man without any attempt to show how the two realities are united in Him. The fruit of the Redemption is the possibility of a reconciliation of man with God of which faith in Christ and obedience to His Precepts are the means, Baptism and the Eucharist.

St. Irenæus, at pains to make clear that philosophizing is not the way to the Gospel, studiously avoiding language which savours of the philosophical, closes an age in the history of Theology—the age when little more is done than to repeat the tradition without attempting to draw out its implications. Nor had the Apologists really attempted this—rather they were concerned to justify philosophically that same tradition. The Gnostics again had not themselves advanced the understanding of tradition. Their aim had been to work in with it a mass of extraneous ideas alleged to be necessary for its understanding. With the next generation the first attempts were to be made, and by Christians, to develop the tradition itself not by any process of external addition, but by an intensive study of the whole field of revelation that was to issue in synthesis—scriptural, philosophical, historical—that only genius of the first order and an encyclopædic learning could produce. This was the work of the school of Alexandria, the achievement of Origen. The synthesis had its good and bad fortune. It affected profoundly all subsequent theological effort, but that effort was the surer for the masterly insistence of St. Irenæus on its most fundamental character. His mind left on Catholic Theology that consciousness of itself as primarily a tradition whose interpreter is Authority that has ever since remained Catholic Theology's most evident characteristic.

Was St. Irenæus a revolutionary in this matter? Did he remake Christian thought? It has been laid to his charge. The answer to this is the study of his second-century predecessors. St. Irenæus did not invent a theory to serve his purpose, a theory so ingenious that all others since have kept it. He is not the inventor of "*Roman Catholicism.*" Every element in his theory is older than himself, every principle there from the beginning.

V. MARCION—MONTANISM

Gnosticism is an interpretation of the Gospel dangerous for the Church because there are Gnostics who work to impose that interpretation from within the Church to the detriment of the traditional faith. The two other deviations from the tradition which troubled this second century are of quite a different character. Marcionism is a deliberate attempt to reform the Church, to reconstitute it on another basis and in another institution, to set up a "true Church," as against the traditional Church. Montanism is an attempt, on the part of Catholics, to impose as a power in the Church, superior to the hierarchy, the authority of private revelation. These two heresies had a great success. More than one great mind fell away to them, e.g. to Montanism, the greatest mind Latin Catholicism had yet known, Tertullian.

Marcion, born towards the end of the first century,

was the son of the Bishop of Sinope. He came to Rome about 135 and taught there for another twenty-five years, a contemporary of the Gnostic Valentine. The details of his excommunication we do not know. Its date was 144. Marcion is not a Gnostic—speculation, the craving for hidden and higher knowledge, the search for knowledge as the sufficient and necessary means of salvation did not move him. His aim was practical, to bring back Christianity to the point at which it had begun to go wrong and to restore to men what alone could save them, the real Gospel.

Struck by the opposition between the Old and New Testaments, the Law and the Gospel, Marcion concluded that the Gospel was meant to displace and reverse all that the Law had approved. The Law, harsh, inflexible, was the work of the Creator, an imperfect God to be abandoned now for the Supreme God, God of love and goodness revealed in Jesus Christ and the Gospel He preached. From the beginning of the Church, however, the ignorance or prejudice or weakness of the Apostles has harassed the Gospel with a wealth of Old Testament ideals.

The one only exception to this is St. Paul. Marcion's devotion to St. Paul as he conceives him—a St. Paul whose preaching of freedom from the Law becomes exaggerated into caricature—knows no limits. In the light of his theory he restores the text of St. Paul's writings, rejecting the "interpolations" made by his until now successful opponents. The same principles lead him to reject the rest of the New Testament except his own—amended—version of St. Luke. A book of his own composition—the *Antitheses*—which sets forth the opposition between the Law and the Gospel, completes the Marcionite "bible." This revolutionary innovator is equally concerned to establish a new morality. The most rigorous asceticism is prescribed as necessary for all, fasts, perpetual abstinence from meat, and, equally for all, perpetual celibacy. Marcion was a capable organiser, and, once excommunicated, set himself to build up a " Church" on the pattern of the one which had rejected him, complete with hierarchy and sacramental ritual. The movement spread, and by the end of the century Marcionite churches were to be found in every province of the empire. A hundred years later it was still flourishing. It had its martyrs in the persecutions, and, in the middle of the fifth century, Theodoret was occupied with the problem of a whole village of Marcionites in his diocese of Cyrrus.

Montanus, the founder of the sect called after him, was a recent convert, and the highlands of central Asia Minor, the neighbourhood of Ancyra, the scene of the movement's origin. With Montanus were associated two women, Priscilla and Maximilla. Montanism began as a "revivalist" movement—the founder fell into ecstasies, and to the accompaniment of bizarre gestures and howlings "prophesied" and taught. The end of the present dispensation was at hand. The heavenly Jerusalem was to descend—and to descend precisely at Pepuza, two hundred miles away and more. Whence a general exodus to Pepuza, and round the sacred place a new town speedily grew up of expectant devotees. The new prophets, except for their assertion that they were the organs through whom the Holy Ghost would henceforward speak, did not at first innovate in matters doctrinal. In works they followed the contemporary current of rigorism, multiplying fasts and prayers, establishing new food-abstinences and prohibiting marriage. The founders died, the Second Coming delayed, but the sect spread and rapidly, while from every part of the Church came protestations—not against the asceticism, but against the novelty that men should claim the authority of the Holy Ghost for things uttered during the extravagances of these ecstasies. When the authority of the hierarchy touched the movement the first suspicions were justified, for it preferred its prophets to the bishops. "The novelty of Montanism was its desire to impose private revelations as a supplement to the deposit of faith, and to accredit them by ecstasies and convulsions that gave rise to suspicion." Montanism is a revolt against an established institution—the role of authority in matters of doctrine.

The attitude of the bishops to these two heresies should be noted, and the effect of the measures they took. There are no councils held—councils are an institution of later date. The dissidents are excommunicated, and their supporters follow them into new organizations they form. The Church, more or less diminished in numbers, goes its own way free of the influence, having rejected by its own power what it could not assimilate. This is in striking contrast to the state of things we see two centuries later, when the foreign body is maintained within the Church by forces external to the Church and the Church suffers from this violence.

Part II

I. THE EASTER QUESTION

From the story of the fortunes of the Church in its first contacts with the thought of the Romano-Hellenistic world we turn to that of its own domestic life. The chief feature it offers to our study is that of its authority in action. What, better than all his predecessors, St. Irenæus had formulated in so many words is taught no less plainly by the practice of his own generation and the one which immediately follows. This section and the next describe the action of the seat of the *potentior principalitas* during the years 189–265.

The first series of events to be noted gathers round the question as to the correct date at which Easter should be kept. In Asia it was the practice to keep Easter on the 14th of the Jewish month Nîsan. At Rome, and generally, it was kept on the Sunday following the 14th Nîsan. The inconveniences due to the lack of uniformity were especially felt in Rome, and as early as 154 the Pope of the day—Anicetus—had endeavoured, but unsuccessfully, to win over the Asiatics in the person of their greatest bishop, St. Polycarp of Smyrna. There was a renewal of trouble in 167—this time at Laodicea. Then, in 190, the Pope St. Victor I resolved to impose the Roman usage uniformly. The resulting controversy is more important than the occasion which produced it.

The facts are simple enough. The Roman bishop wrote a letter to the Bishop of Ephesus—Polycrates—asking him to call together the bishops of Asia and rally them to the Roman usage. Polycrates obeyed in part, summoning the bishops, but he refused to abandon the use traditional at Ephesus. But it was not merely to Asia that the Pope had written. Similar demands had been sent to other provinces too, and these had unanimously agreed to follow Rome in the matter. Whereupon St. Victor notified the other churches that, for the obstinate adhesion to their own local custom he cut off the Churches of Asia from the communion of the Catholic Church. Immediately from all sides there were protestations against the severity of the decision and appeals for mercy—notably from St. Irenæus of Lyons. Whereupon the Pope withdrew the excommunication.

The historical significance of these facts is enormous. From the documents preserved we learn that this assembly of bishops at Ephesus is an unusual thing—nothing less than Victor's authority would have brought it about. Polycrates bases his refusal on the apostolicity of his own Church, its canon of faith. The conflict then is between rival Apostolic traditions. Rome does not argue, but instinctively orders—and the rest of Christendom, realizing Rome's right, can only pray Rome not to exercise it. Note also that it is not from the communion of the Roman Church merely that Victor claims the right to cut off these Asiatics, but from that of the Catholic Church.

II.   EARLY CONTROVERSIES ON THE TRINITY.
ST. HIPPOLYTUS

St. Victor I died about the year 198. His successor was Zephyrinus (198–217). With his reign begins a series of troubles that continue for half a century.

Associated with their beginnings is a cleric of the Roman Church who was later to succeed Zephyrinus, the deacon Callistus. Callistus had had an eventful life. As a slave he was unlucky enough to be a bad business man and lose his master large sums of money. His efforts to recover some of it from Jewish debtors led to them, in revenge, denouncing him as a Christian. Whence a period of penal servitude in the mines of Sardinia. About 190 he was set free, and the accession of Zephyrinus found him at Antium, a pensioner of the Roman Church. Zephyrinus brought him back to Rome, and for the next twenty-five years he was the chief figure among its clerics. He remained to the end a man of affairs. He was an administrator rather than a theologian. Nor was Zephyrinus more learned than his lieutenant—unfortunately, for the Roman Church was on the eve of a theological dispute that was to end in a local schism. If Zephyrinus and Callistus, the rulers, lacked taste for Theology and skill in its discussion, that was emphatically not true of a third personage of the Roman Church, the priest Hippolytus. In him (his writings have almost all perished) the Roman Church had a mind comparable to Origen, a genius with which, alas, there went an impatience of ignorance and a gift for rough and bitter language that recalled Tertullian—his contemporary.

The essence of the controversy that now broke over the Roman Church was the divinity of Christ. In what sense is the Logos God ? In what relation does the Logos stand to the Father ? Hippolytus had his learned theory which explained the difficulty and at the same time allowed for the traditional teaching that Logos and Father are God, that God is one and that the Logos is yet distinct from the Father. But to appreciate and to use that theory called for a trained philosophical mind, and even then a certain good will, if it was to be distinguished from the heresy that made the Logos a second, inferior God (Subordinationism).

What precipitated the crisis was the arrival in Rome of a visitor from Smyrna, Epigonus come to open a school of Theology. On this great question of the relation of the Logos to the Father, Epigonus (and his more famous successor, Sabellius) was a Modalist, i.e. he believed that neither the Fatherhood nor the Logos-ship were absolute divine realities. They were nothing more than temporary roles or modalities of the one, only divinity. Modalism had already met with objections—at Rome under Pope St. Eleutherius (177–189), at Carthage from Tertullian, and at Smyrna. The new school were careful to state their teaching in a more cautious phraseology. Also they gained a certain name as orthodox from their attacks on a second school of heretical theology, that of the followers of Theodotus the Tanner whom St. Victor had condemned but a few years before for teaching that Jesus Christ was no more than a man in whom God dwelt.

Hippolytus had fought against Theodotus and his adherents, and now Sabellius did the same. Whence, for the Roman authorities, a first impression that Sabellius, too, was orthodox, and thence, for Hippolytus (whose theories the authorities would not officially sanction), a disposition to denounce Zephyrinus and Callistus—in whom he professed to see the Pope's bad angel—as patrons of Modalism. Zephyrinus died in 217, and when Callistus was elected in his place the learned, and choleric, Hippolytus left the Church and set himself up as the true Bishop of Rome.

He is thereby the first anti-pope and remained such for nearly twenty years.

Callistus meanwhile condemned Sabellius, but he still refused to give official recognition to Hippolytus' theories. Whence a stream of bitter attacks from the disappointed theologian. On the other hand Callistus did not condemn his rival's theories, and if Hippolytus was not in communion with Callistus that was entirely his own work.

III. TERTULLIAN, ST. CALLISTUS AND THE PENITENTIAL DISCIPLINE

The schism of Hippolytus was not the only trouble Callistus had to face. He was the author of a change in the penitential discipline of the Church which drew down on him all the venom of Hippolytus and of Tertullian as well. The change inaugurated by the so-called "Decree of Callistus" is important and the grounds on which the Pope justified his action important too, for he gives as his authority Our Lord's words to St. Peter. (*Matt.* xvi, 18, 19.) To understand his action and the criticisms it produced we must review the whole history of the subject.

A power over the moral failings of the members of the Church was undoubtedly left by its Founder to the Apostles (*Matt.* xvi, 19; xviii, 18; *John* xx, 22, 23), and we have instances of how they used their discretion in the matter. (1 *Cor.* v, 2 *Cor.* ii.) A generation later, at the end of the first century, we can note a general acceptance of the idea—as an ideal—that baptism being of its nature unrepeatable the Christian should thenceforward keep intact the seal there received. The Church should be a community of

holy people. (*cf. Heb.* vi, 4, 8; x, 26–27; xii, 16–17.)
The witness of everyday life offered a contradiction
of fact to the ideal. There were Christians who
sinned and gravely. Did their lapses matter? According to one opinion, based on Gnostic theories of the gulf
between matter and spirit, not at all. But the more
prevalent opinion judged them with the utmost
severity. Here it is important to notice that current of
rigorist exaggeration in moral matters which, from the
very beginning, had a place in the Church—the
Encratites. These rigorists ignored the Gospel distinction between counsels and precepts and insisted
that the way of counsel was of universal obligation.
Especially were they rigorist in whatever related to
sex-morality, and they made perpetual continency
a condition of salvation. These exaggerations were,
in origin, partly Jewish, partly Gnostic, but they
undoubtedly affected many of the Christians of these
first generations. Nevertheless they did not represent
the official teaching. This finds its earliest expression
in the work of Hermas called *The Shepherd*.

Hermas was a priest of the Roman Church, brother
to St. Pius I (140–54), and *The Shepherd* was written
about 150. It is a practical treatise concerned with
salvation and conduct and its main thesis is that for
sinners who repent there is pardon. How strong was
the Encratite influence against which he wrote may be
judged from Hermas' insistence that his teaching is
that of the Church. No sin is so great that repentance
does not give the sinner a right to pardon. The
pardon, however, is not unconditional. The sinner
turns to God and God heals his soul. Between the
two terms of repentance there intervenes a series of
actions by which the sinner manifests his sorrow and

qualifies himself for pardon. And the forgiveness available through this system is only once available. Forgiveness for any repetition of the sin must be the private affair of the sinner with God. The Church's discipline will help him no further.

The elements of the like system are found in Clement of Alexandria and in Tertullian too. Tertullian's *De Penitentia*, instructions addressed to catechumens, teaches like Hermas, but less hesitantly, that there is a means of pardon for post-baptismal sin. He describes the rite in detail and gives it a name—*Exomologesis*. It is a laborious public act of penance in token of acknowledgement of sin, of repentance and desire for pardon. It involved a special dress—sackcloth; a special penitential regime of fasts and abstinence; relegation, while it lasted, to a special place in the assembly—among the *penitentes*. Tertullian has left us a moving picture of the repentant sinner under-going this discipline—prostrate at the door of the church, in sackcloth, ashes on his head, begging the faithful to pray for his forgiveness and amendment. The duration of the penitential period varied according to the sin. Its value was twofold. Of itself it was simply an offering to God in satisfaction for the wrong done. The Church intervening, associating herself with the offering, made it "efficacious," for the Church is Christ, and His prayer, His mediation, is infallibly efficacious. Some more details are known from Tertullian's later book *De Pudicitia*—an attack on Callistus for his innovations. Not all sins, we learn, are subject to this discipline. Three sins are so grave that whoever commits them the Church will not take it on herself to pardon, but leaves such sinners themselves to make their peace with God. They are admitted

to the Exomologesis, but never receive from the bishop
the official reconciliation. They are penitents for life
for whom the Church will do no more than pray.
The three sins in question are idolatry, murder and
fornication.   Moreover, it is still the rule that once
only can pardon be gained through the Exomologesis.

The origin of these reservations is obviously not
scriptural.   It is a matter of Church discipline and,
apparently, later than Hermas.   Whatever its origin
its stringency defeated its purpose.   Tertullian himself
witnesses to that.   Very few would offer themselves
for the public penance—whence a mass of anxiety and
uncertainty and hidden sinfulness.   Others found a
way out through the intercession of those about to die
for the Faith.   It had become the custom to remit the
public penance, wholly or in part, on their recommendation.

Pope Callistus' innovation consisted simply in this,
that for the future the system of the Exomologesis
would be available for sinners in matters of sex.
Such sinners upon performing due penance would be
readmitted to the communion of the Church.   Had he
degreed forgiveness without repentance Tertullian
could not have been more bitter.

Thirty years later the reservation was modified as
far as it regarded the sin of idolatry.   The new well-
organized type of persecution, official and systematic,
inaugurated by Decius (250-1), led to a host of apostasies, and thence to a serious dispute between the
episcopate and the confessors over the custom of
granting remission of discipline in consideration of a
confessor's recommendation.   The confessors began to
claim these remissions as a right.   *"Communicet ille cum
suis,"* ran a note received by the Bishop of Carthage,

St. Cyprian. St. Cyprian denied the right. Though confessors might, by custom, recommend such remissions it was still the bishop's prerogative to fix the conditions for the reconciliation of sinners. At Rome there were similar troubles, and the Roman Church, apparently, was inclined to be severe. Repentant apostates were not reconciled even on their death-beds, although they might be given Holy Communion. The Church would do no more than allow the supposition that God had forgiven them. They still remained outside her official forgiveness and reconciliation. Nevertheless the disposition to do something for the repentant apostate is evident. With Pope Cornelius it developed into a definite modification of the older practice. Cases of apostasy were to be treated on their merits. All were to be given a hope of reconciliation if repentant, at least at death. None were to be reconciled who refused the discipline of the Exomologesis.

IV. ST. CYPRIAN AND THE ROMAN PRIMACY

It was not merely with repentant apostates that Pope St. Cornelius had difficulties—a more serious trouble was the dispute with the African Primate, St. Cyprian himself. St. Cyprian, Bishop of Carthage, 248–258, was one of the time's most striking personalities. Born of a distinguished family, a highly cultivated man of the world, noted as an orator, wealthy, a wit—his conversion to the Church in middle life was a sensation in polite Carthage. He was henceforward as distinctly a saint as he had been a society figure, and from the first days of his election (which followed very soon on his conversion) a great bishop in every sense. For his ideas he is indebted

most to Tertullian, whom he cites at every turn—
though never by name. St. Cyprian is himself no
theologian, no philosopher.

His brief episcopate did not lack for events. It
saw two of the fiercest persecutions (Decius 250–1,
and Valerian 257–8), his own troubles with the
apostates and a succession of serious disputes with
the popes. The chief features of these must be noted
and their meaning made clear.

At the time when St. Cyprian's troubles with the
apostates were at the full the Roman See was vacant.
Its bishop, St. Fabian, had been martyred (January
20, 250), and, thanks to the persecution, his successor
was not elected for some fifteen months. For the
discontented among St. Cyprian's clergy this seemed
an opportunity by "working" the election of a pope
from the Romans of like mind with themselves, to
overthrow St. Cyprian and replace him with a bishop
who would be more amenable to the wishes of the
confessors. The priests from Carthage arrived then
at Rome, and, allied to the Roman clergy of their
own way of thinking, did their best to elect their man.
They failed. Cornelius (elected March 251) was,
as we have seen, of like mind with St. Cyprian.

The defeated faction proceeded to give him a com-
petitor, electing as bishop the most scholarly member
of the Roman clergy, Novatian. St. Cyprian sided
with Cornelius and thanks largely to his efforts
(especially with the "confessor" party in Rome) the
schism speedily lost much of its first prestige. It was
about this time that St. Cyprian published his treatise
On the Unity of the Church—a work concerned to plead
for unity in the local church, that in each church there
should be but one bishop, *practicé* that since Cornelius

was elected, Novatian, whatever his virtues, had no standing. St. Cyprian's mind here does not go beyond the fact of the innumerable churches that make up the Church Catholic, and he is concerned that in each of the local churches there should be unity. The weakness of a system that fails to provide a more objective unity for the Church as a whole St. Cyprian himself was to demonstrate in the next few years—and practically, by acts.

St. Cyprian's differences with Pope Cornelius began when Felicissimus, an insubordinate Carthaginian priest, one of those who had led the opposition of the "confessors," one of the conspirators responsible for the Novatian schism, and now excommunicated, set up a rival church, and, condemned now by the united African episcopate, appealed to Rome. "Their impudence took them across the seas, to Peter's chair, that chief of churches which is the source of episcopal unity," said St. Cyprian, and St. Cornelius gave them a hearing, intriguers whom, thought the African, he should never have allowed in his presence.

A sudden renewal of the persecution and the exile of St. Cornelius dissipated the cloud on his relations with St. Cyprian. With his next successor but one more serious trouble began. Two Spanish bishops accused of apostasy and other misdeeds had been deposed. One of them appealed to Rome and St. Stephen reinstated him. His people—and the successor they had elected—thereupon appealed to the bishops of Africa, and these when they met (autumn of 254) upheld the deposition. The rights and wrongs of the case as between the Spanish bishops and their accusers are not known. More important is the fact of this difference between St. Cyprian and "Peter's chair, that chief of churches." The occasion produced from St. Cyprian some strange new theology, e.g. that bad bishops are rightly deposed *by their flocks*, and this because a bishop's power of order is linked to his state of grace.

This affair of the Spaniards was still fresh when a second trouble arose. The Bishop of Arles was showing himself an extreme rigorist in the matter of reconciling repentant apostates—contrary to the decisions of 251. The Bishop of Lyons, in the name and at the request of the other bishops of that province, thereupon denounced him at Rome and at Carthage too. St. Cyprian, faced with a fact so inconvenient for his incomplete theory of unity as this of a legitimate bishop in open rebellion against the decision of the universal episcopate, did not act on his other theory that the bad bishop's flock should depose him, but wrote to the pope begging him to intervene and to bring about the deposition of the erring prelate. Finally would the Pope let him know the name of the new Bishop of Arles?

St. Cyprian's attitude in this matter is in keeping with the procedure traditional from the beginning— and in contradiction with all his own new theories. The final controversy of his life sees him back in his own confusion. The disputed point now was the validity of baptism administered by heretics. At Alexandria, in Palestine, it was considered valid. In Asia Minor, at Antioch, in Africa generally it was regarded as null. St. Cyprian asked by one of his people for a decision wrote elaborately defending the African view. He brought the question before the bishops of Africa when they met in 255 and wrote for the council its letter to the bishops of Numidia dealing with the point in the same way. Apparently the known difference between the Roman and the African practices was the occasion of troubles of conscience. The decision of the African bishops was not accepted universally—opposition began even among the bishops. From this controversy we gather that the practice defended by St. Cyprian was a novelty no older than thirty years. Nevertheless, the African council in 256 confirmed its earlier decision and St. Cyprian wrote to Rome to notify the Pope.

The Pope refused even to receive his envoys. They were looked on as heretics—possibly because Rome had already spoken and the African bishops were repeating the mistake of the previous year in the matter of the Spanish bishops. St. Cyprian—who the previous year had been claiming that the African practice was an article of faith—now proposed a compromise. Each bishop being supreme in his own diocese, let each decide for himself which practice he would adopt. The contradictions between St. Cyprian's action and his written theories are many. St. Stephen replied by a decision and an order in form—one of its phrases *nihil innovetur nisi quod traditum est* has ever since been one of the axioms of Catholic Theology.

St. Cyprian had written that he proposed to force no man's conscience, he would not lay down the law. For reply Rome gives him the command that for the future he is not to re-baptize heretics already baptized. St. Cyprian did not submit. He looked around for supporters outside Africa and found a mighty ally in the bishop of one of the chief sees of the East, Firmilian of Cesarea in Cappadocia, a one-time pupil of Origen. Firmilian replied in an anti-papal philippic more violent even than that in which St. Cyprian was now expressing himself. His letter is the last event of the controversy that has come down to us. The tension between Rome and Carthage, between Rome and Asia Minor, ended with the death of St. Stephen, August 2, 257. His successor Sixtus II did not press the point and the question was allowed to sleep. Just a year later St. Cyprian himself died—gloriously martyred, September 14, 258.

He does not show to advantage in these controversies —a practical man a little lost in these theological depths, irritated in proportion as he finds himself in ever deeper waters. There is much more in his life as a bishop, and in his writings—he is the Christian Latin stylist par excellence of the centuries before St. Jerome and St. Augustine—than these discussions reveal. He did not, apparently, see in the controversy on baptism anything more than a matter of discipline. Nor did his opponents. Nevertheless its implications went very far indeed. It implied the question of the validity of the sacraments, of the perpetuity of the power of order once truly possessed, and it raised for the first time the controversy, settled only in our own day, as to the respective spheres of the divinely ordained primacy of the Pope and that of the no less divinely ordained institution of the local episcopate. And, finally, from all sides the parties to the controversy witness to a passionate belief in the unity of the Church as something essential and traditionally so.

THE EARLY CHRISTIAN WRITERS

By the Rev. C. C. MARTINDALE, S.J., M.A.

I. THE FIRST POST-APOSTOLIC WRITERS

THIS lecture seems to me no easy one to write, because it is to deal with personalities rather than with general history or with details of doctrine. Now while a number of names are known to us, as of Christian writers or rulers having lived in the century immediately following the Apostolic Era, they remain but shadowy, even when the writings themselves, for which those who bore them were responsible, were important. Thus I cannot succeed in making an image for myself of St. Clement, whose period actually overlaps with the apostolic one, and whose Letter to the Corinthians is so valuable dogmatically because of its witness to the jurisdiction of the Roman See well outside of Italy and within the "Greek" world. The impression this letter made upon St. Polycarp, of whom we speak below, was so strong that he quotes it continually—forty or so quotations from it are said to be discoverable in Polycarp's sole Epistle to the Philippians. Clement was therefore no doubt a great man and a great Pope: it remains that he does not provide matter for one's visualizing faculty. For this first lecture, then, I have chosen three names only: Ignatius of Antioch, Polycarp of Smyrna, and Justin the first Apologist.

We know nothing of St. Ignatius save what we derive
from his letters, into the literary problem set by which
it is not my business to go. Enough to say that neither
the much abbreviated version nor the much padded
version is authentic, but the intermediate one must
be regarded as being so. His second name, Theo-
phoros, gave rise to the legend that he was the child
whom Our Lord took into His arms: it has its value
in that people felt his age was such as to have made
that possible. He certainly speaks as if he had been
converted in middle life, somehow violently, and had
till then led a life unworthy of the Faith, let alone of
his bishopric; but this may be due to his passionate
way of feeling and writing, which may indeed have
been intensified by, but not originated by, the strain
of his journey under arrest in Rome where he was to
be martyred. Incidentally, he could not have been
a Roman citizen, else he would not have been given
to the beasts. Persecution may have broken out in
Antioch about A.D. 100; he may have been its only
victim, anyway the only one it was worth taking to
Rome, allowing for expense and so forth. But he
does not allude to companion martyrs from Antioch,
though very many were picked up on the way: Rome
could not supply nearly all the human victims needed
for the arenas. The journey was a mixture of misery
and magnificence. He was brutally treated by his
escort, yet, like St. Paul and others, he was able to
receive visits from all the Christians who wished to
see him—and delegations came from even distant
towns, and he was able to keep one deacon, from
Ephesus, for quite some time, so helpful had he
proved. Also, he kept sending letters to the towns
he had passed through, thanking them, and begging

them to write to Antioch to congratulate it on the passing of the persecution. At Philippi, we lose sight of him. We can assume that his martyrdom occurred, certainly in Rome, about A.D. 110.

There are those who have called the style of St. Ignatius hysterical, as though an Asiatic nearly two thousand years ago ought to have talked like a modern Englishman. Of course it involves broken sentences, abrupt transitions from one thought to another, and indeed from one grammatical construction to another. It remains that his great theme, in all the letters save that to the Romans, is the unity of the Church and of the episcopate: when writing to Rome, he was no more giving urgent counsel to hot-headed Orientals, always in danger of schism, but pleading lest a cruel charity should rob him of his martyr's crown and somehow doom him by rescue.

Here is a sentence from his letter to the Ephesians— I translate so far as possible to exhibit the bishop's own style and curious choice of words.

"Yes, for Jesus Christ, our indisseverable existence, (is) the Thought of the Father, as also the bishops, those allocated unto the extremities (of the world), exist in the Thought of Jesus Christ. So it befits you to run together with the thought of your bishops, as indeed you do. For your praiseworthy college of priests, worthy of God, is indeed thus fitted to the bishop, as strings are to a lyre. And so in the oneness of your mind and harmonious love, Jesus Christ is being chanted. And become, each of you, a choir, that being one in voice owing to your oneness in mind, taking on the colour of God in oneness, you may sing with one voice through Jesus Christ to the Father."
. . . "Let no one be set astray! unless a man be inside

the Altar, he is deprived of the Bread of God. . . .
There is but one physician, flesh and spirit, begotten
and unbegotten, God made flesh, true life in death,
both of Mary, and of God, able at first to suffer and
then sufferingless, Jesus Christ, our Lord." And
again: "I am your 'refuse' (victims immolated on
behalf, e.g., of a town and cast away, could thus be
named; later on, the word lost its colouring and
became merely "your very humble servant" . . .), and
consecrate myself sacrifice on your behalf, Ephesians!"
"You are stones of the Temple of the Father, prepared
for the building erected by God the Father, carried
up to its topmost by the machine of Jesus Christ, which
is His Cross, making use, as a rope, of the Holy Spirit:
your Faith is your Crane and your love the track that
carries you up to God. So be, all of you, fellow-
wayfarers, God-carriers and temple-carriers, Christ-
carriers, holy-things-carriers, at all points decorated by
the commands of Jesus Christ." Now and again, he is
epigrammatic almost in the style of the *Imitation*.
"Better to be, and not talk, than to talk and not to be.
. . . He who truly possesses the Word of Jesus, can
understand also His silence. . . ."

In one obscure place he seems to speak of himself as
subject to gusts of indignation that distress him: "I am
in love with my Passion; but I know not whether I
may merit it. For the *zelos*—passion?—(that inflames
me) is invisible to the eyes of the many, but fights me
all the more." Certainly, when he thinks of heresy,
he expresses himself in a score of fierce rebukes.
Heretics are wild beasts in human form; ravishing
wolves; flowers of the devil; tombs, and the monuments over tombs; poisoned ointment; parasite branches
bearing fruits of death. . . . They "stealthily entangle

Jesus Christ by believing awry, as it were providing a deadly poison in honey-wine, so that a man unwittingly drinks death with delight and with perverted pleasure."

"Therefore be careful to make use of one only Eucharist; for one is the flesh of our Lord Jesus Christ, and one the Cup unto Communion of His blood, one altar, even as one bishop together with his priests and deacons, my fellow-servants."

But it is, naturally, his imminent martyrdom that also preoccupies him. In his letter to the Smyrnæans, he says (alluding to the Docetic heresy, that Christ was man only in appearance)—"If that be so, then am I only in appearance chained. Why, then, have I made and given myself over to death, to fire, to steel, to beasts? But near to the sword, near to God; in the midst of the beasts, in the heart of God—only, in the Name of Jesus Christ. I endure all, in view of co-suffering with Him, He giving me strength who became completely man." And to Rome, he writes as to the Church "on whom mercy has been shown in the mightiness of the Father Most High . . . church beloved and illumined by the will of Him who willed all things that are, according to the love of Jesus Christ, our God, church that sits first in the place of the region of the Romans, God-worthy, dignity-worthy, blessing-worthy, praise-worthy, good-fortune-worthy, holiness-worthy, and sitting first in the Love-Church, Christ-ruled, Father-named—Church whom I salute in the name of Jesus Christ." "For me," he proceeds, "it will be difficult for me to make sure ($\epsilon\pi\iota\tau\upsilon\chi\epsilon\hat{\iota}\nu$) of God, unless you spare me."

"Never shall I find such an occasion for making sure of God. If you speak no word about me, then *I*—

the Word of God! But if you love my bodily flesh too much, back I shall be, a mere voice. Let me free to be the food of beasts through which it is for me to make sure of God. I am the wheat of God, and by the teeth of beasts must I be ground, that I be revealed the pure bread of Christ." He asks that the beasts be caressed into leaving no fragment of his body . . . when the world shall no more see his body, then only will he be fully Christ's disciple. "The hour of my birth is upon me—have pity on me—do not fetter me from living; do not will that I should die . . . leave me to lay hold on the pure light—when *there* I shall have come, I shall be man at last."

Naturally it is impossible to offer you any adequate picture, in these few minutes, of the character revealed to us by these Letters which can recall, by their echoes, St. Paul at the one end and papal encyclicals at the other. For you to judge whether you feel a feverish love for martyrdom in what I last quoted: I might be tempted to; but I think I should be right in resisting that temptation. Ignatius lived at a great height of intensity, and his language was utterly sincere. It is indeed a change to turn to the quiet and solitary letter that survives from St. Polycarp. What we know of St. Polycarp is drawn less from his own surviving letter than from the account of his martyrdom that was sent out by the church in Smyrna to the Christians of a Phrygian town called Philomelion, with the intention that it should be communicated to those of the entire Church. However, a certain amount can be gleaned here and there that concerns him.

His martyrdom occurred at latest in 166, and far more probably in 155 or 156, at two in the afternoon of February 22 or possibly 23. His own allusion to

having served Christ for eighty-six years leaves us
still in doubt whether he was born of Christian parents,
and baptized at once, and was therefore, precisely
eighty-six years old; or whether he dates it from his
conversion, if he was a convert: but that would make
him very old indeed, and since he had only just made
a voyage to Rome, it seems strained to put his age
at near one hundred. We can assume, then, that he
was born about A.D. 70, which makes it quite possible
that he knew, or was even the disciple of St. John, as
has been often and perhaps usually maintained.

He can hardly have been a Jew; he practically
ignores the Old Testament, though quoting freely
from apostolic and sub-apostolic writings. He was
already bishop in Smyrna when St. Ignatius passed
through that town early in the century. St. Polycarp
and his Christians had, we saw, received Ignatius
with enthusiastic charity; Ignatius was so touched
that he wrote a long letter of affectionate advice to
Polycarp, of which the tone implies that the Bishop of
Smyrna was considerably younger than Ignatius—
Ignatius must have written many such letters to him,
since when passing through Philippi he had asked the
Christians there to send a letter to his own town of
Antioch, congratulating them on their faith and his
own martyrdom: the Philippians did so, and sent it
to Polycarp that he might forward it to Syria, begging
him also to let *them* read any letters that Ignatius might
have addressed to him.

Polycarp seems to have possessed a regular collection
of them, and added to his own reply "all" the letters
that Ignatius had written to him personally, and
others too that were in his keeping. His reputation
as time went on became so great as to be almost

fantastic: people regarded him as a sort of living relic of apostolic times and of such personal sanctity that there was a sort of rivalry to be in mere physical contact with him; during his martyrdom he tried to take his shoes off but could not, not only because he was old and very weak, but because his friends used simply to refuse to allow him to put them on or off for himself. . . . It was probably in 154 that he visited Rome, to discuss the topic of the date of Easter with the Pope. No decision was reached; but Pope Anicetus held him in such great honour that, says Irenæus, Polycarp's disciple, of whom we speak in the next lecture, he begged him to pronounce the words of Eucharistic consecration in his own presence and in that of the whole Roman Church.

The imperial authorities were seldom anxious to inaugurate persecution. They far preferred that accused persons, even Christians, should be found not guilty, precisely because the offence—refusing to worship the Emperor—marked a flaw within the perfect unity of the State, that is, the Empire. Perhaps there would have been no proceedings against the Christians in Smyrna at all, had not a certain Quintus fanatically produced himself to the authorities and denounced himself as a Christian and persuaded others to come with him, and had got them all arrested. It is noteworthy that the moment Quintus actually saw the wild beasts, his nerve deserted him, and the proconsul had no difficulty in getting him to offer incense. "Wherefore, brethren," said the Smyrnæans, "we cannot approve those who deliberately give themselves up: that is not what the Gospel teaches." The others had held firm: even when their bodies were so torn with the scourge that you saw the very veins and arteries, they uttered not one groan. You realized that they were absent from their bodies, or rather, that Christ was at their side: they were rolled on broken sea-shells; given to the beasts. The governors tried to make their torture last as long as possible. Maddened with the blood, the populace had cried out: "Death to the atheists! Find Polycarp!" Polycarp had wished to stay in Smyrna; they had persuaded him to retire to a small farm-house hard by; there, he waited placidly, praying night and day. One night, he dreamt that his pillow caught fire. "That means," said he, "that I shall be burned." They constrained him to go further into another country house; a slave, captured and tortured, revealed his whereabouts. Late one Friday evening, the mounted police found him, upstairs, having supper: he could still have escaped, but came down, talked pleasantly with them, insisted that they should have a good meal, and asked but that he might be allowed an hour for prayer, and, so overwhelmed were they by the sight of this sublime old man, that they left him praying, standing upright, for two hours, praying for all whom he had ever known, great or small, and for "the whole Catholic Church throughout the earth." Then they put him on an ass and took him back to the city. The governor and his father came out to meet them; they put Polycarp between them in their carriage, and tried to seduce him. "What harm *can* there be in offering incense and—the rest—and so saving yourself?" At first Polycarp said nothing: then he answered that he could not do what they asked. They furiously insulted him, and thrust him out of the carriage so violently that he scraped the whole of his shin. But he did not even hesitate, and walked rapidly forward, and they reached the stadium where there was such a noise that no one could hear what was happening. When they realized that he had been arrested, the noise redoubled. The proconsul asked him if he were indeed Polycarp, and he said that he was. Then he was ordered to renounce Christ, and call: "Away with the atheists!" He looked sadly at the frantic crowd, and sighed, and said: "Away with atheists!" "Curse Christ," said the proconsul, "and I will set you free." "Eighty-and-six years have I served Him," said the martyr, "and He has never done me wrong. How then should I blaspheme my King who has saved me?" The proconsul was urgent; let him but swear by "Cæsar's Luck." Polycarp said that the magistrate could not realize that he meant what he said—he was a Christian. If the proconsul wanted to know what *that* meant, let him allow him but one day, and he would explain. But to that ferocious multitude, it were idle to offer explanations. . . . The proconsul threatened to give him to the beasts: "Let them come," said the bishop. "If you despise the beasts, I have fire to burn you with. . . ." But why threaten a fire that burns but for an hour? You cannot realize what the unquenchable fires of hell shall be. . . . The words were stern; but the record says that throughout his long interrogatory, Polycarp was full of courage and good cheer; nothing could upset him or make him "collapse." Finally, a herald was sent out, who cried three times that Polycarp had owned to being a Christian. The crowd became quite delirious and shouted that Polycarp must be thrown to the beasts. The president of the games said that the wild-beast shows were over: they then demanded that the bishop should be burnt.

An enormous pyre was built all in a moment; Polycarp himself took off his clothes and it was now that he tried also to unloose his shoes and could not. They were about to nail him to the wood; but he said: "He who shall give me strength to endure the flames will also strengthen me so that I remain immovable at the stake, without being nailed." His hands, however, were tied to it behind him. He then prayed aloud and the fire was lighted. The eye-witnesses insist very strongly on what follows—the flames arched themselves, like sails swollen by the winds, and the martyr was seen standing upright in their midst. As though seized with a nervousness and fearing a reaction, the authorities ordered the "confector," whose business it was to kill criminals unable to die, to drive a dagger into him. He did so; and a torrent of blood poured from the wound. The fire went out; the Faithful were about to remove the body according to custom, but at the instigation of the Jews the body was refused to them, and burnt. These men, in their bitter and quite characteristic antagonism, had urged that the Christians would be capable of transferring their allegiance from Christ to Polycarp and worship *him*. "They did not know," says the record, "that never, never shall we be able to desert Christ, who suffered for the salvation of all who shall, throughout the world, be saved, sinless on behalf of sinners, nor yet worship any other. For Christ, being the Son of God, we do adore; but the Martyrs, being the disciples and imitators of the Lord, we love, and rightly, because of their insuperable devotion to their King and Master. May we together with them learn the same lesson and share the selfsame destiny." The bones of the martyr were then collected, "more precious than precious stones," more treasurable than gold, to put them where it should be appropriate. "There, so far as it may be possible, and with the Lord's help, we shall assemble in joy and gladness, to celebrate the Birthday" of the Martyr Polycarp.

We retain, therefore, the picture of this aged man, so simple, so loyal; so firm, so friendly; so able to win the passionate devotion of his Christian flock and to be felt as their supreme enemy by Pagan and by Jew, and yet so humble as he tries to loosen his shoe-strings, so strong when he refuses to be nailed. May he pray for us.

With St. Justin, you pass into a new world—the world of deliberate systematic defence of our Faith. Persecution, too, was becoming more self-conscious and thought-out. To refuse worship to the Emperor implied disloyalty to the State; moreover, Pagan imagination was becoming corrupted—fantastic tales were told about the Christians. There is a curious partial parallel in our own history: under Henry VIII, Catholics refused to admit the absolute Monarchy as having full spiritual power as well as civil, but so far, Catholics were not seen as *monstrous*. Under Elizabeth, the question of loyalty still existed, but grotesque legends about the Pope, Rome and Catholics were fastening on to over-heated brains.

Besides this, the Christians had to confront more definite attacks from philosophy, which at first had contemptuously passed by on the other side; and the false mysticism associated with the names "Gnostic" and "Neo-Platonist" had, though to a less degree, to be answered.

After Hadrian had enacted that none must falsely accuse a man of being a Christian, and that a trial must precede execution, a breathing-space seemed provided. As from about A.D. 125, "apologies," i.e. reasoned defences of Christianity, began to appear. But their authors remain shadowy: at most you can detect that some of them tried to stay on the purely philosophic terrain, and even kept the name of Our Lord so far as possible out of what they wrote; they tried just to show that the Christian ethic was harmless, in keeping with the best philosophic ideas, and even civically valuable. Others tried to turn the tables, and to mock at Paganism: this method never does much good, if any. But the movement can be summed up in St. Justin, born about 100, of Pagan parents, in Samaria, and beheaded in 167. He describes his intellectual history as a real travelling from one school of philosophy to another, and certainly I think he tried them nearly all. But they dissatisfied him. He found the Stoics "agnostic" about God; the Aristotelians, "on the make"; the Pythagoreans seemed to want him to know astronomy, music—every science, before he could contemplate the Good. Platonism got him furthest on his way. Then, says he, he met a mysterious old man who turned his mind to the Hebrew prophets: they were old, sublime, and full of strange foreshadowings of the future: moreover, the lives, and still more, the deaths of the Christians impressed him, and he adopted their faith. He did not, however, lay aside his academic dress, but opened a lay lecture-room in Rome, discussed the Faith with Jews and Pagans, wrote his two "apologies" (which he naïvely fancied the Emperor might read) about 150, and a dialogue with a Jew, Tryphon, about 152. None of this seems to have endangered him—perhaps the simple old man was not sufficiently successful. However, a Cynic philosopher is said to have been annoyed by him, and he denounced him. "If I scourge and behead you," asked the prefect, who really wanted to frighten Justin and his companions in chains, "do you really think you will go to heaven?" "Not only I think it; I know it." So they were all of them condemned, flogged and executed.

Without entering into any detail about Justin's method of defence, for that, as I said, lies outside my scope, I can just indicate its main line. He begins from a *fact*—the Christian Life. To be proved a Christian, says he, is to be proved *guilty*. But why? Not only, when a man becomes a Christian, do his general morals improve, but . . . he pays his taxes better; he is *more* loyal than many a Pagan always on the look-out for a new Cæsar. . . . Moreover, he insists again and again, Christians cast out evil spirits. Justin is nothing if not objective: he must have had some experience to convince him of that. The whole topic of "spiritualism" in the earlier Christian centuries, no less than in backward lands to-day, would bear much more looking into. In one place, he waxes hot: Christian worship and morality were accused of frightful horrors by the Pagans: no—it is the Pagans, he affirms, who practise openly what we are falsely accused of doing in secret, and he provides an invaluable description of the Holy Eucharist.

He starts then with an appeal to observable fact, and feels that this should not only prove to the authorities that they were not guilty, but should actually make them think well of the Christians: he was psychologically right thus to "prepare the will" before embarking on theological arguments. "God knows the mood," he says to the Jew, "in which you have put forward your difficulty!" When the Jews keep bursting into laughter whatever Justin says, he sees in that an *antecedent* contempt; when the Pagans condemned the Christians without evidence, that implied an antecedent hatred. No such mentality would ever understand!

Then he appeals to the accessible fact of prophecy. Neither he nor the contemporary Jew nor Pagan could "criticize" the Old Testament as we now do. He felt you could lay your finger on sheer predictions. Hence, while he believes in Our Lord's miracles, he uses them less—*you could not actually witness them*—save indeed, the supreme one, the conversion of so many, and their readiness to die for Him. "Who died for Socrates?" Hence he established definitely, and in face of a man like Celsus, the first anti-Christian systematic enemy of Christianity, who urged that the Faith was nothing else save faith, and a blind one at that—the great truth that Christianity can be defended *reasonably:* that though it *is* a Faith, and we receive it as taught, yet we *have reason* to believe the Teacher, and to be satisfied with results.

He proceeds to the Christian notion of God—above all, He is spiritual, and hence, should be worshipped spiritually, not as the Pagans did; and, of course, He is One, and polytheism stands condemned. He had not much difficulty here, for the world was coming round to a belief in a God who was one, of whom all else was at best a symbol or a name. But soon he embarks on the nature of Jesus Christ, and makes great use here of the well-known Greek term *logos*. In a word, *logos* meant the "plan" of a thing, either in the mind of the maker of that thing or as "incarnate," so to say, in the thing itself. Now God's Thought can be fully expressed (in one sense) in the Universe and fragmentarily in each part of it; and (in another sense) fully in Christ, and partially in any good man whatever. Hence he can actually say that the old philosophers, even when men called them atheists, were Christians before Christ, in so far as they possessed any fragment of truth at all. This, in the sober, unimaginative Justin, was really a great effort of the intelligence and imagination, and a true and happy audacity in speech. He is correspondingly severe on those who distort the traditional Faith; and rather caustically remarks that while Pagans profess to class heretics along with orthodox as "Christians," somehow it is, precisely, the heretics who don't get persecuted. I need not give further details about his actual work. First, he and his fellow Apologists at any rate disentangled the spiritual idea of God, and kept it free from Pantheism. Paganism could never manage that, save at the cost of severing God altogether from the world. Second, they made a bold attempt to state our Faith in terms of philosophy, even, of some one contemporary philosophy, but always correcting or amplifying the latter when it needed it. St. John had set the example by himself using the word Logos: St. Thomas was to pick up Aristotle and restate the Catholic religion in his terminology. Finally, all these men, but especially Justin, insist on the striving of God's Spirit in all parts of the world and of human history, yet so as always to work up towards Christ: their world, like St. Paul's, was Christocentric. These are permanent gifts to Europe and mankind. But if a Tatian, Oriental and detesting the supercilious Greeks against whom he argues, likes to flay them with his bitter onslaught; if a Minucius Felix offers honeyed bait to pagans and almost says that *cultured* folks will find very little to object to in Christianity, if only they will come and listen to him explaining it—Justin, a laborious, honest pioneer, unflexible, not subtle, but so courteous, so earnest in his request to be at least treated fairly, and so scrupulous in his fair treatment of others, Jews no less than pagan—Justin, then, with his transparent simplicity, has written what he thought might help his generation, but what is still of help, as well as of interest, for ours. Yet I expect he was glad when all that remained was to roll up his many parchments and to die for Him on whose behalf he had argued.

We pass in the next lecture to a very different set of men.

II. THE NEW GENERATION

My difficulty about the great figure of St. Irenæus is that which I experienced about St. Clement: I cannot visualize him. And since this paper is not intended to contain mere lists of books, nor, what is far more important, a coherent statement of doctrine drawn from them, I cannot treat Irenæus as he deserves. We cannot, however, pass him over, because, after all, he was a man who at last tried to take a comprehensive survey of the Christian Faith and the Catholic Church, and did not write only as occasion suggested, in the way in which we have seen Polycarp and Ignatius writing; and even the kind of *scheme* we made of Justin's work was built up out of his writings rather than built *them*.

There was, however, an "occasion" because of which Irenæus wrote—a man does not do the kind of work that he did, all in the air. A theory, or system, or religious tendency existed on a very large scale, which opposed itself quite definitely to Catholic orthodoxy. This was Gnosticism. There has always been a sort of human instinct towards breaking through the limitations that appear normally to be imposed upon us. Thus we all agree that a man should free himself to some extent from the tyranny of the senses and lead an intellectual life. The man who scorns ideas, who can attach no spiritual values to anything, is, we feel, a limited man, even, a humanwise crippled man. But there have also always been those who want to escape beyond the frontiers even of ideas, however clear and abstract: they are in search of some more direct intuition or vision of reality than what even artistry can give them. The true artist probably aches with woe when he perceives the parody which the work that he has done provides of the thing as he has thought it, let alone of the elusive reality as intermittently he visions it. All the various schools of Gnostics professed that their ideal was some such sort of vision, and that they could provide a method by which it could be achieved. This method was usually one of asceticism, and a progressive denial of the value of material things—e.g., food, especially meat, or marriage. There was a double tendency— either to practise an extreme austerity, so violent that a no less violent reaction followed it; or, to declare that your body was not really "you," so that what it did could not matter; the divine spark, your Real Self, within you was what alone you need trouble about. A convenient doctrine for those who wanted the best of both worlds, or of all three—the world of sense, that of intellect, and that of mystical union with the "really Real," the One. Two consequences that concerned Christianity followed from this. First, men became, really, individualists. Each followed his lonely path towards the Divine. Second, the Gnostics quite allowed that "religion"—*any* religion—could be a valuable discipline for second-rate people, and that each religious system had a symbolical value, but no more. This is pretty well what modern Theosophy teaches, though no more vulgar a misuse of ancient and sometimes venerable ideas than it is can well be imagined. Now historical Christianity, however much it may lead up to a supernatural destiny of direct Vision of God, is essentially an authoritative Teaching, is primarily a collective *Didache*, not an individual *Gnosis*. And it claims to be unique, by no means just symbolical, and, as a divine revelation, final. It was this that Irenæus confronted.

He was a much-travelled and a singularly "all-round" man. Palestinian, Asiatic, Greek, Roman and even Gallic elements entered into his composition, for about 180 A.D. he became Bishop of Lyons. He knew, by experience, the facts; and also, true to his name, the Pacific, he wanted to reconcile opposing parties and to get rid of quarrels based on misunderstandings. Therefore he did not merely attack the Gnostics, proving that they were wrong. He aimed at exhibiting the Truth, the whole Truth organically interconnected within itself, all its origins, its parts, and its consequences in a beautiful and living whole. Certainly the task was, and at any time would be, colossal, and probably beyond the force of the intelligence of any one man. He supplies then a mass of material, by no means accurately distributed or elegantly ordered, but a solid foundation none the less for almost all that came afterwards. His work is like a very fine, strong piece of architecture, overlaid with a quantity of very bad decoration, much of which should fall off, given time, or could be chipped off without any harm to the building. To my mind, what is so valuable is his sense of vital continuity between Christ, the Apostles, and contemporary Catholic authority. Substantially, this is what he says: "If you want to know what Christ says, which is what God says, enquire from the bishops. And since it would be interminable to wander round whole scores of dioceses, go to Rome, with which everyone from anywhere has to agree." There you will get the Christian teaching, which, he insists, is that of the Incarnate God, in its totality, and without need of further comparisons. I know well how scholars have struggled to elude the manifest implications of this; but I fear that their translations are bad, and their deductions due to an unconscious determination that Romanism shall not have existed so early. Yet it did. The historical foundations, walls, and roof of Roman Catholicism are solid.

It remains then that Irenæus attempted two things that were difficult: he tried to present his Faith as a whole, and an authoritatively "given" whole, and to retain and foster kindliness in regard of his adversaries without ever compromising. I do not mean that (e.g.) Justin was harsh; but plenty of religious controversialists both had been and were destined to be so.

Titus Flavius Clemens of Alexandria in Egypt makes a bridge between those whom we have thus far mentioned, especially St. Justin, whom however intellectually he transcended, and the Africans, of whom below. He may have been born about 150 A.D., possibly in Athens. Thence, anyhow, his mental pilgrimage is said to have begun. It took him, even after his conversion to Christianity, from Asiatic Greece to Sicilian Greece, to Syria, to Egypt, to Assyria, to convert Palestinian Jews, for his higher instruction. Finally, he settled in the enormous, commercial, cultured, speculative and vicious city Alexandria. Both the Jews and the Christians of that city had for long had an "allegorizing" tendency which was the exact opposite of, for example, the more eastern schools to which men like St. Basil and the two St. Gregories were to belong: these were literal, realist and scientific. Clement was trying, not always with success, to follow the most difficult course of all—a middle one—he wanted to be as sympathetic as possible with Pagans (who were actually admitted to the lecture-rooms that he shared with his master Pantænus) without succumbing either to them or to the semi-Paganism and fusion of ideas proper to Gnosticism. His probably earliest writing is an "Exhortation to the Greeks." He freely uses their mythology—Amphion and Arion sang so sweetly that they drew after them the beasts and the very stones; but Christ sang sweetlier still, with men's souls for His harp from which by the Holy Spirit He draws the perfect music—nay, Himself He is the perfect Song. Clement then seeks to prove this, by showing the poverty of Pagan guesses and dreams compared with Christianity. Much that he wrote has perished: his " Miscellanies" may not be much more than a collection of notes for his lectures, though the theory running through them is, that Truth is given wholly to man through Revelation, but also, in a different way, and in part, through sheer reasoning—Philosophy.

He who would be the "perfect Gnostic"—the true Know-er—must be the perfect Christian. He carries

H

on, in his own way, those passages of St. Paul where the Apostle keeps praying for his converts an ever-deeper Knowledge of their Faith—Paul was "sensing" already the imminence of Gnosticism. His other great work, the "Tutor" ("pedagogue" was a word emigrating from its original meaning—the person (usually a slave) who accompanied lads to school, and had more or less continual care of them—towards what we more definitely mean by "Tutor"). Christ was the soul's tutor; no detail of man's life was beneath His notice; His method is orderly and calm. Thus the Christian character is formed. This shows, maybe, that Clement was morally sympathetic as well as intellectually so; and his treatise on the Rich Man who Can be Saved insists in its turn on the fact that wealth is not bad in itself: all depends on the use you make of it.

In 202, persecution broke out: men under instruction to be Christians were legislated against with separate severity: at last Clement was persuaded to flee; he went to Cappadocia where an ex-pupil of his was bishop, but in prison. Clement shepherded the Christians, but died before 215 or so, when the bishop, Alexander, then released, alluded to him in terms that prove that he was no more alive. Clement's reputation has suffered severely: his name was indeed removed from the Martyrology on the advice of Baronius. He should not at any rate be criticised for having used inaccurate language about the Holy Trinity or the Person of Christ, since the controversies properly concerned with these had not yet ripened.

What one must confess is, that he succumbed to the Alexandrian allegorizing school far too completely, at least so far as the Old Testament was concerned; that he was coloured with Stoicism in that the Christian calm he praised seems all too like an annihilation of the passions rather than their control; and that he went too near Gnosticism in his distinction between the faith of the enlightened Christian and that of the average God-fearing orthodox man. But it was his sympathy and desire to see the best in things that made him run this risk, and I think that he went wrong, if at all, verbally rather than really. Not that he was not bold.

The Greek Mysteries deserve a paper to themselves. They were at all points different from the Christian Mystery. They imposed a ritual purification on the neophyte; then, a preliminary initiation, and then promised an enlightenment which should stand the soul in good stead in its journey through the underworld, at the end of which it should become a god. But this whole process was mechanical and magical— what you became depended wholly on the ritual things you had done: no new ideas were conveyed by the Mysteries; still less was any theology about the nature of the soul's union with God provided. Clement audaciously took the terminology of the Mysteries, put new meanings into it till it suited Christianity, and offered the triple series (Purification: Enlightenment: Union) as the route of the Christian's Godward Progress. One meets in him an audacity not less than St. John's and St. Justin's in their adoption, and adaptation, of the expression *Logos;* and a charm that exceeds the naïve attractiveness of Justin, as that of a modest, yet cultured man can exceed that of one honest, yet less urbane. It is a pity that his disciple Origen has almost quite eclipsed him, as the dazzling snow-clad Alps can eclipse the more modest foothills, with their fragrant vegetation and their wild flowers.

The writers we have mentioned wrote in Greek. Latin Christian literature was inaugurated by Tertullian, who was, as we could expect, an African. For the centre of gravity of Latin literature had shifted somewhat earlier to Spain, and thence back to the north African coast. Here an extraordinary diction had formed itself, of which the best examples are Appuleius and Fronto. They used the *elocutio novella* —a strange development of Latin full of rhymes and assonances and dainty diminutives and boldly invented or modified words. This African-Latin reached, shorn of its affectations, a high state of perfection in St. Augustine, and in fact in him and St. Jerome had produced a real non-hybrid Latin which had but little to do before it turned into the sonorous splendid Latin of the medieval hymns. Tertullian wrote it, only harshly, almost savagely, in keeping with his temperament. Born about 160 at Carthage of military parentage, and having become a lawyer, he stamped his personality upon his writings; for, having lived as a Pagan till middle-life, indulging in the fierce vices of that scorched and violent land, when he became a Christian he conceived of his religion as a Warfare, and a Law. The Christian fought, and obeyed. Hitherto it had been conceived of as a Knowledge— anyway as something for the Mind. A whole new mood, with its appropriate metaphors, was provoked among Christians: attention gravitated from the intellect to the will, from ideas to behaviour. The colossal Carthaginian, Augustine, whose brain was quite big enough to contemplate all sides of truth, leaned definitely to the arena where Grace and Will fought out their struggle and made their happy marriage.

Who knows why, Tertullian became a Christian about

190, and at once embarked on a fierce but legally-drawn-up indictment of the Pagans. He put the Pagans definitely on trial. . . . In refuting charges against the Christians he turned the tables on themselves. "You say Christians adore a semi-ass, semi-goat god—such is the caricature colported by a Jew. They do not: but you *do* adore beasts and semi-beasts. Look at Egypt!" He tried to write serener works in defence of his Faith: but again invective bursts out; a fine but clattering rhetoric cannot be suppressed; epigrams rattle off like machine-guns. Terse as Tacitus (and not less obscure for very brevity) he can yet roll off magnificent phrases like a military march. His great book is on Heresies, and how they have no *right* to be listened to.

About the year 200 we begin to detect in him an austerity too severe to remain well-balanced. His treatise on the Theatre, to which he urged that a Christian could not possibly go, was perhaps justifiable in his day, and anyhow gorgeous denunciation. His pages on women's dress are superb: if men, to-day, denouncing fashions, were only half as funny, they might be more effective. But you begin to see that his appeal to his wife not to marry again, should he die, is leading up to his later idea that second marriage was but fornication. At last, you see him turning towards the Montanists, a sect believing in individual inspiration and rejecting all Church discipline, and preaching a fierce asceticism, and denying that all sins could be forgiven.

In 211 or a year or two later he definitely apostatized. He writes a whole pamphlet to show that a Christian soldier cannot wear a wreath, and indeed that no Christian can be a soldier. He calls the

Montanists "spirituals," and the Catholics mere
"psychics." He sneeringly rejects all philosophy—
Philosophers are the Patriarchs of Heretics. After a
while he left the Montanists and founded a sect of his
own, the relics of which were received back into the
Church by St. Augustine. He died, very old, and
unreconciled. His was a great tragedy. He was
undoubtedly a genuine Christian: his earliest work is
the best. Some of his epigrams, like the immortal
Anima naturaliter Christiana, Credo quia impossibile, are
imperishable: future generations would quote him,
taking care not to name him. At least, he is an invaluable witness for what the Catholic Faith of his
days really was at worst; he was a headstrong, em-
bittered, individualist who, quite possibly under stress
of unwarrantable criticisms, turned against the Church
the very weapons that he had denounced the Pagans
for condescending to use against her.

The far less feverish Cyprian of Carthage, converted
about 246, was his disciple. Wealthy patrician, cultured and open-minded, he smoothed Tertullian's
jagged style and turned, so to say, his diamonds into
opals. He too was over-stern, and disallowed the
validity of baptism by heretics and joined issue over
that with the contemporary Pope (who, as always,
was right). Yet they died friends, both of them
martyrs, and there was nothing to cause an ultimate
rupture save Cyprian's characteristically African tendency towards (i) nationalism, and (ii) individualism.
It is impossible for me here to indicate how this
African current swept the Western world towards
St. Augustine.

It would take me beyond all due limits if I spoke
of Origen, successor of Clement, successor of Justin,

somewhat as Cyril of Alexandria stepped into the shoes of Athanasius as he did into those of Origen. His too was a tragedy, and much less deserved than Tertullian's. What I have tried to do is to exhibit some *men*, whom we know hardly at all save by their *books*, and to indicate the nature of their work, but even so, subordinating what they did to what they were. The history of dogma is grateful for the books: those who are fond of, anxious about, hopeful for mankind may feel even too forcefully drawn to attend to the men, who lived, thought, made efforts, were tormented—not worst by the persecutor's engines, but too often by themselves, their temperament, their restive souls—or who, again, by the Grace of Christ surmounted all these things. Do not allow yourselves to think of the living Church as an affair of this century or that; of the New Testament, or of Pius XI, or of the thirteenth century or of the Renaissance. May the flow of her life, which is Christ's, be discerned within the growing of her body, which is also Christ's. May never your idea of the Church be that merely of an organization, a very large and very ancient sect. It is the Living Vine, from which some tendrils, alas, have been snapped off, while others have borne rich clusters: the Temple, of which some columns, alas, have fallen, whereas others stand upright and support the whole, among which, please God, shall be you.

PAGANISM AND CHRISTIANITY: LEGAL RELATIONS

By the Rev. Paulinus Lavery, O.F.M., B.A.

A study of the legal relations between Paganism and Christianity during the Pre-Nicene period may well be considered as part of the ever-present question of the relations between Church and State, but with this accidental difference, that the Church in this period did not show externally in the same degree those attributes and qualities by which it could be easily recognized as a complete and independent society. This study, then, necessarily entails some consideration of the general attitude of Roman civilization towards the newly-founded religion of Christ. It is a difficult matter to determine, largely owing to the vagueness of contemporary literature on the subject, and it is necessary to presume that later writers who deal with this subject are presenting substantially the same ideas as existed one hundred years before.

It is in reference to the beginnings of the persecution of the Christian community that we get our first inklings of the official attitude to Christianity. Before the time of Claudius no direct act of Roman officialdom against the Christians is recorded; on the contrary, Felix and Festus showed themselves to be rather favourable than otherwise (*Acts* xxiv, 6). In Rome itself the Christians seemed to enjoy the same status and privileges as the

Jews. Claudius expelled the Jews from the city because of disturbances which had arisen (Suetonius, *Vita Claudii*, 25, 4), and some Christians were involved in this exile. There is no doubt that in the popular mind there was a good deal of confusion of the Christians with the Jews,[1] and this confusion was to be found as late as the reign of Domitian, who, according to Dio Cassius, was moved to persecute the Christians because of their adoption of Jewish ways of life.

Contemporary or almost contemporary writers refer to them as *"invisos per flagitia,"* *"sontes et novissima exempla meritos"* (Tacitus, *Annales*, 15, 44), *"genus hominum superstitionis novæ ac maleficæ"* (Suetonius, *Vita Neronis*, 16, 2); their religion Tacitus calls *"exitiabilis superstitio,"* their Founder put to death by order of a Roman Procurator. But the real causes of suspicion of the Christians at this time could hardly differ greatly from those alleged against them in the second century and so well described by Tertullian in his *Apologeticum* and Minutius Felix in his *Octavius*. They may be summed up as follows.

Two general considerations: conversion to Christianity meant a real change in one's mode of life, a necessary withdrawal from society and attendance at theatres, public spectacles, etc.; secondly, the ceremonies of Christianity were little known, conducted secretly in the early morning and in the evening, and therefore very liable to an interpretation that they were superstitious. These two general conditions would both tend to bring suspicion on the Christians. Specific calumnies were divided into public crimes such as atheism, that the Christians were the cause of public calamities, and that they were unprofit-

[1] Tertullian, *Apologeticum*, xxi, 1.

able members of society, and private crimes, amongst which were numbered infanticide (Thyestian banquets), incest and adoration of an ass's head. It can be easily seen how belief in these accusations could breed suspicion, hatred and fear of the Christians as a secret sect, lacking in respect to the Emperor, especially at a time when there was a distinct tendency to increase the divine prerogatives of his person. It was in such an atmosphere and in such circumstances that the Christians were first subjected to persecution, and official action, raising the question of a legal basis for that action, began. The actual motives which initiated the First Persecution are rather difficult to determine. The general idea is that Nero, sensing that he himself was suspected of being responsible for the burning of Rome, diverted the suspicions of the people from himself to the Christians, but the problem is not material to our subject.

We have to discuss and endeavour to determine under what law or laws this persecution was effected. It is a complicated problem which still remains unsolved as far as all persecutions of the Christians are concerned up to the time of Decius (249–51). From then onwards we have clear and definite legislation, largely by imperial decrees, which leaves us in no doubt as to the juridical status of the Christian community. We shall consider the problem as it presents itself under Nero and his successors, and then the legislation from Decius onwards.

The question may be stated thus: Were the Christians persecuted under ordinary criminal justice or by the coercive power of the magistracy? Criminal justice here means laws already made with acts contemplated to come under them without any direct reference to the Christians at all. To put such laws in force the ordinary processes of law (*delatio, cognitio, sententia*, etc.) were necessary. The coercive power of the magistracy signifies the power enjoyed by the magistrates of punishing a crime immediately without any formal process. It is a form of summary justice and was governed by no fixed legislation but rather was left to the discretion of the officials. These, then, were the alternative solutions: ordinary criminal justice or the coercive power of the magistrates.

Until the beginning of the present century the general opinion was that the Christians suffered under the processes of ordinary criminal justice, but in the year 1900 Mommsen advanced the theory about the coercive power of the magistrates. Harnack accepted this theory, but Callevaert opposed it strongly. There is little or no evidence to be found in favour of this theory in the writings of Tertullian, who, of course, in his *Ad Nationes* and above all in his *Apologeticum*, must be considered one of the chief authorities regarding the legal basis of the persecutions. Its chief support is to be found in the famous letter of Pliny the Younger addressed to the Emperor Trajan about the year 112, and Trajan's rescript. Supporters of this theory argue that Pliny was concerned about the Christians, not so much because they were Christians, but because of their disobedience in refusing to sacrifice to the gods (cf. his statement "*Perseverantes duci iussi*"). On the other hand the letter makes it quite clear that they had also to speak evil of Christ, which, of course, involved far more than mere external conformity with the official Roman sacrifices.

Again, it is argued that Pliny, in proposing his doubts to Trajan, used the expression "*non modicum hæsitavi*," which would imply that the matter had been left to his discretion, and that it was therefore a question of coercive power. But one can trace in the mode of procedure which he describes the various acts mentioned above which formed the normal process of criminal justice and would be absent in the exercise of the magistrates' power. Finally they use a very strong argument from Trajan's rescript, viz., "*Neque enim in universum aliquid, quod quasi certam formam habeat, constitui potest*," implying that the whole matter was to be left to the discretion of the officials. Whatever we may think about the force of these arguments, it is clear that those who hold this opinion are not faced with any further difficulties, as the question is sufficiently answered if one admits the coercive power of the magistrates to have been the legal basis of the persecutions.

If, however, it is maintained that the Christians were persecuted under ordinary criminal justice, a further question presents itself. Was it by force of some common law already in existence or by a law specially directed against the Christians? For a long time the general opinion was that it was by some common law such as the *Lex Iulia maiestatis*, which was aimed against anything which in any way endangered the safety of the Roman people. The profession of Christianity could also be easily considered as the *crimen læsæ religionis* or the *crimen læsæ augustæ maiestatis*. However, many authorities, as Allard, Callevaert, Duchesne and Leclercq, maintain that there was some special law directed against the Christians, as witness Tertullian's "*Non licet esse vos*" or "*Christiani non sint.*" The upholders of both opinions unfortunately rely largely on the same source for their arguments, Tertullian's

Apologeticum, so that it is difficult to see how any finality of judgement can be secured.

There is another opinion about the legal basis of the persecutions, put forward by Prof. A. Profumo, which is not widely known but certainly deserves serious consideration.[1] According to Tacitus in his *Annales* the Emperor Tiberius, who was well versed in law, set up a certain juridical institute. In this he was actuated by political motives and directed this institute against the Patricians and against the very large number who were coming from the east and were affected by superstition (in the Roman legal sense) or who might be considered anti-imperialistic. This institute linked together with an indissoluble bond three laws which were already contained in common law and which, by the force of this institute, constituted a juridical unity. This triple class of laws was made up of (1) the *Leges Sumptuariæ* against crimes of immorality, harmful superstition, excessive luxury, etc.; (2) the *Lex Iulia de Peculatu* against crimes referring to religion; (3) the *Lex Iulia de Maiestate*, a law of very wide application which related to anything which might in any way endanger the Emperor or the Roman people. As will be noticed these laws referred respectively to domestic life, religious life and public life. This institute was not a new written law, but rather a system or juridical form (process of legal procedure), and, according to Profumo, that was the precise meaning of an *institutum*. As a result it was not to be found in the codes of law, though it had the same force as a law. Tacitus alludes to other institutes in his *Annales*, II, 14, as does Tertullian in *Apologeticum*, VI.

[1] Cf. Attilio Profumo: *Le Fonti e i Tempi dello Incendio Romano*, Roma, pp. 229.

The effect of this particular institute was this, that if anyone were found guilty of an offence against one of the three classes of laws, whether by confession or otherwise, he was immediately guilty of offence against the other two in the eyes of the law. The reason for this was to be found in the fact that, in the mind of the legislator, violation of any of these laws denoted a state of mind opposed to the existing order of things and anti-imperialistic. As regards its history, Tiberius was its author. After his reign it was not enforced by Caligula nor by Claudius nor even in the first years of Nero's reign. It was revived by the latter about the year 62 and was the basis of the persecution of the Christians till the time of Septimius Severus. The very nature of the institute explains how it was that, though all the acts of Nero were rescinded after his death, persecution could continue, for the institute was one of the acts of Tiberius and was therefore not revoked. It also explains the lament of the Apologists that the law was not administered fairly in that it was only put into operation against them and not against the Pagans, though they were equally guilty of offences against it.

That concludes our brief exposition of the various theories about the legal basis of the persecutions. The question is certainly a very difficult one, and it is quite impossible to give a definite solution. The more probable opinions at the present time seem to be the existence of a special law or Profumo's theory.

We pass now to a consideration of the actual legislation of the emperors regarding Christianity before the year 249. Persecution under Domitian was due most probably to causes which would be most easily explained as coming under the *Institutum Tiberianum.*

He was the first Emperor to assume divinity during his life. Rome had been deified and he considered himself the *Vicarius Deæ Romæ*. Thus failure to practice the Roman religion could be much more easily construed as an act, not only against religion, but also of lèse-majesté towards the Emperor. Under his successor, Trajan, the position of the Christians was clarified, particularly by the rescript of the Emperor to Pliny. It was certainly not a very clear piece of legislation and was inspired largely by motives of expediency. Tertullian sums it up in the words *"O sententiam necessitate confusam!"* and gives full play to feelings of righteous indignation in his commentary on it. Yet it is of extreme importance for the history of the persecutions. There it was laid down that Christians were not to be sought out nor were anonymous lists of supposed Christians to be accepted in the tribunals. Probably Trajan did not regard Christians as a danger to the State and further wished to calm down the feelings of the populace against them. One effect of the rescript, however, was to give pardon to those who denied the Faith. Before this time denial of the Faith after conviction was useless: now, on the other hand, apostasy meant also freedom from any penalty. Hadrian followed more or less the same trend of legislation in his rescript (dated about 124–5) addressed to Minutius Fundanus, Proconsul of Asia. In it he defined (i) that it was not lawful for Christians to be brought to judgement by a tumult of the people ; (2) that accusers of the Christians had to prove their accusations; otherwise they laid themselves open to the penalties for false accusers.

Antonine the Pious certainly sent some rescripts in the same sense as the rescripts of Trajan and Hadrian,

but there was no change in the juridical status of the
Christians under him nor under his successor, Marcus
Aurelius. The decree attributed to the latter (*Dig.*,
XLVIII, tit. 19, 11, 2) is too vague to be considered as
applying to the Christians only, but seems rather to
be a general act of legislation against superstition.
It is true that Tertullian refers to Marcus Aurelius
as a protector of the Christians, largely, it would seem,
because of the alleged miracle of the production of
the rain.[1] It is possible, however, that he is thinking
of the fact that Marcus Aurelius increased the penalties
for false accusers (not specifically of Christians), an
act which would indirectly benefit the Christian community by making people more chary of bringing
accusations against them.

There is nothing relevant to our subject in the reigns
of Commodus and his successors until we come to
Septimius Severus. His legislation was directed, not
against the Christians as such, but against those who
desired to become Christians. In or about the year
202 he issued a rescript forbidding anyone to become a
Jew or a Christian (Ælius Spartianus, *Vita Severi*, 17, 1).
This was the first direct prohibition of a change from
paganism to Christianity; circumcision and its implications had frequently been the subject of legislation.
The immediate result of this rescript was the dispersal
of the Catechetical School of Alexandria and the
martyrdom of SS. Perpetua, Felicitas and their Companions, who were all catechumens at the time of their
apprehension.

From this time onwards to the accession of Decius
there followed a long period of quiet and peace for
the Christians, due in great part to the desire of the

[1] Cf. *Apologeticum*, ed. Rauschen, Bonn, 1912, p. 25, n. 5.

so-called Syrian emperors for religious syncretism. During this period Christianity influenced, rather than was influenced by, the imperial authorities, as we shall see later.

Decius became Emperor in the year 249. Fired by a genuine patriotism which urged him to restore the unity of the Empire by bringing the Romans back to the altars of their fathers, he decreed that all Christians should sacrifice to the gods and written testimony to the fact of this sacrifice having been performed was to be obtained. Those testimonies, known as *libelli sacrificationis*, which have come down to us, do not show clearly in any instance whether the person concerned was a Christian. The penalty for non-observance of this decree was torture, imprisonment or even death, and it constitutes the first piece of legislation under which we know the Christians to have suffered. From Decius to Diocletian it is a mere matter of mentioning the anti-Christian legislation. In 257 Valerian issued a decree (to be found in the Proconsular Acts of the Martyrdom of St. Cyprian), directed chiefly against the clergy, but it has a special interest for us in that it forbade entrance into the cemeteries, a question which will arise later. His second decree, of 258, was very much more severe and imposed the death penalty on the clergy, the higher ranks of nobility, and confiscation of goods and degradation for other classes if they refused to retract their religious tenets. All goods, land and cemeteries confiscated under Valerian were restored by a decree of Gallienus.

Finally, we come to Diocletian, the last of the great persecutors of the Church, a man in himself allied to justice and right, yet tenacious of Roman traditions

I

and principles. Swayed by the enemies of Christianity he issued a decree in the year 303, ordering the destruction of Christian churches, the burning of the Scriptures, the degradation of the higher ranks of Christians, the reduction of the plebeians to slavery and the denial of the right of manumission to slaves. A second decree ordered that all bishops should first be cast into chains and then compelled to sacrifice to the gods; a third offered liberty to all prisoners provided they would sacrifice; otherwise they were to be subjected to great tortures. The fourth and final decree, similar to that of Decius, ordered that all Christians in every part of the Empire should be compelled, under pain of death, to sacrifice to the gods. This persecution continued, at least in parts of the Empire, long after Diocletian had retired, and did not come to an end until the issue of the edict of Galerius, in association with Constantine and Licinius, in the year 311. Maximin Daza, although he ceased open persecution, did all in his power to restore the Pagan religion. He also tolerated secret persecution of the Christians up to the very eve of the issue of the Edict of Milan, when a letter from Constantine impelled him to send a rescript to Sabinus in favour of them. The edict of Milan is the last imperial legislation of note which we shall consider, but we shall defer examination of it to the end of this lecture.

So far we have considered the legal relations between Paganism and Christianity only in direct reference to the persecutions. We shall now pass to other points which present a certain amount of difficulty in this same period.

The phrase "The Church of the Catacombs," though perhaps a picturesque way of speaking of the

Early Christian Church in Rome, has little historical basis and has often led to the impression that the Christians almost habitually used the catacombs as places of worship. In fact it was only in times of the very severest persecution that that was so. Normally the Sacrifice of the Mass and other meetings of the Christians were celebrated in the houses of the more wealthy members of the community. In Rome one thinks immediately of the house of Pudens (now S. Pudenziana), the house of Clement (S. Clemente) and the house of Pammachius (now SS. Giovanni e Paolo). Nevertheless the difficulty arises as to how the Christians could possess the cemeteries, as they undoubtedly did, and how they could visit them unmolested, though such visits must have been known to the imperial authorities and could hardly be concealed, considering that most of the catacombs were situated along the great highways such as the Via Appia. We know that Valerian forbade the Christians to enter the cemeteries and that Diocletian confiscated them, but that was sporadic legislation and does not affect the general difficulty.

The answer would seem to lie in the fact that certain societies or guilds, as they were called in the Middle Ages, were recognized in Roman Law as corporate bodies (*collegia*), set up for a definite purpose and protected by law in the fulfilment of that purpose. Generally speaking, even under the Republic, the Government had been opposed to such societies because they afforded an opportunity for political organization, and a *Lex Iulia*, systematized under Augustus, had forbidden such associations unless they were exempted on the grounds of antiquity or had received recognition from the Senate. But it is quite

certain that many *collegia* continued to exist or came
into existence despite that law. Many of these had
some sort of religious foundation or background and
increased in numbers so quickly that it was almost
impossible to keep a check on all of them. As a result
the word unlawful, as applied to them in the *Digesta*,
implied the existence of political activity as opposed
to the simple fact that they were unlicensed. Thus
collegia funeratitia, whose object was the burial of the
dead and the care of their tombs, did not attract
attention. On the contrary, in the year 133 a *senatus
consultum* seems to have more or less sanctioned religious
or charitable *collegia* ("*sed religionis causa coire non
prohibentur*") and allowed them rather wider scope
than merely the burial of the dead.[1] It was under
this sanction, according to de Rossi and others, that
Christian *collegia* developed and escaped interference
from officials, except when persecution was particularly severe. We know from Pliny's letter to Trajan
that the latter had forbidden "*hetæriæ*," associations
which involved a good deal of social activity and even
conviviality, but this edict would not much affect
Christians as they could easily retain the purely
religious side of such associations.

With the development of the *collegia* came the recognition of their corporate rights, which explains how the
Christians of Rome, for example, possessed burial
places of their own, such as the cemetery of Domitilla,
the burial-place of the Glabriones, etc. That their
collegia were so recognized is clear from the action of
Pope Zephyrinus who, in 199, put Callistus at the head
of the cemeteries of Rome, though their beginnings

[1] For the whole question of *collegia* cf. E. G. Hardy, *Studies in
Roman History*, First Series, London, 1910, pp. 128-49.

were of a much earlier date. It was thus that the Christians, apart from the decrees of Valerian and Diocletian, were enabled to take advantage of Roman law in obtaining burial-grounds, and, when necessary, meeting-places.

The influence of Christianity on Roman law and religion is a vast subject, and concerns more the period subsequent to Nicea, yet there are some interesting points to be mentioned even during this period, especially towards its close. It is first noticeable under the so-called Syrian Emperors, Caracalla (211–17), Eliogabalus (218–22) and Alexander Severus (222–35), under whom the Christians enjoyed a long period of peace. They were all descendants of Bassianus, a High Priest of the Sun, and aimed at a religious syncretism which would abolish all distinct sects and incorporate a modicum of many religions into one satisfactory to all. The instigator of this syncretism was Iulia Domna, a Syrian, wife of Septimius Severus and mother of Caracalla. According to Ælius Lampridius (*Vita Heliogabali*, 3, 5) Eliogabalus wished to unite the Jews, Samaritans and Christians and to become High Priest of them all. Alexander Severus went still further: he tolerated the Christians, placed in his lararium statues of Apollonius, Christ, Abraham and Orpheus, and sacrificed to them: he also wished to build a temple to Christ (cf. l.c. *Vita Alexandri Severi*, 22, 4 ss.). Alleging that he was copying the custom of the Jews and Christians in their mode of selecting their priests, he ordered that in the appointment of procurators and other officials the names of the candidates should first be proposed to the people, so that if they had any objection to their taking office, they could make it known. In other ways also he showed clearly that he was under the influence of Christianity.

After his time there is little or no evidence of such influences until the time of Constantine. As an interesting sidelight, however, it is worthy of note that when an appeal was made to the Emperor Aurelian to remove Paul of Samosata from the episcopal palace at Antioch, from which see he had been deposed, the Emperor answered that the building should be handed over to him whom the Italian bishops of the Christian religion and the bishop of Rome should designate (Euseb., *H.E.*, VII, 30).

With Constantine a new era began, and it will be well to consider first the exact legal bearing of the Edict of Milan. It must be borne in mind that Constantine was not a Christian at this time: he was almost certainly baptised on his death-bed by Eusebius, the Arian bishop of Nicomedia. This explains certain things in his life which would seem inexplicable if the work of a baptized Christian.

The Edict of Milan, issued by Constantine and Licinius in the year 313, may easily be epitomized as follows. Firstly, it granted religious liberty to all the inhabitants of the Empire. It did not, as is so often said, make Christianity the official religion of the Roman Empire. In fact, the Pagan religion continued to be practised, the altar of the goddess Victory remained unmolested in the Senate, and the fire of the Vestal Virgins burned for long afterwards. Secondly, places of worship (which had been confiscated under Diocletian) were to be restored to the Christians: likewise other property where possible. Failing restoration, compensation could be had from the imperial treasury. This latter part of the Edict recognized the corporate rights of the Christian community in Roman law.

Following this great change in the legal status of the Christians, Constantine introduced many changes in law which show a distinct Christian influence. He legislated clearly that Christians could inherit property left to them by will: priests, and later, minor clerics were exempted from public offices which involved possession of property and administration of material things. He issued a decree enjoining worship for all on Sundays (this, and his retention of the title *Pontifex Maximus* show that he was not yet entirely a Christian in sentiment), but he expressly exempted Christian soldiers from worship of the Pagan gods. Judicial courts were not to be held on that day. Ecclesiastical courts, in which Christians placed their causes before bishops, were given State sanction and their judgements were binding on both parties, even if one were a Pagan. The Christians were protected against the Jews and Christians becoming Jews were punished. Jews were forbidden to circumcise Christians or to have Christian slaves. The death penalty by crucifixion or in the arena was abolished: penalties such as branding, which were inflicted on slaves, were abrogated. In the field of morals, severe punishments were established for assaults on children: bigamy, which had become very prevalent, was forbidden by law: divorce was made more difficult. The laws against restriction of births, which had fallen heavily on priests and virgins dedicated to God, were somewhat relaxed in favour of the Christian ideals of celibacy and virginity.

By this legislation Constantine assisted greatly in the spread of Christianity and Christian ideals. Yet such a close bond between Emperor and the Church as began to develop had its dangers, which were to appear later. Towards the end of his reign he played a still greater part in the life of the Church, witness the Council of Nicea, and though there was no conflict with him, yet the seeds of Cæsaro-Papism were sown at this time. The full fruits of this tendency, disastrous to the independence of the Church, were to flourish later.

With Constantine we conclude this survey of the legal relations between Church and State in the pre-Nicene period, and have endeavoured to indicate the main points which arose in the first three centuries of the existence of the Church on a question of admittedly perennial importance and one which was never more real and actual than at the present time.

THE PAGAN APOLOGISTS

By the Rev. P. G. N. RHODES, D.D., M.A.

MODERN psychologists tell us a good deal about rationalization, i.e. the tendency of the human mind to find convincing logical justification for actions which are in fact motived by some instinctive or scarcely conscious desire. So a hypnotist may impress upon his subject that at eleven o'clock he is to place the ink-pot on the carpet. Accordingly as the clock strikes eleven the victim, if he is sufficiently impressionable, will place the ink-pot there, but the curious thing is that he will have a quite rational and sufficient reason ready to explain why he does this curious act. The hypnotist knows quite well that the reason alleged is not really the cause of the action, it is simply the rationalization of it.

It is a commonplace to say that mankind is prone to deceive itself, and this process of explaining one's actions to oneself in a favourable light by means of a rationalization is far more consoling to human vanity than the unpleasant task of penetrating down to the secret reality which has supplied the actual motive. It is not surprising, therefore, that in religion, which claims to affect the most secret springs of human activity, we find this method of self-protection widespread. It is hard indeed for us to welcome the truth, when by so doing we involve ourselves in a cataclysm of worldly disaster. Yet, on the other hand, there are few who will cynically admit to themselves that they are maintaining falsehood against the known truth. Rationalization is the solution; those queer arguments appear, those strange difficulties which are triumphantly produced as conclusive reasons why the distasteful truth should be shunned as if it were dangerous error. Again it is a commonplace to say that argument seems to have little effect in securing conversions. No matter how convincingly the alleged objection is refuted, no result seems to follow; at the best, a fresh difficulty is substituted for the former one. And naturally so, for one is not dealing with reasons, but with rationalizations. The really impelling cause why adhesion is not given to what seems to us to be so plain may be something quite different, some fear or longing which the enquirer cannot explain even to himself. When such hidden urges are not working, and the difficulty is genuinely an intellectual puzzle of which a solution is sought, the response to an adequate answer is quite different.

It would be absurd to suggest that all objections to the Catholic Faith are of the nature of mere rationalizations. Without the grace of God the human intellect will find insuperable difficulties in teaching that which is so mysterious and so supernatural. There are symptoms usually present, when rationalization is taking the place of reason. One suspects this to be the case when furious bitterness takes the place of a calm spirit of enquiry. Plainly something of immense personal importance is felt to be endangered; there is no need for anger in an unprejudiced discussion about the ultimate realities of the universe. One can also plainly see rationalization at work, when what is defended is quite obviously an absurdity. This is verified most easily at a later date; looking back through the pages of history one is amazed to see how grotesque have been the alternatives to the Christian Faith that excited controversialists have been led to propound.

It is here that for us the interest of the Pagan Apologists is to be found. The question is now a dead one; not even the enemies of Christianity would suggest the Paganism of Rome as a serious alternative. The verdict of the whole of humanity has been given against them. But men of education and intelligence in their time entered into the lists against the champions of the Church to defend the fairy-stories of the ancient world. We find in them the prototypes of the anti-Catholic propagandist; we can trace there in the beginning the methods by which the human mind will find a method to protect itself against a religion which so mortifies the inclinations of fallen nature.

We may best begin by reminding ourselves of the grotesque nature of the task that the Pagan Apologists undertook. The Pagan religion had become ridiculous, considering the state of civilization to which the Empire had attained. One could not call the primitive spirit-worship of the early Romans ridiculous, with its vague tutelary gods in charge of even the smallest human operation. We cannot resist a smile on reading of the extraordinary specialized activities attributed to some of these deities; but the simple-minded peasants, little raised above the level of the Bantus in culture, accepted it all without criticism. Still less could we find the gracious fairy-land of the early Greek civilization ridiculous, though we should not shut our eyes to gravely evil tendencies found there. We still find such legends among primitive peoples; the Greeks with their innate artistry had produced them in a strikingly beautiful form. But legends and beliefs that may have their appeal when we find them among simple-minded primitives become ridiculous in surroundings of higher culture. So the superb mythology of the ancient Germans becomes an outrage when it is seriously proposed as the spiritual food of modern Germany. Now in the second century after Christ the civilization of the Roman Empire had attained a peak that has never been surpassed save by the Chinese, and by our own culture during the last hundred years. It was not only a high material civilization that was attained, but the intellectual standard was a very high one, and from our point of view a very modern one. The great age of poetry was passed; poetry requires a certain substratum of sincerity for its greatest manifestations. Perhaps we can see the spirit of the time most clearly in Lucian, witty, cynical, utterly disillusioned, the Anatole France of his age. But the official religion of the Romans had not progressed beyond a childish polytheism. There had been a syncretism between the Greek and Roman beliefs; Roman gods had been identified with Greek ones, Mars with Ares, Venus with Aphrodite, and the Greek legends had been accepted as part of the Roman belief. There was also a tendency to incorporate exciting new beliefs from the Orient; Attis and Anubis might find themselves admitted to the much more respectable company of Hera and Athene. Picturesque and exciting the established religion might be, but to regard it as *true* should have been as absurd in that state of culture as it would be in ours.

How far did people really believe it all? The Pagans

did not exactly demand religious faith in their gods. They required a respectful attitude towards the religion of the State, and a willingness to participate sometimes in the official sacrifices. More especially must the loyal citizen share in the veneration of the genius of the Emperor. No one was concerned with the interior mental attitude of their fellow-citizens. But probably most Pagans more or less believed their religion. At any rate they were convinced that misfortunes fell upon the State because the gods had not been sufficiently appeased, and this was one of the chief reasons for popular hostility towards the Church.

We have then a people in a high state of civilization still endeavouring to believe a religion that had taken form among primitive agricultural folk. They were now faced with the true religion, completely adequate both for the simplest and the most highly trained intelligence, and one that, while supernatural, offered no impossibilities or absurdities to the intellect. In the end the contest proved too unequal; Paganism collapsed and was replaced by Christianity. But this did not take place at once; the change was one from which the Pagans shrank, and a desperate attempt was made to find reasons for declining the new religion. Hence the interests of the Pagan Apologists.

There are two main methods by which an obsolescent form of religion may attempt to maintain itself. One way is to explain away the old religion, surrendering literal belief in its statements, and interpreting them as allegories or poems. This is the means of defence that in recent times the Modernists offered to the Catholic Church, which was not however in need of such defence, and declined it as suicidal. Their representatives in ancient times were the neo-Platonists,

who made use of the ancient mythology to give
an orthodox religious flavour to their mystical philosophy. We will return to this attempt to solve the
problem.

The other method is simply that of hostile propaganda. The new truths must be so misrepresented
that the dying religion may appear in a favourable
light by comparison. "The national cult may have
its faults and difficulties, but then no educated man
can possibly accept the absurdities put forward by
the Catholics."

This latter method was precisely that adopted by
Celsus, the father of all anti-Catholic propaganda.
He is the earliest writer of this kind of whom we have
information, and his work has proved a quarry for
all his successors. The later Pagan Apologists did
little but repeat his slanders, nor have later opponents
of the Church succeeded in getting much fresh
ammunition. We can then fittingly consider his
attack in some detail.

Celsus brought out his book, the *True Account*, i.e. of
Christianity, about the year 178. He seems to have
moved in the best literary circles, as the great writer
Lucian dedicated his *Alexander* to him. To-day Celsus
would certainly have been a journalist, with a flair
for the sensational and bizarre. He seems to have
made his reputation by a book on witchcraft, a popular
subject at the time. (A weakness in the otherwise
high culture of the Empire was this belief in witchcraft, due to the fact that the physical science of the
time was in a rudimentary condition. There was a
tendency to look for preternatural causes for phenomena
they found inexplicable). Lucian's *Alexander* is on a
kindred subject, and so was naturally associated with

the name of Celsus, as the recognized authority. Celsus completely accepted the alleged phenomena of witchcraft, and we can well imagine that his work was full of sensational experiences at the hands of sorcerers. Having dealt adequately with this topic, Celsus looked round for fresh material. Christianity suggested itself to him, as a subject as obscure and queer as witchcraft itself. He set to work to acquire information. He seems to have worked hard at this, and he himself was quite convinced that there was nothing worth knowing about Christianity that he did not know. "I know everything" is the remark that he makes continually. He did know rather more than the average Pagan; but this is saying little. His writings were so full of astonishing misconceptions that it is not easy to see whence his knowledge could have been derived. In the first place he seems to have consulted the Jews, who were delighted to give him the reasons for their intense hatred of Christianity. He treats the Christian religion as being a heresy from Judaism, and devotes one book to the objections of the Jews against the Church.[1] He had access, it would seem, to the Bible, at any rate to the Old Testament. In addition he seems to have come across some queer Gnostic sect, and makes much of "the genealogies and old wives' fables" with which they regaled their followers. He has some queer anti-Christian legends, of unknown origin. He does not seem to have any personal contact with Catholics, or at any rate to have gained their confidence sufficiently for them to have explained the true Christian teaching to him.

[1] Quotations from *Celsus* express his meaning, and are not necessarily literal. (Origen, *Contra Celsum*, book II.)

However, the whole work is written in a furiously hostile manner, and he gives the preference to heretical caricatures of the Faith, as more promising material than the sober doctrines of the Church. It is therefore possible that he may have known more of the Catholic Church than would appear. Had Christianity really appeared to him as silly a business as he pretends, there could be no explanation of the attraction that he admits it possesses, nor of the fearful hatred that he displays towards it. The same remark holds good of some of the more recent enemies of the Faith.

The work in question is now, parodoxically enough, only preserved for us in the quotations from it in Origen's reply. What influence it had in its time is hard to say; there is no reference made to the work by other contemporaries, and every manuscript has perished. Origen decided, with some hesitation, that the work did sufficient harm to need a refutation, and later anti-Christian writers follow very similar lines to those of Celsus, which suggests that he was to some extent the founder of a school. Origen deals with the book thoroughly, chapter by chapter, often quoting the original, and the possession of the original could add little to our knowledge of Celsus' line of argument.

Perhaps the chief difference between Celsus and his modern followers is in his attitude towards the miraculous. Marvels cause him no difficulty ; he was a specialist in such things. Miracles of healing, miracles over nature, Old Testament and New Testament miracles, he accepts them nearly all. He rejects some of the greatest, such as the Virgin Birth; but he is quite prepared to agree that strange things happened. As a good journalist, he is not going to throw over such excellent copy. But he attributes them all to witchcraft and incantations; they are performed through the power of spirits.[1] Nor, in his opinion, can Christian and Biblical miracles hold a candle to the far more exciting wonders of the Egyptian jugglers, who can cast out evil spirits, blow away diseases, show fine banquets not really existing at all, and so on.[2] Christianity is in fact rather a tame affair, in comparison with the witchcraft he had investigated before, and with the amazing legends of the Greek mythology. But in other respects he is quite modern.

We have, for instance, the modern depreciation of the importance of man. The Christians say that man is the crown of creation, that he surpasses in value all the material universe. Celsus declares that man is but an animal like the rest, and that there is no justification for the belief that the world was made for him, rather than for the ants and flies.[3] Modern unbelievers take the same line, though they would not follow Celsus in asserting that eagles can practise sorcery, and other birds, as known to the augurs, can foreknow the things of God.

Very familiar to us still is the complaint that the Church would substitute credulity for a reasoned intelligence. This ancient slander survives from the writings of Celsus. "We must follow reason," he says, "and a reasonable leader. The Christians say: ' Do not enquire, only believe. Thy faith shall save thee. The wisdom of this world is evil, and folly is good.' "[4] He continually states that Christians seek their converts among the ignorant, and do all they can to depreciate education. This probably to some extent reflects a real

[1] Origen, *Contra Celsum*, book II, i, 6.　　[2] *Ibid.*, i, 68.
[3] *Ibid.*, iv, 74.　　[4] *Ibid.*, i, 8, 9.

K

difficulty of the Christians of the time, namely that the only available higher education dealt with the pagan literature, which seemed to imply an acceptance of belief in the gods. Later on the apostate Emperor Julian tried to debar Christians from higher education, on the ground that they ought not in conscience to study classical literature. In later times still Catholics have had to renounce opportunities of education offered them at the expense of their faith. But Origen has no difficulty in making the correct reply, that the Church desires wise and educated men for her members, provided that no risk is caused to their souls by their studies, and that no barrier is placed in the way of the poor and ignorant who may desire to hear the Gospel.

"The Christian religion is one of terror; its adherents are overcome with dread, but there is nothing behind it all. It is much the same as in Egypt, magnificent temples, and nothing in them except a dog to worship."[1] Again a curiously Protestant criticism. It is still more curious that in the second century the Catholic Church, hiding in catacombs and secret places, should have caused that profound emotion of awe which indignant Protestants have attributed to magnificent architecture and unearthly music.

Celsus is shocked at the invitation to sinners, of notoriously evil life, to join the Church.[2] It is impossible, he says, to effect any real modification of character in the adult. This is brought against us to-day: the lethal chamber is the scientific substitute for the sacrament of penance. He is particularly annoyed with the Christian desire to influence children,[3]

---

[1] Origen, *Contra Celsum*, book II, iii.
[2] *Ibid.*, iii, 59.   [3] *Ibid.*, iii, 55.

interfering with parental rights. Origen indignantly asks why the young should be left without assistance in the midst of the fearful evils of that time.

"Christianity is a rite of foreign and barbarous origin. The Apostles were worthless individuals, tax-farmers and low-class sailors."[1] Here we are touching the real objection that the Roman Empire felt towards the Faith. It was a humiliation to them to suggest that the Empire needed to go to Judea for its religion. The established religion had sufficed for their fathers, it had been unquestioned during the glorious days of old, it must not be rejected in favour of this exotic sect. The established religion was in fact the religion for gentlemen; the true Roman could not be expected to listen to these strange foreigners of no social or educational prestige.

"Christianity is against the law."[2] Here again we have a real objection, the fearful personal risk taken by any citizen who joined the Church at that time. At hardly any time has the attraction to the Church been greater; the standard of holiness was very high; many great Saints to whom we now erect cathedrals and dedicate cities were then walking the earth. Yet at no time has the convert had to make greater sacrifices. No wonder that the Pagans looked for any excuse to serve as a rationalization.

"Christianity is unpatriotic.[3] We must help the Emperor with all our might, labour for him, fight for him and under him. We should take office in the government of the country; yet Christians selfishly disqualify themselves for all such responsibilities." Origen is frankly pacifist in his reply to this, and

---

[1] *Ibid.,* i, 65.   [2] *Ibid.,* i, 1; v, 26.
[3] *Ibid.,* viii, 73, 75.

refuses to do more for the Emperor than pray for him. It is, however, plain that the Church did not in reality forbid the taking of arms by Christians for imperial defence; she preferred the Empire as it was to Gothic barbarity and Persian cruelty. The Pagans themselves had precluded Christians from most offices by their requirement of the adoration of the Emperor's genius. Catholics in England have found themselves in the same ambiguous position.

"The Roman Empire has been founded and preserved under the protection of the old national religion. Other parts of the world may have been assigned to other protecting spirits; for the true Roman there can be nothing save the old Roman faith. Look at the Jews, who have lost their country through not asking for the help of our gods. If we give up our religion, our fate will be the same."[1] It is safe to say that every anti-Catholic controversialist has repeated this argument down to the present day, with, of course, slight changes.

"The Christian Church is so narrow-minded. God is the God of all men; it is absurd to think that He would insist on being worshipped in the Christian way alone. Christians ought at any rate to join with us in our public feasts."[2] An equally familiar complaint to-day.

"After all there are so many kinds of Christians, disagreeing with each other, that the sensible man will take no notice of any of them."[3] The scandal caused by heresy was then felt in the second century. It was at the height of Gnosticism, and an enquirer who had only come across those sectarians might well

---

[1] Origen, *Contra Celsum*, book II, viii, 69.   [2] *Ibid.*, viii, 21.
[3] *Ibid.*, iii.

be excused for some confusion. But one suspects that
Celsus knew quite well that there was a greater Church
than theirs. He uses Gnostic silliness as an excuse
to attack Christianity, but most of his arguments seem to be directed rather against Catholic
Christianity.

The above are the general arguments of Celsus
against Christianity. He attacks Christianity in detail
on a number of points.

He dislikes the Mosaic account of creation, without,
however, offering any explanation himself of the
existence of the world. He jeers at the stories of the
Pentateuch, and twits the Christians for attempting
to avoid the difficulty by allegorical interpretations.[1]
Origen is at a disadvantage here, as he made great use
of allegory in explaining the Old Testament. Probably
Celsus has Gnostic evasions in mind. He has a poor
opinion of Moses; the sorcerers of the East could put up
a finer show in the way of wonders. Above all, why
call God Adonai? Why not call him Jove? A happy
via media between Paganism and Christianity might
perhaps thus be found. Origen replies that Jove
cannot be dissociated from Saturn and Juno.

He makes a venomous attack on Our Lord, and
inevitably attacks our Lady too. He has a curious
story, perhaps derived from the Jews, about the
Nativity. Mary, he says, was a poor sempstress, who
was seduced by a soldier named Bar-Panther. She
secretly gave birth to Jesus, and was cast out by her
husband. Jesus went as a servant to Egypt, and there
learnt magic. This He practised on his return, and so
got himself regarded as a god.[2] This concoction

---

[1] *Ibid.*, i, 17, 18.　　　　　[2] *Ibid.*, i, 28.

deserves no further notice, though it may easily turn up again (minus the magic) in the future.

The descent of the Holy Spirit as a dove for some reason especially annoys Celsus. The incident neither suggests the trickster nor the magician, and Celsus is uncomfortable about it. He has a new version of the Passion. Jesus, after His condemnation, succeeds in hiding Himself, and tries to escape, but is betrayed by His disciples.[1] This again looks like a Jewish account of the matter. The Gnostic view, that Jesus had no real body and did not really suffer, does not appear in Celsus, so that his views of Christianity were not derived exclusively from that source. On the contrary, he argues that Our Lord's divinity is disproved by the fact that He ate and drank as a man. A god would require a god's food, ambrosia and nectar presumably.[2]

As has been stated, Celsus regards Christianity as a corruption of Judaism. He devotes a section of his work to reproaching them for having deserted the faith of their fathers. This part of his attack need not delay us long, as he is simply repeating the arguments of the Rabbis against Christianity, and with these we are not now concerned. It may be noted that the greatest objection on the part of the Jews was that it was inconceivable that the true Messias should have been crucified between criminals. The Cross was the stumbling-block.

The above are the arguments of Celsus, he paid them out plentifully with abuse and jeers at the illiteracy of converts to the Faith. There are his Plain Reasons for not joining the Catholic Church, and they have

---

[1] Origen, *Contra Celsum*, book II, ii, 9.   [2] *Ibid.*, i, 68.

proved, nearly all of them, to possess a sort of immortality. They are still extant to-day. They have been refuted for seventeen hundred years, but are not dead. Why? Because they are not reasons, but rationalizations of an antecedent determination not to join the Church, whatever may be true.

It soon became plain that in spite of the labours of Celsus the attraction of the Nazarene was greater than of the pagan gods. An ingenious attempt was now made to meet this by adding a fresh god to the pantheon. A certain Philostratus, early in the third century, brought out a life of Apollonius of Tyana, who is represented as a miracle-worker and saint, a demi-god who in the end leaves the earth for heaven in a mysterious manner. It was hoped that this would fill the gap; a miraculous life, attractive personality and no unpleasant demands for any change of religion. The disadvantage was that Apollonius was an imaginary god. There may have been some person of that name, about which the story is woven, but nobody takes seriously the romance produced by Philostratus. Perhaps we should except the modern Theosophists, who claim Apollonius as an adept or Mahatma. Modern rationalists are also apt to couple his name with that of Christ; not through any belief in Apollonius, but to suggest that the life of Our Lord is equally imaginary. Even the Pagans knew better than this; some small cult of Apollonius was started, under the influence of the Empress Julia Domna, but the unreality of the whole business became too apparent. This, too, melted away before the rising sun of the true religion. A similar failure attended other attempts to provide Paganism with a Saint, by idealizing the philosopher Pythagoras. By this time it was apparent that it was hopeless to renew the faith of the world in Jove and Juno. The plan was to invent new and more attractive doctrines, hoping that the old cult might be allowed to survive as a sort of appendage to which attention need not be explicitly drawn. The same process is not unknown to-day among obsolescent sects.

We can now pass to the last stage, in which belief is refined away into vague mystical emotionalism. In the fourth century, after the establishment of Christianity under Constantine, and still more after the grotesque attempts of Julian to revive the old religion, it became inconceivable for the educated classes to believe in the ancient myths as literal accounts of true facts. Julian had made himself ridiculous in the eyes of the whole world by his endeavour to galvanize the old beliefs back into activity. A modern psychologist would find no difficulty in understanding his case ; he was endeavouring to rationalize the hatred and terror he felt for the Arian surroundings of his childhood, during which scarcely for an instant had he been free from the fear of a violent death. To him Paganism brought a sense of escape and liberty; the mentally normal of his contemporaries had come to see that Paganism was a degrading enslavement of the soul. It may be interesting to sum up briefly the main heads of his attack on Christianity. He follows more or less the usual lines, but as an ex-Christian he has a better knowledge of the matter than Celsus. His work is that of a typical apostate, plenty of inside information, but everything maliciously distorted. He attacks the Old Testament as attributing human passions, as jealousy and vindictiveness, to God. He says that only in the Fourth Gospel is deity attributed to Christ (a modern touch this), who was really an insignificant figure. Christianity has nothing to offer in comparison with the superb Greek literature, and the magnificent Empire of the Romans. It is rather anti-social and unpractical. If Christians literally gave to whoever asked them, trade would become impossible. But no Christians do practise their religion, they have been given to immorality from the beginning, as Paul himself found at Corinth. They are intolerant persecutors of the Pagans and other Christians. He denies that the Messianic prophecies have any reference to Jesus; the Bible is full of contradictions (e.g. the two genealogies of Christ), and so cannot be inspired. He mocks the Christian veneration of relics and of the Cross. Against this he tries to exalt the Pagan religion, to make it a source of holiness, led by its priests, who were to be models of the spiritual life. Nobody was less enthusiastic than the priests themselves at this prospect, and at Julian's death the Empire was simply relieved to be rid of a crank. Somehow the episode acted as a *reductio ad absurdum;* literal Paganism never again had a serious chance of acceptance.

There were, however, still many who still hated Christianity, and they were now reduced to their last resort, to waive the historicity of the Pagan myths, but to treat them as allegories of mystic truths. For this purpose the neo-Platonic philosophy was used. We cannot now deal with this very important philosophic school. It had considerable influence on the Catholic scholastic philosophy, and has claims to be treated with respect. One may, however, suspect that there were two classes among its adherents, firstly, those whose main interest was the philosophy itself, and secondly, those who adopted neo-Platonism to provide themselves with an escape from Christianity. The first class were sincere enough in their desire to produce a system of universal application, and in pursuit of this ideal endeavoured to reconcile their philosophical views with religion, as manifestly a factor in human affairs. This Plotinus, in the third century, was a Pagan of the best type, upright in character and sincere in belief. But Porphyry of Tyre, his successor, is stated by St. Augustine to have been an apostate Christian, and he certainly used the philosophy as a method of defence against Christianity. He wrote no less that fifteen anti-Christian works, in the usual style, attacks on the anthropomorphisms of the Old Testament, denials of the miracles of Our Lord, belittling of the teaching of the Apostles. His special phobia was about the Catholic doctrine of the eternity of Hell. In opposition to the Faith he set up the mystical neo-Platonic philosophy, and tried to find a revealed basis for it in the Pagan Oracles. The ancient myths of the gods he explained away as allegories. Later the emperor, Theodosius II, ordered his anti-Christian works to be burnt, and no copy now remains. But Porphyry had given a twist to the neo-Platonic school, from which it did not rid itself for a long time. Iamblichus carried on the tradition. By the beginning of the fourth century, the effect of Christian teaching had been to make polytheism appear absurd; Iamblichus now admits that there is only One Supreme Being, though the gods, goddesses and heroes find their place as intermediate spirits. The legends of Paganism are still further explained away, and even pagan fatalism is modified in a Christian direction. The main preoccupation of Iamblichus is a kind of magical mysticism, by which the initiate may find himself in personal intercourse with the great spirits of the universe. Although he is unconsciously influenced by the teachings of the Church, he relaxes no whit his hostility. During the fourth century a division of opinion among the neo-Platonics; some remained frankly hostile, as Proclus; others endeavoured to find a *via media* between neo-Platonism and Christianity. Ammianus Marcellinus is a good example of this latter tendency. Part of his writings survive; it seems harsh to call them anti-Christian, as he speaks with respect and even amazement of Christ and His teachings. But for all that, he adheres to Paganism, which has now become reduced to a belief in oracles and auguries. He still tries to believe in the gods, but attempts to identify them with the Platonic Ideas, an amazing transformation. The Neo-Platonic school at Athens was suppressed by the Emperor Justinian in 529. The elements of truth in the system came to find a more congenial home in Christianity; the anonymous and probably semi-Monophysite writer who assumed the name of Dionysius the Areopagite was certainly influenced by the school, and through him, as has been stated, the great scholastic philosophers were affected.

It is interesting to note how in the end the more superstitious elements of Paganism, augury and oracle-mongering proved to have the greatest vitality. One may compare the tendency of the sceptical modern world to find its solace in mascots and spiritism. Paganism still retained much power over the rustic population, but more and more degenerated into witch-craft. Even in the Middle Ages the witches venerated Janus and Diana; the sorcerers' Sabbath, with its

worship of the "devil," was the lineal descendant of the
Ephesian worship of the Magna Mater. But we have
no literary account, from the witches' point of view,
of their reasons for preferring their strange cult to
Christianity; the Apologists of Paganism had ended.

THE ORIGIN OF THE EPISCOPATE

By the Rev. HUGH POPE, O.P., S.T.M., D.SS.

I. THE DOCTRINE OF THE CHURCH. DIVERGENT VIEWS ON THE SUBJECT. THE PROBLEMS TO BE DISCUSSED.

The teaching of the Church on the Hierarchy as a divinely established thing is familiar. The Council of Trent felt compelled to enunciate it with emphasis because it had then become the fashion to call it in question:

"If anyone says that all Christians without distinction are 'priests of the New Testament,' or that all alike are endowed with the same spiritual powers, of such it can only be said that their views are destructive of the Ecclesiastical Hierarchy which is like 'an army set in array'. They imply too that, in contradiction to St. Paul's teaching, all are Apostles, all Prophets, all Evangelists, all Pastors, all Teachers. (1 *Cor.* xii, 29.) This Holy Synod therefore declares that, besides the other Ecclesiastical Orders, Bishops, who have succeeded to the position of the Apostles, hold the chief position in this Hierarchy and are, as the same Apostle says, 'set by the Holy Spirit to rule the Church of God' (*Acts* xx, 28), and that they are superior to the Priests, confer the Sacrament of Confirmation, ordain the Church's ministers, and can do many other things which those of an inferior Order have no power to do."[1]

[1] The Council of Trent, Sess. xxiii, cap. iv., Denz., no. 960.

Whence the following Canons:

Can. 6. If anyone shall say that there is not in the Catholic Church a divinely instituted Hierarchy comprising Bishops, Priests and Ministers, let him be anathema. Can. 7. If anyone shall say that Bishops are not superior to Priests, or have no power to confirm or ordain, or that if they have they have it only in common with Priests . . . Let him be anathema.

The Vatican Council, too, when emphasizing the Primacy of the Pope as the successor of St. Peter, was at pains to point out that "so far is it from being the case that this power of the Supreme Pontiff is any prejudice to that ordinary and immediate power which belongs to Episcopal jurisdiction—a power whereby the Bishops, successors of the Apostles in whose place they have been set by the Holy Spirit, do each of them individually rule and govern as true Pastors the several flocks which have been entrusted to them, that, on the contrary, their power is asserted, safeguarded and vindicated by the Supreme and Universal Pastor."[1]

So, too, Pope Leo XIII:

"Since Bishops are the successors of the Apostles, they inherit the 'ordinary' power of the latter, so that the Episcopal office necessarily belongs to the inmost constitution of the Church. And while they have not full, universal or supreme authority,

[1] "Tantum autem abest ut haec Summi Pontificis potestas officiat ordinariae ac immediatae illi episcopalis jurisdictionis potestati, qua Episcopi, qui positi a Spiritu Sancto in Apostolorum locum successerunt, tanquam veri pastores assignatos sibi greges, singuli singulos, pascunt et regunt, ut eadem a supremo et universali Pastore asseratur, roboretur ac vindicetur." (Sess. iv, cap. iii.)

yet they are not to be considered merely vicars of the Roman Pontiffs."[1]

Finally, the *Codex of Canon Law* says:

"Bishops are the successors of the Apostles, and by Divine institution are set over their particular churches which they govern with 'ordinary' power under the authority of the Roman Pontiff."[2]

More than a hundred years before Trent John Huss had taught that

"there is not the slightest evidence that there ought to be one Head to rule the Church in spiritual matters . . . without the assistance of such monstrosities Christ could govern His Church much better through the medium of His true disciples throughout the world. . . . In all important matters the Apostles and the Lord's faithful Priests governed the Church well long before the office of the Pope was introduced, and they would do so now to the Day of Judgement were the Pope—as is possible— to cease to be. . . . Nor does anyone validly wield civil authority or be a Prelate or a Bishop so long as he is in mortal sin";

for all which Huss was condemned by the Council of Constance, A.D. 1414–18.[3]

---

[1] "Sic Episcopi, quod succedunt Apostolis, horum potestatem ordinariam hereditate capiunt, ita ut intimam Ecclesiæ constitutionem ordo episcoporum necessario attingat. Quanquam vero neque plenam neque universalem ii, neque summam obtinent auctoritatem, non tamen vicarii Romanorum pontificum putandi," (Encycl. *Satis cognitum*, June 29, 1896.)

[2] Canon 329, § 1. "Episcopi sunt Apostolorum successores atque ex divina institutione peculiaribus Ecclesiis præficiuntur quas cum potestate ordinaria regunt sub auctoritate Romani Pontificis."

[3] Denzinger, Nos. 653–656.

While, so far back as the middle of the fourth century, Pope Cornelius I, A.D. 251–253, writes to Fabian, Bishop of Antioch, that

"Novatian failed to realize that in the Catholic Church (viz. the church of the city of Rome) there must be one Bishop, and in that Church, as he could not have failed to know, are forty-six priests, seven deacons, seven sub-deacons, forty-two acolytes and fifty-two Exorcists, Lectors and Ostiarians, as well as more than fifteen hundred widows looking after the needy."[1]

But is this traditional view well-founded? Can it be traced back to apostolic days? Nonconformity and "Presbyterianism" are based on the supposition that such traditions are purely human, in no sense primitive, and incompatible with the plain teaching of the New Testament. Quite apart from the interpretation to be attached to certain passages in the Pastoral Epistles to Timothy and Titus, certain facts are, so it is alleged, fatal to the notion that a hierarchy, consisting of bishops, priests, deacons and the rest, ever formed part of Christ's designs for His Church. There is, for example, the cherished notion of the universal priesthood of all the faithful,[2] as though Moses' words on this subject were not to be read in conjunction with his very positive statements about the peculiar priesthood of the sons of Aaron,[3] and as though St. Peter were not singularly explicit in saying a holy priesthood to offer up *spiritual* sacrifices. There

[1] Pope Cornelius I, A.D. 251–3, to Fabian Bishop of Antioch, A.D. 251, Denzinger, No. 45.
[2] *Exodus*, xix, 6; 1 *Peter* ii, 5, 9; *Apocalypse* i, 6, v, 10, xx, 6; cf. Lightfoot, *Christian Ministry* (Philipp.), p. 185.
[3] *Exodus* xxviii–xxix; *Leviticus* viii, xxi; *Numbers* xvi–xviii.

are also two statements by St. Jerome and St. Clement
of Rome which at first sight seem to imply that the
Episcopate was a post-apostolic afterthought; these
we shall examine below.

The Presbyterian and Nonconformist bodies have
quite made up their minds on this point; for them
the Presbyterate is, in one form or another, everything,
and bishops are not only no essential part of the
Church's constitution but are not even necessary for
its *bene esse*, or well-being.

The Church of England has committed itself to the
doctrine of Apostolic Succession as one of the four
points in the so-called "Lambeth Quadrilateral" of
1920: Holy Scripture, the Creeds, the Sacraments and
the Historic Episcopate. But even on this last point
they are divided into two camps:

"Two views prevailed in the Church (of England).
According to one view the bishops were the successors
of the Apostles, and, like them, were an Order
divinely appointed, deriving their authority, not by
delegation from the presbyters or congregation,
but from above. It was intended by God that
there should be an authoritative stewardship of
the grace and truth which came by Jesus Christ,
and a recognized power to transmit it, derived from
above by Apostolic descent. For a valid ministry
and the true performance of the Sacraments this
succession and transmission by Ordination was
necessary.

"The other view of Apostolic Succession was that
the Episcopate was not originally formed out of the
Apostolic Order, but out of the presbyterate by
elevation; and that there was no essential connexion

L

in the early Church between the Apostolic Succession and the validity of the Sacraments."[1]

Even the Archbishop of York, Dr. Temple, stated in a Charge to the clergy, June, 1931, that "the Christian society had adopted the Episcopate as its sole channel of ministerial order as early as A.D. 200."[2]

The negotiations for reunion of the "Free" Churches with the Church of England are hampered by the refusal of the former to accept the Episcopate as a divine institution, and by the inability of the latter to prove that it is so. This impasse clearly appears in the following:

"In a Manifesto recently addressed to the Free Churches by a number of respected and influential members of the Church of England the words occur: 'We hope that Episcopacy may commend itself to the Free Churches as a method of Church order of ancient tradition and historic value.' It may well be asked, If this be all, what justification can we have in making the acceptance of even what we may deem to be 'the wisest and most efficient form of Church order' a condition of union when we know that but for this condition union might be achieved? Such a position can only be justified by belief that here there is a divine provision for the right ordering of the Church to which we must be loyal. . . .

". . . There are signs of a similar danger in regard to order—the other element in our Catholic heritage. Here the issues may not go so deep, but they have

[1] The Rev. T. Tatlow, D.D., see *Church Times*, May 24, 1929.
[2] Certainly a precarious statement. See a curious effort by Dr. Goudge to interpret it in an orthodox fashion, *Church Times*, June 19, 1931.

an importance of their own. They have come to centre round what is called the historic episcopate. Various theories have been and are held as to the origins of episcopacy. But there is no question that by the end of the second century of the Christian era it had secured a place in the life of the Church which even in the midst of the controversies of the fourth and fifth centuries remained unquestioned. Its position historically is analogous to the Canon of Scripture and the Creeds. All alike emerged through a process of gradual growth into a place of accepted authority. Let me quote the words of the Lambeth Committee of 1930: 'If the Episcopate was the result of a like process of adaptation and growth in the organism of the Church, that would be no evidence that it lacked divine authority, but rather that the life of the Spirit within the Church had found it to be the most appropriate organ for the functions which it discharged.' These functions were of great importance to the life and unity of the Church—among them the guardianship of the Faith and the Sacraments and the provision of a duly commissioned ministry. Thus—to quote again the same Report—'we are persuaded that the historic continuity of the episcopal ministry provides evidence of the divine intention such as to constitute a stewardship which we are bound to discharge.' "[1]

Two wholly distinct questions present themselves: (a) What was the origin of the Episcopate? (b) Were bishops always distinct from priests?

There are three possible answers to the question: Whence came the idea of bishops?

[1] *The Church Times*, July 3, 1934.

(*a*) They are a comparatively late institution, a purely human arrangement for the *bene esse* or well-being of the Church, and are in no sense an essential part of the Church's constitution.

(*b*) They are of apostolic origin; for the Apostles speedily realized that for effective government some such institution was necessary; hence bishops do not—as above—pertain to the essential constitution of the Church, though being of apostolic origin the Episcopate will have a peculiar claim to our veneration without, however, being a divine institution.

(*c*) Their appointment formed part of Christ's concept of His Church and was to take place as the Apostles whom they succeeded gradually disappeared, or in cases where the Apostles themselves were unable to govern the local churches—as must indeed generally if not always have been the case.

Further, even supposing that the Episcopate was instituted by the Apostles on their own initiative—though there is not the slightest foundation for such a supposition—would that mean that the Episcopate was therefore a purely human and not a divine institution? Such an idea would argue a curiously inadequate notion of the position of the Apostles who were—after Christ—the foundation of the Church (*Ephesians* ii, 20).

At the First Œcumenical Council of the Church held at Nicæa, A.D. 325, three hundred and eighteen bishops met to investigate a heresy which had recently arisen. Now, on the theory which has prevailed since the Reformation not only among the Presbyterian bodies but even among the Episcopalian churches, these men were "bishops" by no divine institution but by a purely ecclesiastical arrangement. But on that supposition how comes it that nowhere in the history of the Church do we come across instances of the "inferior clergy" protesting against Episcopal authority as such? St. Jerome provides us with a graphic account of the attempt made by the deacons at Rome to arrogate to themselves precedence over the priests.[1] How much more natural it would have been had the priestly body from which—according to certain theorists—the Episcopal body had developed, claimed as much right to a seat in the Church councils as any bishop?

II. THE POSITION OF BISHOP LIGHTFOOT

In his dissertation on *The Christian Ministry*[2] Bishop Lightfoot maintains that in the Old Testament as well as the New the Kingdom of Christ is presented as unfettered and free communion of every individual with the Head of that Kingdom: "It has no sacred days or seasons, no special sanctuaries. . . . Above all it has no sacerdotal system. It interposes no sacrificial tribe or class between God and man." This, the bishop acknowledges, is but an ideal which, owing to "the necessary wants of human society, will, if crudely and hastily applied, only lead to signal failure." He would explain the rise of the sacerdotal system, then, by suggesting that under the Old Dispensation the priests were "representatives of the whole nation, delegates of the people. . . . Direct relationship with God was (thus) partly suspended but not abolished by the appointment of a sacerdotal tribe." The Christian

[1] See below.
[2] A dissertation attached to his *Commentary on Philippians*, 1868, pp. 181–269; reprinted in his collected *Dissertations on the Apostolic Age*, 1892, pp. 137–246.

ideal, he continues, was the restitution of such direct
relationship with God, but the necessity for organization made its realization impossible in practice, and
he concludes that "history seems to show decisively
that before the middle of the second century each
church . . . had its bishop, its presbyters and its
deacons." Whether, he adds, this was due to a divine
ordinance or not "history is obviously the sole upright,
impartial referee."[1] Lightfoot therefore enters into
a careful and detailed investigation of all the data
provided by history, arriving at the conclusion that
"it is plainly competent for the Church at any given
time to entrust a particular office with larger powers,
as the emergency may require";[2] in other words, the
Episcopal office was not of directly divine institution
but due to the growing need of organization. In
accordance with this, when speaking of Timothy and
Titus, Lightfoot, while acknowledging that "the
position occupied by these apostolic delegates fairly
represents the functions of the bishop early in the
second century," refuses to allow that the title of
"bishop" in their case is anything more than "a
conception of a later age."[3] Nor will he allow that the
expression "Angel of the Church" (*Apoc.* ii, 1, etc.)
means its "bishop," though he acknowledges that "this
explanation is as old as the earliest commentators";
one of his arguments is interesting: holding the early
date of the Apocalypse "with most recent writers,"
he feels that "it is scarcely possible that the Episcopal
organization should have been so mature when it
was written . . . probably not more than two or
three years have elapsed from the date of the Pastoral

---

[1] *Dissertations on the Apostolic Age,* pp. 181–7.
[2] *Ibid.,* p. 244.   [3] *Ibid.,* p. 199.

Epistles, and this interval seems quite insufficient to account for so great a change in the administration of the Asiatic churches."[1]

Some of Lightfoot's arguments are sufficiently astonishing: for example, he states that in 1 *Corinthians*, xii, 28, and *Ephesians* iv, 11, where St. Paul "briefly sums up the offices in the Church . . . the permanent government is kept in the background,"[2] yet in the former we have "government," R.V. (and margin "wise counsels"—a very arbitrary rendering of κυβερνήσεις), while in *Ephesians* iv, 11, we have "pastors and teachers" where "pastors" is the equivalent of ποιμένα.[3] Again, he remarks that despite St. Paul's "express directions as to the qualifications of deacons . . . we may perhaps infer from the instructions which he sends about the same time to Titus in Crete, that he did not consider it (the diaconate) indispensable, for . . . he is silent about the diaconate." (*Titus* i, 5 ff.)[4] His argument, too, that since St. Clement's Letter to the *Corinthians* "does not proceed from the Bishop of Rome, but from the Church of Rome . . . the name and personality of Clement are absorbed in the church of which he is the spokesman,"[5] and that since in Ignatius' "letter to the Church of Rome there is not the faintest allusion to the episcopal office . . . therefore the original primacy (is) a primacy not of the bishop but of the whole Church"[6] has become classic with anti-Roman controversialists. But what a delicately balanced pyramid it is!

[1] *Ibid.*, pp. 200–201.
[2] *The Christian Ministry*, dissertation appended to *Philippians*, p. 185; in the collected *Dissertations*, p. 142.
[3] Cf. *John* xxi, 16; *Acts* xx, 28; 1 *Peter* v, 2.
[4] Lightfoot, *Philippians*, p. 192; *Dissertations*, p. 149.
[5] *The Apostolic Fathers*, 1 *Clement*, i, p. 69.
[6] *Ibid.*, p. 71.

III.   THE WITNESS OF HIPPOLYTUS

To sift all the evidence between the Ascension and the Council of Nicæa would be impossible here, indeed unprofitable; to discuss adequately the views held by St. Cyprian alone would demand a separate paper. So, basing ourselves on Tertullian's dictum *"Id verius quod prius"* or "the older evidence is the truer," we shall deal only with Hippolytus' *Apostolic Tradition*, the Letters of St. Ignatius, St. Clement's *First Epistle to the Corinthians*, and the evidence afforded by the New Testament.

Working backwards, then: it is only in comparatively recent years that attention has been called to the importance of the evidence enshrined in the so-called "Church Orders."[1] These seem to have originated in the endeavour to secure unity of practice in faith and ritual and are based on the principle that the regulations of the Apostles as the depositaries of all revealed truth must be our guide in such matters. The oldest of these "Church Orders" is the *Didache* or *Teaching of the Twelve*, before the middle of the second century. It is now generally conceded that the rest, e.g. the *Didascalia*, c. A.D. 250, the *Apostolic Constitutions*, c. 375, and the *Apostolic Church Order* are based on either the *Didache* or the writings of the still enigmatic Hippolytus, among whose voluminous works *The Apostolic Tradition* has now been conclusively shown to be the groundwork of subsequent Church Orders.[2] Writing not

[1] See A. J. Maclean, *The Ancient Church Orders*, 1910; also *The Position of Clergy and Laity in the Early Church in relation to the Episcopate*, 1930.

[2] Dom R. H. Connolly, O.S.B., *The so-called Egyptian Church Order, Texts and Studies*, viii, no. 4, 1916; see also *Notes on the Egyptian Church Order* in *J.T.S.*, April, 1918, pp. 137–42. Burton

later than A.D. 220 Hippolytus' aim is "that the Churches may hold fast that tradition which has continued up to now,"[1] prayers, for example, at certain definite hours because "those very elders who gave us the tradition taught us that at this hour . . ."[2] And again: "I counsel that these things be kept by all who know aright, for over all who hear the apostolic tradition and keep it no heretics will prevail. . . . For the many heresies have increased because their leaders would not learn the purpose of the Apostles."[3] Now, amongst other things, Hippolytus takes the existence of a graduated hierarchy for granted: "Each of the deacons, with the sub-deacons, shall be alert on the bishop's behalf. . . . Let the deacons and the presbyters assemble daily at the place which the bishop may appoint."[4] For Hippolytus, too, the terms "high priest" and "bishop" are convertible: "The bishop must be informed if any are sick . . . for a sick man is greatly comforted when the High Priest is mindful of him."[5] Hippolytus also gives minute regulations for the Ordination of bishops, priests and deacons.[6]

IV. THE WITNESS OF ST. IGNATIUS OF ANTIOCH

St. Ignatius of Antioch, on his way to martyrdom at Rome,[7] wrote seven letters, viz. to the churches at Ephesus, Magnesia, Tralles, Rome, Philadelphia,

Scott Easton, *The Apostolic Tradition of Hippolytus, translated into English with Introduction and Notes*, Cambridge, 1934. See, too, C. H. Turner, *J.T.S.*, July, 1915, pp. 542 ff., W. H. Frere, *J.T.S.*, January, 1915, pp. 323 ff.

[1] *Apostolic Tradition*, 1.   [2] *Ibid.*, xxxvi, 12.
[3] *Ibid.*, xxxviii.   [4] *Ibid.*, xxx and xxxiii.
[5] *Ibid.*, xxx.   [6] *Ibid.*, 2–9.
[7] It is apparently impossible to decide whether Ignatius' martyrdom took place in A.D. 107 or 116.

Smyrna, and to the bishop of the latter place, St. Polycarp, then a young man. Throughout all these letters, save that to the Romans, which stands quite apart from the rest,[1] the plea is for unity[2] and for detestation of all heresy[3] and schism.[4] The one efficacious means for securing this unity is subordination to the hierarchy of bishops, priests and deacons the existence of which is taken for granted throughout, and which, moreover, is expressly said to have been "ordained according to the disposition of Christ."[5] Again and again come such sentences as "Be subject to the bishop and the presbytery" or priestly body;[6] "the presbytery is knit to the bishop as the strings to the harp";[7] "let us strive not to withstand the bishop that so we may be subject to God."[8] So, too, the laity are urged to be "subject to the bishop as to God's command, and likewise to the presbytery"[9] . . . "as to Christ's command";[10] the priestly body stands in the place of the Apostles, for the bishops stand in the place of God or of Christ;[11] the flock is to be "subject to the bishop and to one another as Christ in His human nature was subject to the Father, and the Apostles to Christ, to the Father and to the Spirit";[12] the priestly body itself is to treat their bishop, despite his youth, with reverence as "to the Father of Christ

[1] See J. S. Phillimore in the *Journal of Theol. Studies*, January–April, 1918, for a discussion of the text of the opening clause.

[2] *Magnes.* i, vi; *Trall.* xii; *Philad.* iv.

[3] Especially the Docetes who taught that Christ was only apparently a man and did therefore suffer in reality, *Trall.* x, xii; *Smyr.* ii, v, vii; also the Judaizers, *Magnes.* viii, x; *Philad.* vi, cf. *Acts* xv.

[4] *Philad.* iii, v, viii.

[5] *Philad.* Proemium.

[6] *Ephes.* ii; *Philad.* vii; *Smyrn.* vi.

[7] *Ephes.* iv.

[8] *Ephes.* v.

[9] *Trall.* xiii, cf. *id.* iii.

[10] *Trall.* xiii.

[11] *Magnes.* vi; *Trall.* ii–iii ; *Philad.* v, viii.

[12] *Magnes.* xiii; *Philad.* viii.

Jesus, the bishop of all."[1] Hence nothing is to be done without the bishop[2] without whom indeed or his delegate there can be no valid Eucharist, nor Baptism nor Agape, "for where the bishop appears there let the multitude be, just as where Christ is there too is the Catholic Church."[3] "Therefore let us strive to make use of but one Eucharist, for one is the Flesh of our Lord Jesus Christ, and one chalice in the one-ness of His Blood, one altar, too, just as there is but one bishop with the priestly body and the deacons."[4] It would be difficult to find teaching more explicit and positive. Nor is Ignatius promulgating anything new. He is but reiterating something which was elementary and basic in the minds of all who received his Letters.

Various attempts have been made to discredit the Ignatian epistles. D'Ailly attempted this long ago because he objected to the teaching on the episcopate.[5] Later Volter did the same. But the able defences by Zahn,[6] Lightfoot[7] and Rackl[8] have established their authenticity. Those who are unable to repudiate the Letters take unworthy refuge in abuse of their author.

Ignatius, says Canon Streeter, has the " 'neurotic temper,' and he is writing under circumstances of great nervous strain. Hence whatever he writes is

[1] *Magnes.* iii.
[2] *Magnes.* vii; *Trall.* ii; cf. *Philad.* viii.
[3] *Smyrn.* viii.   [4] *Philad.* iv.
[5] Ably dealt with by J. B. Cotelerius, *SS. Patrum qui temporibus Apostolicis floruerunt,* 2 Vols. Antwerp, 1698, a work which still retains its value.
[6] *Ignatius von Antiochien,* 1873.
[7] *Ignatius of Antioch;* see, too, his Preface to the 6th edition of his *Commentary on Philippians.*
[8] M. Rackl, *Die Christologie des hl. Ignatius von Antiochien,* Freiburg im Breisgau, 1914.

instinct with excitement and exaggeration, and must be interpreted with due allowance made for the mentality of the writer."[1] It is hard to resist the obvious retort that the same might be applied to the Canon who is patently suffering from an "anti-Episcopal" complex! "The most obvious evidence that Ignatius was a man of abnormal psychology is the prophetic seizure he alludes to";[2] "he had an overwhelming conviction of possession by a personality other than his own . . . he believes himself to be under a control";[3] his self-depreciation "is not humility, it is egoism repressed";[4] his yearning for martyrdom is even compared with "masochism"![5]

When St. Ignatius says (*Trall.* iii), that

"without Bishop, Presbyter, and Deacons there is not even the name of a Church,"

Canon Streeter is content to remark that

"this proves too much, for this threefold ministry clearly did not exist, when St. Paul wrote, in the churches he addressed; it did not exist at Rome and Corinth in the time of Clement; nor apparently at Philippi even in the time of Ignatius. Ignatius here convicts himself either of deficient information or else of gross overstatement; and this weakens our confidence in his knowledge of primitive conditions in Antioch."[6]

---

[1] *The Primitive Church*, p. 163.   [2] *Ibid.*, p. 165.
[3] *Ibid.*, p. 166.   [4] *Ibid.*, p. 171.   [5] *Ibid.*, p. 172.
[6] An article in defence of his *The Primitive Church*, in the *Church of England Newspaper*, June 17, 1930; a fine example of the way in which too many students of Church history feel free to handle inconvenient evidence.

Having thus "poisoned the wells" Dr. Streeter is able to deal in summary fashion with St. Ignatius' evidence on the Episcopate:

"The neurotic temperament," he says, "is frequently characterized by an obsessive concentration on certain dominant ideas. To Ignatius, the monarchical Episcopate is literally an *idée fixe*. It may easily happen that an *idée fixe* is an idea intrinsically valuable. In the circumstances of the time, it was probably true statesmanship to strengthen the authority of the episcopate. A policy may in itself be sound, and yet in a particular individual become neurotically an obsession."

Further, Dr. Streeter assumes that St. Ignatius based his idea of the Episcopate on St. Clement's letter to the Corinthians; this letter, he remarks, would have been

"valuable to the High Church party of that day. . . . Like many an Anglican Vicar in the last three quarters of a century, Ignatius, during his tenure of office, changed his church from Low to High."[1]

A vivid imagination is out of place in a student of Church history. Anyone unfamiliar with Ignatius' letters would imagine that they give us copious information on the Saint's life, whereas all we know of him is derived from those seven very brief letters and Eusebius' summary of them.[2]

---

[1] *Ibid.*, p. 173.
[2] *Hist. Eccles.*, III, xxxvi.

V. THE WITNESS OF ST. CLEMENT OF ROME

The Epistle ascribed to St. Clement by universal and unshaken tradition opens with the words: "The Church of God which is at Rome to the Church of God which is at Corinth"; apology is then offered for unforeseen delays in answering the "questions you have put and[1] concerning the schism which a few rash and bold spirits among you have started." Though writing in the name of the Church, the writer is of course an individual who writes in the name of the whole body to the whole Corinthian body, perhaps because the argument turns on the unity of the body corporate, cf. ch. xxxviii. After depicting the charity and unity which had formerly prevailed in the Corinthian Church: "you were subordinate to your prelates[2] and gave due honour to the priests[3] among you,"[4] Clement dwells at great length on the enormity of the schism which has now arisen in their midst. The remedy is simple:

"we should do all things in order, those things which the Lord bade us perform at stated times, viz. the oblations and the public services[5] which He bade us perform, and that neither hastily nor out of due order but at definite times and hours. For He

[1] The text seems to imply that a series of questions had been sent to the Church in Rome and that the latter is about to reply to these and also to deal with the schism of which it has heard from other sources, cf. ch. xlvii; as a matter of fact Clement's Epistle deals only with the question of schism.

[2] Ἡγουμένοις, cf. *Hebrews* xiii, 7, 17, 24.

[3] πρεσβυτέροις, probably "elders" here by contrast with the "juniors" who immediately follow, cf. ch. iii "the juniors rise up against the seniors."

[4] Clement, ch. i.

[5] Λειτουργίας

by His super-excellent will decided where and by whom these things should be carried out, so that, all things being thus religiously performed in accordance with His good pleasure, they might thus prove acceptable to His good will. Those, then, who make their oblations at the appointed times are acceptable and blessed, for they cannot go wrong when carrying out the Lord's behests. To the Chief Priest[1] are assigned his public services, to the priests their due place, while the Levites have their own duties and the laity the duties incumbent on the laity."[2]

"The Apostles preached to us the Gospel by the Lord's command, and Jesus Christ by God's command. Christ, then, was sent by God, and the Apostles by Christ, both in due order by the will of God. Having received His commands, then, and, through the Resurrection of Our Lord Jesus Christ, being filled with complete certainty, confirmed too by the Word of God, with full confidence in the Holy Spirit, they went forth and preached the coming of the Kingdom of God. And when they had preached the Word in various districts and towns they appointed the first-fruits of their preaching —men whom they had proved by the Spirit—to be bishops[3] and deacons of such as were about to embrace the faith. Nor was this an innovation, since many centuries before the Scripture had spoken of bishops

---

[1] τῷ γὰρ ἀρχιερῷ . . . καὶ τοῖς ἱερεῦσιν . . . καὶ λευίταις ἰδίαι διακονίαι In the N.T. ἱερεύς is used only of the Levitical priesthood except in the *Epistle to the Hebrews*, where it is used of Christ, and in *Apocalypse* i, 6, v, 10, xx, 6, where it is used of Christians.

[2] Clement, Ch. xl.

[3] The word "bishops," ἐπισκόπους, is here apparently used generically for the priestly class, cf. *Philippians* i, 1; yet *cp*. Ch. xliv where πρεσβύτεροι seems to stand for bishops and priests alike.

and deacons: *I will establish their bishops in justice
and their deacons in faith.*" (*Isa.* lx, 17.)[1] Clement
goes on to instance the case of Moses and the rod of
Aaron, and then concludes:

"So, too, our Apostles knew from our Lord Jesus
Christ that contentions about the title of 'bishop'[2]
would arise, and hence, endowed with complete
foreknowledge, they appointed the aforesaid bishops
and afterwards laid it down that on the death of these
latter other approved men should succeed to their
ministry. We, then, reckon that men thus appointed
by the Apostles or, subsequently to them, by others
of approved virtue, with the consent of the entire
Church, men who have blamelessly ministered to
Christ's flock in humility, peacefulness and gener-
osity, and who have during long years met with the
highest approval from all, cannot justly be deprived
of their office. For it will be no small sin on our part
if we remove from the episcopate[3] men who have
in holy and blameless fashion offered the gifts.
Happy those priests[4] who have already completed
their course and have met death after a fruitful
and perfect ministry; for they have no reason to fear
lest some one should remove them from the position
assigned to them. But we see that you have
removed from office men who have fulfilled it
honestly, blamelessly and honourably. . . . It is a
truly grievous thing, and altogether unworthy of

[1] According to the LXX version; the Vulgate and Douay: *I will
make thy visitation peace and thy overseers justice;* the Rev. Version:
thy officers peace and thine exactors righteousness.

[2] τῆς ἐπισκοπῆς. It is difficult to understand how Lightfoot
can say that there is "no mention of Episcopacy properly so-called
throughout the Epistle"; for in the language of Clement, "'bishop'
and 'priest' are still synonymous terms." (*Commentary of Philipp.*,
p. 205, see his *St. Clement of Rome*, i, p. 69.)

[3] *Ibid.*   [4] πρεσβύτεροι.

Christians, that we hear of you, namely, that the ancient and long-established Church of Corinth should, through the influence of one or two men, have started a sedition against the priests."[1]

Certain conclusions seem clear: (*a*) According to St. Clement Christ had not only left definite arrangements about liturgical services but—so at least chap. xl would imply—about the hierarchy of "chief priest," "priests" (ἱερεῖς) and "deacons," all of them totally distinct from the laity. (*b*) This enactment of His the Apostles carried out when they set up such a hierarchy of "bishops and deacons," chap. xlii, where "bishop" seems to be used as a generic term for those superior to the deacons, a passage which must of course be read in the light of chap. xl, where we read of "chief priests" and "priests." (*c*) Christ had also foretold that difficulties would arise about the Episcopate; hardly about the mere "name," as the text has it, but perhaps about the dignity attaching to it, perhaps even about superiorship in general, the need of which would speedily become apparent. To preclude such disputes, then, the Apostles themselves were to appoint such "chief priests" and to arrange that others were to succeed those whom they had appointed as death called these latter. (*d*) That all bishops were priests is evidenced by the use of the words "chief priests" and "priests," chap. xl; conversely that not all priests were bishops appears from chap. i: "You were subordinate to your prelates and gave due honour to the Elders among you," where, to judge by chap. xliv, "happy those priests . . .",

[1] *Clement*, ch. xliv.

M

we should hardly do justice to the context if we rendered πρεσβυτέρους by "elders."

Clement's letter, then, written at the close of the first century, shows that the Church both at Rome and Corinth took it for granted that the hierarchy of bishops, priests and deacons was due to a divine ordinance, though the Corinthian Church had allowed itself to forget this.

Apropos of this command left by Christ, Rothe,[1] a Presbyterian, maintained that the practically simultaneous deaths of SS. Peter, Paul and James called for immediate steps to secure definite organization, now that so many of the original rulers of the churches had departed. Such a step, he urges, could only have been due to the surviving Apostles, e.g. St. John and St. Philip, who, he thinks, met in a council shortly after the fall of Jerusalem in A.D. 70. Of this second Council he would see traces in the meeting held for the appointment of Symeon as the successor of James at Jerusalem, also in a fragment somewhat doubtfully attributed to St. Irenæus, perhaps with greater probability in St. Clement's statement given above that the Apostles "afterwards laid it down that on the death of these latter (viz. the bishops appointed by them). . ."[2] Rothe thinks that up to that date the Church had been governed by presbyter-bishops and deacons only and that the institution of bishops as now understood was due to this apostolic enactment.

Quite apart from other reasons this theory seems to us to fail because based on a false conception of the nature of the Church. Even when all the Apostles

---

[1] See his arguments summarized by Lightfoot, *Philipp*. pp. 201–207; also Hefele, *Patres Apostolici*, 2nd ed. 1847, on 1 Clement xliv.

[2] Rothe's argument depends on his rendering of the word ἐπιτομή by "codicil," on which see Lightfoot and Hefele, *l.c.*

were still alive they were not "the Church," for the Church is a living organism of which the Apostles were the propagators.   Presbyterian and other writers seem rather to regard the Church as an organization which depends for its vitality and persistence on the character of its rulers at any given date.   As St. Optatus remarked of the Donatist schismatics of his day: "*Inde est, quod ignoras, et quae sit sancta Ecclesia: et sic omnia misruisti*,"[1] they fail to understand what Augustine so constantly repeats "*In Christo loquitur Ecclesia, et in Ecclesia loquitur Christus.*"[2]

VI. THE WITNESS OF THE NEW TESTAMENT

To what does the New Testament evidence amount? Taking the *Gospels* first, it is noticeable that Christ says singularly little about the government and administration of the Church He is founding.   But He does form a body of Apostles quite distinct from the general body of disciples and He does give us most positive statements about the one who is to be chief amongst them.   The *Acts of the Apostles* deals not so much with the organization of the Church itself as with the foundation by individual Apostles of a number of local churches which are perfectly conscious that they form but parts of a whole—the Ecclesia, or Church; and this "Church" is not regarded as an organization but as a living organism, a "new creature," as was Christ Himself its Founder; the "soul" of this organism is the quickening Holy Spirit, and this same Church is even personified as the living Body of Christ which He loves even as a husband loves his wife.

Similarly in the all too brief Epistles nothing is laid

[1] *De Schismate Donatistarum*, i, 10.
[2] *Enarr.*, 4, ii, on *Psalm* xxx.

down in doctrinal fashion about the administration
of these local churches; it is taken for granted that
each church has its ministers; nowhere does it say
that they are to have them. How striking in this
connexion is the opening sentence in *Philippians* i, 1,
"to the bishops and deacons." Where did they come
from? Who appointed them? So, too, in St. Paul's
address at Miletus: the "Bishops who rule the Church"
by the appointment of the Holy Spirit are not a detail
of administration which the Apostle is now instituting,
nor a happy thought on the part of the Asian churches
who fancy that for the *bene esse* of their church it would
be a good idea to have "overseers." It is the same
with St. John's churches in Asia: bishops there are
regarded as a matter of course.

On thing, then, is certain: bishops are in recognized
possession as early as the date of St. Paul's address
at Miletus. Nor is there the remotest hint that the
idea of having such bishops emanated from the
Apostles; it was part of the *"esse"* of the Church, not
simply of its *"bene esse."*

Further, we must disabuse ourselves of the notion
that the Apostles only acted "corporately" or as a body.
Throughout the *Acts* and *Epistles* they are depicted as
acting on their own individual initiative; they found
churches and administer them as circumstances permit.
Yet those churches all work on the same general lines;
surely an indication that there was a general and well-
understood norm. Why, for instance, did St. Paul
feel it necessary to go and consult St. Peter? (*Gal.* i, ii.)

But it is claimed that the New Testament evidence[1]

---

[1] We give the chief references again for convenience: *Phil.* i, 1;
Acts xx, 17, 28; 1 *Peter* v, 1–2; 1 *Timothy* iii, 1–7 on bishops, whereas
iii, 8–13 deals with deacons, and there is no mention of priests until
we come to v, 17–19; *Titus* i, 5–7.

shows that "bishop" and "priest" (presbyter) are convertible terms, and that the same appears in St. Clement's Epistle, but that with the opening of the second century the distinction between the two offices is "more modern."[1] Others maintain that Ignatius is indebted to Clement for his ideas on hierarchy.[2] Lightfoot would even maintain that by "the close of the second century" the notion of their identity had disappeared, only to be recovered by the Fathers in the fourth century who "began to examine the apostolic records with a more critical eye," and he quotes St. Jerome,[3] Ambrosiaster, Chrysostom, Pelagius, Theodore of Mopsuestia, etc.

Quite apart from the fact that totally divergent conclusions are here deduced from the same premisses it is somewhat startling to learn that between Clement, A.D. 98, and Ignatius, A.D. 107–16, there should have occurred so remarkable a change of outlook on a vital question. Further, these views seem based on a false conception of the letters of Clement and Ignatius. One would gather from a perusal of the many learned disquisitions on them that these writers were concerned with the doctrinal questions attaching to the episcopal office, whereas nothing was further from their minds. They both take the position of bishops for granted, and their teaching on the dangers of schism are based on the universally accepted ideas of the Episcopate which they rightly presume that their readers have; if those ideas were being ventilated for the first time both Clement's and Ignatius' arguments against schism would lose their force.

To us it seems perfectly clear that the evidence of

---

[1] Lightfoot, Dissertations on the Apostolic Age, p. 193.
[2] H. B. Streeter, The Primitive Church.
[3] On St. Jerome, see below.

the New Testament and of the apostolic fathers all points to the time-honoured traditional position, viz. that whereas every bishop was a priest, not every priest was a bishop in fact, though he was so potentially. The New Testament evidence is, it must be remembered, extraordinarily meagre, consisting more of a series of allusions to facts rather than of dogmatic pronouncements on the subject. It is the same with the apostolic fathers. On many points they are "didactic," concerned to make the teaching of the Church perfectly plain; but nowhere do they "teach" us about the relation between the Episcopate and the Presbyterate. It should never be forgotten in dealing with this and similar problems that tradition is as much an historic fact as some precise statement in a document. Indeed it is far more valuable as a guide to the truth than precise documentary statements. For whereas these latter may be and often are isolated facts which have to be interpreted, and their relation with similar statements carefully weighed, tradition is of its very nature not "*a* fact" but a series of facts, not something isolated but something persistently "handed down"; it is the "isolated facts" which have to be brought into harmony with tradition; to attempt the converse, to try and square tradition with such "facts," only leads to confusion, while the endeavour to sweep tradition on one side and regard it as something quite distinct from historic evidence is futile. Yet this is precisely what Lightfoot insists on doing. "In this clamour of antagonistic opinions," he says, "history is obviously the sole upright, impartial referee; and the historical mode of treatment will therefore be strictly adhered to in the following investigation."[1]

[1] *l.c.*, pp. 143–4; *Commentary on Philipp.*, p. 187.

To enter into details :

The use in the New Testament and in the apostolic fathers of the word "bishop," ἐπίσκοπος, with the verb ἐπισκόπεω and the abstract noun ἐπισκοπή, "Bishopric," will replay investigation. First of all we have the verb and the abstract noun with the sense of "overseeing" or supervision. St. Paul, for instance, says it is the duty of the faithful *to be looking diligently* (ἐπισκοποῦντες) *lest any man be wanting* . . . (*Heb.* xii, 15; similarly *the ancients* (presbyteri) are told by St. Peter to *feed the flock of God, taking care of it* (ἐπισκοποῦντες) . . . *not as lording it over the clergy.*[1] (1 *Pet.* v, 2, 3.) Similarly St. Ignatius remarks that Christ alone will *take care of* (ἐπισκοπήσει)[2] the Church of Antioch since Ignatius their bishop is now removed from them, while he addresses Polycarp as "Bishop of the Smyrneans, though more correctly *watching over them* (ἐπισκομένῳ) under God the Father and the Lord Jesus Christ."[3] The abstract ἐπισκοπή appears in the familiar quotation by St. Peter from *Psalm* cviii, 8, *his bishopric let another take* (*Acts* i, 20), but more particularly with the meaning of "visitation," e.g. in Christ's lament over Jerusalem *because thou hast not known the time of thy visitation,*[4] with which compare St. Peter's *Glorify God in the day of visitation.*[5] But the same terms are also used by St. Paul of a definite office: *If a man desire the office of a bishop,*[6] and he proceeds to state the qualifications for this office. Precisely the same twofold usage occurs in St. Clement, "they shall be made manifest in the visitation (ἐπισκοπῇ) of Christ,"[7] though just previously he had said that

[1] κατακυριεύντες τῶν κλήρων.   [2] *Romans* ix.
[3] *Ad Polycarpum*, Proemium.   [4] *Luke* xix, 44.
[5] 1 *Peter* ii, 12.   [6] 1 *Timothy* iii, 1.   [7] 1 *Clement*, l.

"the Apostles knew from Our Lord Jesus Christ that disputes would arise concerning the name of bishopric, ἐπισκοπῆς."[1] Finally Ignatius prays that Polycarp "may abide in union with God and the episcopal office (ἐπισκοπῇ)."[2]

The concrete term, ἐπίσκοπος, appears in St. Paul's charge to "the ancients of the Church" of Ephesus,[3] whom he warns to *take heed to yourselves and to the whole flock wherein the Holy Ghost hath placed you bishops*, ἐπισκόπους, *to rule the Church of God*,[4] words which find their echo in St. Peter: *Feed the flock of God which is among you. . . .*[5] Of the fifty-nine times the word occurs in the apostolic fathers no less than fifty-one are to be found in the Epistles of St. Ignatius.

Further, we have a significant word, ἡγούμενοι, "rulers" or "prelates." St. Paul, for instance, tells us to "remember," "obey," and "salute" our prelates,[6] ἡγουμένοις ; Clement speaks of the priests and Levites of the Old Testament, of the kings, princes and leaders, ἡγούμενοι[7]; he speaks too of the military leaders, as illustrating that subordination to constituted authority which should characterize the Christian body, and, in words reminiscent of St. Paul, he praises the Corinthians because in the past "you have been subject to your prelates, ἡγουμένοις, and have given due honour to the presbyters who are among you; you have bidden the younger people observe modesty and reverence, and the women . . ., etc."[8] It is very doubtful

---

[1] *Clement*, xliv. [2] *Ad Polycarpum*, viii.
[3] *Acts* xx, 17. [4] *Ibid.*, 28.
[5] 1 *Peter* v, 2; cf. 1 *Timothy* iii, 2, *Titus* i, 7.
[6] *Hebrews* xiii, 7, 17, 24.
[7] 1 *Corinthians* xxxii, xxxvii, li, lv; cf. lxi.
[8] *Ibid.*, i, cf. xxi, "Let us then venerate our prelates, προηγουμένους, honour our presbyters and instruct our young people in the discipline of the fear of the Lord."

whether, because it can be rendered "elders," the word "presbyteri" here should be limited to those who are seniors merely in age; we have to bear in mind the many passages in the Pastoral Epistles which imply more than this.[1]

The Greek "presbyter" means, of course, "an elder," e.g. "the elder son." (*Luke* xv, 25.) But while these "elders" occupy a prominent position in the early Church,[2] clearly not every man of a certain age held this position merely by right of grey hairs; when St. Peter beseeches the "ancients" that are among them, adding *who am myself also an ancient*,[3] when St. John styles himself "the ancient,"[4] neither of these Apostles can mean that they too are old men like their readers and can therefore appeal to them on the equal footing of old age, as St. Paul does when he says to Philemon, *Thou art such an one as Paul, an old man.*[5] Old age may have been a desirable requisite for admission to an office, but it did not necessarily confer a right to it. Hence the very definite and early statement that Paul and Barnabas *ordained to them priests* (elders, presbyters) *in every church*;[6] these same "priests" are said to *rule well*[7] and are styled *the priests* (elders) *of the Church*;[8] they are teachers of whom is demanded definite qualifications[9] and they are *ordained in every city* for this purpose.[10] In this connexion it is well to

[1] No need to insist on Clement's repeated quotations from *Hebrews;* his familiarity with the Pastoral Epistles is no less marked, cp. for example, ii with *Titus* iii, 1; xxi with 1 *Timothy* v, 21; xxvii with *Titus* i, 2; xliii with *Titus* i, 3; xliv with 2 *Timothy* iv, 6; see Eusebius, *H.E.*, III, xxxviii, 1.

[2] *Acts* xi, 30; xv, 2; xvi, 4; xx, 17; xxi, 18.

[3] 1 *Peter*, v, 1.   [4] 2 *John* 1, 3 *John* 1.

[5] *Philemon* 9.   [6] *Acts* xiv, 23, *Titus* i, 5.

[7] 1 *Timothy* v, 17.   [8] *James* v, 14.

[9] *Titus* ii, 2.   [10] *Titus* i, 5.

note how St. Paul is said to have called the ancients (elders, presbyters) of the Church to Miletus[1] and in the course of his address—an episcopal "charge"— says to them: *Take heed to yourselves and to the whole flock wherein the Holy Ghost has placed you bishops* (ἐπισκόπους) *to rule the*[2] *Church of God.*[3]

These passages point to the conclusion that while every "elder" was not therefore a "priest" yet every priest had to be an elder, at least by his moral character. Timothy was clearly a young man,[4] so, too, was the Bishop of Magnesia,[5] as also St. Polycarp when St. Ignatius wrote to him, whether in A.D. 107 or 116, for Polycarp was not martyred till A.D. 155 when, as he says, he had been serving the Lord for six-and-eighty years.[6]

The terms ἱερεύς, hiereus, "priest," and ἀρχιερεύς, high priest, are used in the New Testament only of the Jewish priesthood save in the *Epistle to the Hebrews*, where they are used of the Jewish priesthood, of Melchisedec and of Christ; in *Apocalypse* i, 6; v, 10; xx, 6, they are applied to the whole Christian body. Clement uses ἱερεύς of the Egyptian priesthood,[7] also of the Levitical priesthood,[8] but it is important to note that he transfers all the terms used of the Levitical hierarchy to the Christian body: "To the high priest are assigned his own functions, to the priests their peculiar task, and the Levites have their own ministry."[9]

---

[1] *Acts* xx, 17.

[2] ποιμαίνειν, a most significant word, cf. *John* xxi, 16, 1 *Peter* v, 2.

[3] *Acts* xx, 28. St. Irenæus, *d.* A.D. 202, read in his text of xx, 17: "Having summoned from Miletus the bishops and priests who were from Ephesus and the other neighbouring cities." (*Adv. Haer.*, III, xiv, 2; *Patrol. Graeca*; Migne, vii, col. 914.)

[4] 1 *Timothy* iv, 12; 2 *Timothy* ii, 22; cf. *Acts* xvi, 1–3.

[5] St. Ignatius, *Magnes.*, iii.

[6] *Martyr. Polycarpi*, ix.

[7] 1 *Corinthians* xxv.   [8] *Ibid.*, xxxii.   [9] *Ibid.*, xl.

Similarly Christ is "the high priest"[1] as in *Hebrews*, but once more the term is transferred to the Christian hierarchy.[2] The same usage appears in St. Ignatius: "Priests are good, but more excellent is the high priest to whom alone was entrusted the holy of holies and the hidden things of God, for He (Christ) is the door of the Father."[3]

Apropos of the term "clergy" in 1 *Peter* v, 2, 3, "not lording it over the clergy," Lightfoot, who is a sturdy opponent of "sacerdotalism," repudiates the notion that "the clergy" here denotes the priestly caste: "the earliest instance," he says, "of 'clerus' meaning clergy, seems to occur in Tertullian (*De Monogamia*, 12)," and he argues that the priesthood of the ministry springs from the priesthood of the congregation.[4] Moulton and Milligan remark that "the difficult κλήρων of 1 *Peter* v, 3, is probably best understood of the 'portions' or 'congregations' ('parishes,' Tindale and Cranmer) of God's people assigned or allotted to the presbyters, while an example of the later ecclesiastical term may be found in a Macedonian inscription, not earlier than the second century A.D.: 'We therefore beseech the esteemed bishop of the holy church at Amphipolis and its well-beloved κλῆρον,' where Ferguson (*Legal Terms*, p. 60) thinks that κλῆρον is best understood of 'the clergy' taken collectively."[5]

But as a matter of fact when priests are mentioned it is always in their ministerial, administrative capacity as "elders," "the priests that rule well" (1 *Tim.* v, 17); their sacerdotal functions are taken for granted, or

---

[1] *Ibid.*, xxxvi, lxi.   [2] *Ibid.*, xl–xli.
[3] *Philadelph.* ix, cf. *John* x, 7.
[4] *The Christian Ministry, Commentary on Philippians*, pp. 242 and 257.
[5] Vocabulary of the Greek Testament, *s.v.* κλῆρος.

rather do not come into the picture. This silence, has, we think, led Lightfoot astray, for he maintains[1] that in the New Testament sacerdotal claims are absent and are even doubtfully present in the writings of the Apostolic Fathers. He minimizes, too, the references to the "oblation," would even regard St. Paul's "We have an altar" (*Heb.* xiii, 19) as "an extension of a metaphor . . . on which a false superstition has been erected."[2] This silence about the purely sacerdotal functions of the priests may explain the expression "bishops and deacons" in *Philippians* i, 1, for, to repeat: all bishops were priests so far as sacerdotal functions were concerned, but not all priests were bishops when it was a question of administrative and ministerial work.

VII. THAT THE EPISCOPATE SUCCEEDED TO THE APOSTOLIC BODY

The Councils of Trent and the Vatican stated as an acknowledged fact that the bishops were successors of the Apostles.[3] This was the opinion also of Theodore of Mopsuestia:

"Those who are nowadays termed 'Bishops' were of old called 'Apostles' . . . for as the holy Apostles departed this life those who were ordained subsequently to them to preside over the churches, since they felt themselves far from equal to those predecessors of theirs—not only not having the testimony of miracles to support them as the latter had had, but being in many other points their inferiors—they deemed it unfitting that they should claim the title

[1] *Commentary on Philippians*, pp. 244–250.
[2] *Ibid.*, p. 261.
[3] See above, pp. 151–2.

of 'Apostle.' They therefore split up the title and, while leaving to the priests the title of 'Priest,' termed the others 'Bishops,' those, that is, who were endowed with the power to ordain, so that these latter might realise that they had full authority over the churches."[1]

The same is said by Theodoret;[2] Lightfoot speaks of this as an "opinion hazarded" by him, yet, not quite consistently, adds in a note that Theodoret "has borrowed it from Theodore of Mopsuestia." Lightfoot, however, rejects the identification of the Episcopate with the Apostolate as "baseless," on the grounds that the two offices are not identical, that the Apostles "held no local office," and that since "bishop was at first used as a synonym for presbyter and afterwards came to designate the higher officer under whom the presbyters served, the Episcopate properly so called would seem to have been developed from the subordinate office. In other words, the Episcopate was formed not out of the apostolic order by localization but out of the presbyteral by elevation."[3]

Now these post-Nicene writers are only stating what was to them traditional. They knew, as well as we, indeed better than we, that Hippolytus had spoken of the bishops as "successors of the Apostles and partakers of the same grace both of high priesthood and of teaching, and accounted guardians of the Church."[4] The same expression occurs too in the Prayer for the Consecration of a Bishop given by Serapion, Bishop of Thmuis, c. 350: "make him a

[1] *Comment,* on 1 *Timothy* iii, ed. Swete, 1882, ii, pp. 123–4.
[2] *Comment* on 1 *Timothy* iii.
[3] *Commentary on Philippians,* pp. 195–6.
[4] Proem. to *Adv. Haereses,* iii.

living bishop, worthy of the succession of the holy
Apostles."[1]

VIII. OF THE SUPPOSED "PRESBYTER-BISHOPS" OF THE ALEXANDRIAN CHURCH

Much stress is laid by some writers on the fact that
at Alexandria the bishop was, until a comparatively
late date, elected by clergy and people.

And it is presumed that the clergy, the presbyters,
elected one of their number as their bishop and then
consecrated him. But the question then arises: How
could men who were not themselves bishops "consecrate"? Some have been so impressed by this that
they have even gone so far as to coin the term "presbyter-bishops" over whom there was no church-officer
and who had due authority to appoint and ordain
their own successors. "They were, in fact," says Gore,
"all bishops—there was poly-episcopacy, not mon-
episcopacy; what was temporarily lacking in these
churches was the presbyteral office pure and simple,
such as we read of in the New Testament, and in
later history, which had not these powers."[2]

This seems to us a most gratuitous supposition. As
a matter of fact neither Eusebius nor St. Jerome say
that these clergy "consecrated" their bishop. When
Dr. Streeter writes: "When the see was vacant, we are
told, the twelve presbyters chose one of themselves,
and the remaining eleven, laying their hands on his
head, blessed him and created him patriarch"[3]

---

[1] Given by Scott Easton, *The Apostolic Tradition of Hippolytus*,
1934, p. 68.

[2] A Paper read at Sion College, November 4, 1930; cf. *The Church
and the Ministry*, pp. 177 ff.

[3] *The Primitive Church*, pp. 253–4. See St. Jerome, *Ep.* cxlvi;
Eusebius, *Hist. Eccles.*, VII, xxx, 17, and M'Giffert's notes; Light-

his only authority is the Arabian Eutychius who was
Patriarch in A.D. 933–940. Even supposing that they
did consecrate we have a possible analogy in the case
of the election of the Pope by the Cardinals who elect
him and then consecrate him as Pope. No one concludes that the Pontiff thus consecrated is inferior to
those Cardinals nor that his office is a purely human
one. The analogy fails, of course, owing to the fact
that the consecrators are themselves bishops. The
truth is that the whole argument rests on the supposition that there was not at Alexandria a complete
hierarchy from the very days of St. Mark who consecrated Anianus as his successor[1] and, as the author
of an ancient *Vita S. Marci* says: "also ordained
three priests and seven deacons."[2] The same Patriarch Eutychius referred to by Canon Streeter says
that "the Evangelist St. Mark appointed twelve Priests
to be with the Patriarch Anianus."[3] It is significant,
too, that the very Heraclas, in whose day it is maintained that the method of election now prevalent
first began, was a disciple of Origen who has left us
the clearest indications of the existence at Alexandria
in his day of a fully constituted hierarchy: "Neither
Bishop, nor Priest, nor Deacon, nor widow can be
digamists",[4] or again: "More is demanded of me than
from a deacon, more from a deacon than from a
layman; while a person who is over the whole Church
will have to render account for the whole Church."[5] It

foot, *The Christian Ministry*, pp. 188–95, in *Dissertations on the
Apostolic Age*; Cotelerius, *Patres Apostolici*, II, ii, p. 327; Hippolytus,
Apostolic Tradition, i, 2nd ed. Easton.
  [1] Eusebius, *Hist. Eccles*.
  [2] See Cotelerius, *l.c.* ii, p. 319.   [3] *Ibid*.
  [4] *Hom*. xvii on Luke, Delarue, iii, 953; cf. *Hom*. xiii, also *Hom*.
xi on Jeremias and *Contra Celsum*, iii, 48.
  [5] *Hom*. v on Ezechiel.

was the same with Origen's predecessor in the school at Alexandria. "I reckon," says Clement of Alexandria, "that the ecclesiastical grades amongst us, Bishops, Priests and Deacons, are imitations of the glory of the Angels."[1]

IX. OF ST. JEROME'S TEACHING ON THE POSITION OF BISHOPS IN THE CHURCH

A famous letter written by St. Jerome[2] has caused much heart-burning. A correspondent, Evangelus, had written to ask him whether there was any foundation for the notion that deacons were superior to priests. In reply, St. Jerome, who characteristically opens with the words *A fool will speak foolish things* (*Isa.* xxxii, 6), says: "I hear that some one has been silly enough to prefer Deacons to Priests, that is to Bishops." In support of this bold statement, viz., that bishops and priests are the same, he quotes all the familiar passages from the New Testament (viz. *Phil.* i, 1; *Acts* xx. 28; *Tit.* i, 5; 1 *Tim.* iv, 14; 1 *Peter* v, 1–2; 2 *John* i, 3; *John* 1), and then says:

"But that afterwards one was chosen to be over the rest was simply done to provide a remedy against schism lest some individual should break up the Church of Christ by drawing it to his side," and he instances the case of Alexandria where, from the days of St. Mark until Bishops Heraclas and Denis, "the Priests chose one of their own body, assigned him a superior position and styled him 'Bishop'. . . . For with the exception of ordaining what can a

---

[1] Strom. vi, 13; cf. *Paedag.* iii, 12.
[2] Ep. cxlvi. The date is uncertain.

Bishop do that a Priest cannot"? "Rome," he adds, "is not to be regarded as a different kind of Church from that in the rest of the world; Gaul, Britain, Africa, Persia, the East and India, as well as the other barbarous peoples, adore one and the same Christ and hold to the same rule of truth. If you make it a question of authority, then surely the World is greater than the City (*Orbis major est Urbe*). Wherever you find a Bishop, at Rome, Eugubium, Constantinople, Rhegium, Alexandria or Tanis, his merits are the same as those of a Priest."

If, he continues, there are abuses at Rome where— though this is not the general rule even there— deacons, as Jerome himself has witnessed, sit while the priests stand, and if the deacons there even venture to give a blessing to priests, well, that is Rome's concern and it is idle to allege the customs of an individual city against universal practice.

"The titles 'Priest' and 'Bishop'," he concludes, "signify age and dignity respectively; hence though in the Epistles to Titus and Timothy we read of the ordination of Bishops and Deacons, not a word is said about the ordination of a Priest, for the Priesthood is contained in the Episcopate. . . . To realize that these Apostolic traditions are based on the Old Testament it will be sufficient to note that what Aaron, his sons, and the Levites were in the Temple, that the Bishops, Priests, and Deacons claim to be in the Church."

Making every allowance for St. Jerome's vehemence and his tendency to exaggerate a case it is clear that his sole idea here is to remind the deacons of their

N

subordinate position: *"Sciant quare Diaconi constituti sint,"*[1] and that he is emphasizing the position of the priests at the cost of the deacons, not at the cost of the bishops. Nowhere in this letter does he suggest that every priest is *ipso facto* a bishop, but merely that every bishop is a priest. The statement, however, which immediately concerns us is that "afterwards one was chosen to be over the rest simply to provide a remedy against schism." Yet is this any more than a reminiscence of St. Clement's "and afterwards laid it down that on the death of these latter (the Bishops appointed by the Apostles) other approved men should succeed to their ministry"?[2] Jerome in this very letter speaks of this as "Apostolic tradition." Moreover, he speaks of the power of ordaining as something inherent in the episcopal office, hardly as something due to their priestly powers. In many other passages he shows unequivocally that he regarded the hierarchy as a divinely instituted thing. He insists, for example, that "the titles 'Bishop', 'Priest' and 'Deacon' do not refer to merit but to offices. Nor does it say *if a man desire the office of a Bishop he desires* a good favour, but *he desireth a good work*, since, placed in a higher position, he can if he likes make it an opportunity of practising virtue."[3] And again: "The Bishop is the light of the Church . . . his function is to keep people from error . . . the salvation of the

---

[1] Ep. cxlvi, No. 4.   [2] 1 *Corinthians* xliv.

[3] "Episcopus et presbyter et diaconus non sunt meritorum nomina sed officiorum. Nec dicitur: Si quis Episcopatum desiderat, bonam desiderat gratiam; sed bonum opus desiderat; quod in majori ordine constitutus, possit, si velit, occasionem exercendarum habere virtutum. . . . Cernis igitur quod Episcopus, presbyter et diaconus non ideo sunt beati quia episcopi vel presbyteri sint aut diaconi sed si virtutes habuerint nominum suorum et officiorum." (*Adv. Jovinianum*, i, 34–5.)

Church depends on the position of the High Priest whose extraordinary and supereminent power is given him lest. . . . Hence it comes that without the Bishop's chrism and permission neither Priest nor Deacon has the right to baptize."[1]

Again, after saying: "Put not your trust in rulers, not in Bishop, Priest or Deacon, nor in any human dignity," Jerome carefully adds: "I do not mean thereby that you ought not to be subject to these Ecclesiastical dignitaries, for *He that curseth father or mother*, says Leviticus, *dying let him die*, xx, 9, and the Apostle himself bids us obey our Prelates in the Church, all I mean is that it is one thing to honour rulers, quite another to put our trust in them. So, let us honour the Bishop, pay reverence to the Priests and stand up when the Deacon enters, but let us not put our trust in them."[2]

Once more: "Bishops should remember that they are Priests, not masters; if they would have the clergy pay them the honour due to them as Bishops then they must honour the clergy as clergy";[3] while when John of Jerusalem implied, at least by the action he took, that "there was no difference between Bishop and Priest; the sender and his messenger are of like standing," Jerome's comment is brief: "A sufficiently ignorant statement; by it you, as the saying goes, have made shipwreck before leaving harbour."[4]

St. Chrysostom's teaching is precisely the same:

---

[1] "Ecclesiæ lumen est Episcopus . . . sacerdote enim fidem veram prædicante ex omnium corde tenebræ discutiuntur . . . ideo Episcopus in Ecclesia constituatur ut populum coerceat ab errore . . . Ecclesiæ salus in summi sacerdotis dignitate pendet cui si non exsors quædam et ab omnibus eminens detur potestas tot in ecclesiis efficientur schismata quot sacerdotes. Inde venit ut sine chrismate et episcopi jussione neque presbyter neque diaconus jus habeant baptizandi." (*Dial. contra Luciferianos*, 9.)

[2] *On Mich.* vii, 5–7.   [3] *Ep.* lii, 7.   [4] *Adv. Joann. Hierosolm*, 37.

"There is not much difference between Bishops and Priests; for the latter have received a commission to teach and exercise leadership in the Church, while what he (St. Paul) says of Bishops applies also to Priests, for Bishops are only superior to Priests by ordaining power,[1] in this alone do they seem to excel them."[2]

St. Augustine seems to regard the question as having no more than an antiquarian interest, for he is content to say of the Aerians that they derive their name from "a certain Aerius who is reported to have regretted that though he was a Priest he could not get ordained a Bishop. . . . He also maintained (presumably in consequence of his disappointment) that there was no discernible difference between Bishops and Priests."[3] On the question whether elders (presbyteri) and priests were convertible terms he merely remarks that "whereas every old man is an Elder (Presbyter) not every Priest (Presbyter) is an old man."[4] Again, when writing to St. Jerome and almost apologizing for being a bishop while Jerome is only a priest, he says: *"Quanquam enim secundum honorum vocabula quæ jam Ecclesiæ usus obtinuit,"*[5] which should surely be rendered: "Although according to the honorific titles which Church-usage has long maintained," but which Lightfoot, we think unfairly, renders: "Although according to titles of honour which the practice of the Church has now made valid."[6]

[1] χειροτονία.   [2] *Hom.* xi, 1, *on* 1 Tim.
[3] "Aeriani ab Aerio quodam sunt, qui cum esset presbyter doluisse fertur quod Episcopus non potuit ordinari . . . Dicebat etiam presbyterum ab episcopo nulla differentia debere discerni." (*De Hæresibus*, liii.)
[4] "Proinde omnis senex etiam presbyter, non omnis presbyter etiam senex." (*Quæstionum in Heptateuchum*, i, 70.)
[5] Ep. lxxxii, 33.
[6] *Dissertations on the Apostolic Age*, p. 193.

THE EUCHARIST DURING THE FIRST THREE CENTURIES

By the Right Rev. Dom Fernand Cabrol, O.S.B.,
Abbot of Farnborough

During July, 1922, from the 24th to the 29th, the Summer School assembled at Cambridge, devoted itself wholly to the study of the Eucharist. The result of this study was a book, *Catholic Faith in the Holy Eucharist*, which may be said to have achieved a decided success.[1] It treated of the Eucharist under every one of its aspects, but especially from the dogmatic point of view. This year the general subject of our Summer School is the study of the Church, of Her life and of Her development, during the period between the years A.D. 33 and 325; that is, the epoch called *Ante-Nicean*. Like the other Sacraments the Eucharist would naturally take its rightful place here, but this time its study must have a more specially historical character; it cannot and must not be a mere repetition of the Conferences given in 1922. But the Eucharist is so vast a subject that many Conferences might be devoted to it without our fearing to repeat ourselves.

In the present Conference I intend to show:

(1) That the history of the Eucharist during this period is based on the testimony of numerous witnesses of very different kinds.

[1] Third edition, enlarged in 1928, Heffer, Cambridge.

(2) That in the life of the Christians of that age the Eucharist occupies the most important place.

(3) To such an extent that it may be said that Christian piety in the first three centuries is specially concentrated, specially expressed in the Eucharist.

(4) The various ways of treating the Eucharist are another proof of this.

I

Since we are on historical ground we must first examine the documents (texts or monuments) on which is based the history of the Eucharist.

It may be said at the outset, that of all the Seven Sacraments the Eucharist is the best documented during that period. Baptism itself, which has a fine literary history, as well as Holy Orders, are less well known than the Eucharist; and the testimony of contemporary authors in their regard is less frequent. As to the other Sacraments—Confirmation apart, because at that time it was usually connected with Baptism— that is to say, Penance, Extreme Unction and Marriage, we know something of the obscurity by which they are surrounded, and what difficulty the theologian finds in discovering clear and precise texts as regards the use and practice of these Sacraments. Thus from the very first step we take into this history, we see that the Eucharist has a place all its own. Let us mark this place in starting, for we shall have to return to it.

The texts which give us information about the history of the Eucharist are, first, those which we find in the New Testament: the famous text of St. Paul in his First Epistle to the *Corinthians*, the story of the Last

Supper in the three synoptic Gospels, and the sixth chapter of *St. John*. Then we have the texts of the Apostolic Fathers from the time of St. Ignatius: St. Polycarp, St. Irenæus, up to Tertullian, Origen, and St. Cyprian; the apocryphal writings, which are not very orthodox witnesses, but yet are often precious; and lastly, heretical writings, which in their own way bear witness in favour of the Eucharist, and even by their errors—like those of the *Aquarians* or the *Artorytrites* —throw light upon one rite or another.

Naturally it is impossible to quote all these texts here; even a large number of Conferences would not be sufficient for that. I shall content myself with referring those who are willing to undertake the task to the Conferences of 1922, united in the volume *Catholic Faith in the Holy Eucharist*, where a part of these texts will be found; and also to some works published since that date, like those of Lietzmann, Wetter, and Brilieth, and especially to the masterly work of Goossens, which, with a bibliography of the subject, discusses the most recent theories upon the origins of the Eucharist, the study of the New Testament texts, and the refutation of Réville's, Lietzmann's, Vetter's, etc., books.[1]

It is also necessary to remember that besides written books, the Eucharist is represented on numerous monuments, such as the frescoes in the Catacombs, inscriptions, epitaphs, chalices, or pyxes. The number of these monuments is considerable for the first three centuries, and what we have already said with regard to quotations from writers must here be repeated: these witnesses are far more numerous in the case

[1] Werner Goossens, *Les origines de l'Eucharistie, Sacrement et Sacrifice*, Paris, 1931. See also the bibliographical Note A.

of the Eucharist than in that of any of the other Sacraments, even Baptism.

It will be enough for me to mention the frescoes in the Catacombs which represent the miracle of the multiplication of the loaves, and the miracle of Cana. In most cases these pictures contain a clear allusion to the Eucharist.

The sacrifice of Abraham is also a symbolic figure of the Sacrifice of Christ. This tradition is maintained in these words of our Canon: *et sacrificium patriarchæ nostri Abrahæ* (*accepta habere*).

The famous fresco called the *Fractio Panis* (in the *Capella Græca*, Catacomb of St. Priscilla) represents as taking part in the rite, seven persons—a mystic number which indicates the whole assembly of the faithful. The figure in the middle holds in his hands a loaf; while before him is a chalice, and two dishes with two fish and five loaves. On either side of the table stand the seven baskets mentioned in the miracle of the multiplication of the bread. This painting, which goes back to the second century, is quite clearly an allusion to the Mass.

In another place we see a man standing, draped in his mantle, his hands extended towards a tripod on which rests a loaf and a fish, while on the other side of the table stands a woman, her hands raised like those of an *Orante*.

The numerous reproductions of the fish, or symbolic *ichthus*, of loaves and wine, of the vase of milk, of thirsty deer drinking at a spring, are also symbols of the Eucharist which are explained to us in the two famous inscriptions of Abercius and Pectorius.

But for all those developments which such a subject demands, I must again refer those interested to a bibliographic note, in which they will find all the materials to enable them to study it more profoundly.[1]

Taken together, these texts and these monuments confirm as a whole that which I said at the beginning: no Sacrament in the first three centuries is described in greater detail than the Eucharist; to none are more frequent allusions made by contemporary writers.

This is an incontestable advantage which gives to this Sacrament a privileged place, and allows us to describe and to study it under various aspects, both as Sacrifice and as Sacrament. We shall do this in the following paragraphs.

II

From the abundance of these texts and monuments regarding the Eucharist in the first three centuries, we arrive at our first conclusion, namely: that they reveal the importance attached by Christians of those days to the Eucharist, and the place which it held in their spiritual life.

To-day a non-Catholic who is asked what, according to his ideas, is the most important act of Christian worship, might hesitate. Could it be the Benediction of the Blessed Sacrament, processions, pilgrimages, the dedication of a church, the ceremony of Baptism, that of Marriage, of Holy Orders, or the celebration of such and such a Feast?

I said a *non-Catholic*, meaning one who would only observe things in a superficial way. As for a Catholic, he would not hesitate one instant in replying that it was the Mass.

In the first three centuries the non-Catholic himself

[1] See Note B.

would not have hesitated, for he would have seen, as Renan has done, that the Mass is the centre of Christian worship, and that everything must be referred to it.[1] At that time indeed there existed only two public and official ceremonies: the *a-liturgical* synax, and the *liturgical* synax.

We know the term *synax* (σύναξις) means assembly or meeting. From the very beginning of the Church meetings were held, in which passages of the Old Testament were read, and also the books of the Gospels, the Acts of the Apostles, or even other documents like the letter of St. Clement. Psalms and canticles to Christ as God were also sung. We have a description of these assemblies in a letter of Pliny's and in St. Justin.[2]

In very early times—let us say from the second century—the *a-liturgical* synax was united to the celebration of the Eucharist, and soon became its necessary prelude. So much so indeed that the name of Pre-Mass, or Mass of the catechumens was bestowed upon it. As in the earliest times, it is to-day composed of readings and the singing of psalms, introit, gradual, *Alleluia* or tract, with the Epistle or other lessons, the prayer of the collect, and finally the Gospel. Thus this part of public prayer which primitively formed what we call the Breviary, and which contained the germ of the Office of Mattins or Vigils and the other Hours, adhered so closely to the Eucharistic Sacrifice that it ended by uniting with it, for to-day we cannot imagine a Mass which is not preceded by this preparatory prayer.

[1] Renan, *Les origines du Christianisme*, t. VI, "L'Eglise chrétienne," 1883.
[2] All these texts are given in our book *The Mass of the Western Rites*, Sands and Co., London, 1934, p. 10 *seq*.

Apart from the Mass, all the other Sacraments are scarcely conceivable. To be convinced of this with regard to Baptism, Confirmation, Order and Matrimony, it is sufficient to have studied the liturgical history of that period. In the case of Penance and of Extreme Unction the proofs are less striking, nevertheless it is not very difficult to show that they are closely attached to the Eucharist.

The *agape*, vigils and services for the dead were also usually celebrated in union with the Mass.

Thus by the history of the primitive Liturgy that word of Renan is verified, that the Mass was the centre of Divine worship during the first centuries.

Another conclusion derived from these texts, which we can but indicate here in the most summary manner, is that all of them, in spite of the difference of time as well as of their authors, describe a rite which is substantially the same everywhere, and in which we find the characteristics of our Mass—Sacrament and Sacrifice.[1]

III

To-day the history of Catholic devotion is a subject of much study. It may be asked which of all these devotions is the most popular? The answer to such a question would not be easy to give. It would seem that there are great varieties of opinion on this point. Some are specially drawn by devotion to the Blessed Sacrament; others by that to the Sacred Heart; others again by that to our Lady, to St. Joseph, or to some other Saint.

---

[1] To make this clear I must again refer to my book, *The Mass of the Western Rites*. The work of Mgr. Batiffol on *L'Eucharistie* may also be consulted.

But for the first three centuries it would appear that such a question could not even have been asked. Most assuredly the fervour of the first Christians was not less than our own—far from it, indeed. But their devotion did not take the same form; it was more unified; it was not spread over different objects.

Most decidedly I have no intention of discussing these modern devotions, but it must be confessed that some of them arose from the fact that such or such a Feast had fallen into disuse for a time, and on its revival men believed it to be a new one! I will give but one example of this: that of the devotion to the Holy Name of Jesus, so zealously preached in the fifteenth century by St. Bernardine of Siena and St. John Capistran. Now it is enough to read St. Paul, or other writers of the earliest centuries to understand clearly that devotion to the Name of Jesus was at that epoch universal, and that the acclamation *In Nomine Domini nostri Jesu Christi* (In the Name of Our Lord Jesus Christ) was most widely diffused. Thus the Feast of the Holy Name of Jesus more recently introduced has done little more than accentuate, by throwing a stronger light upon it, that other Feast of the Circumcision, which was already a Feast of the Holy Name.

There is, indeed, nothing more curious to study than the evolution of piety in the Church; and recently much interest has been aroused upon this point. Latterly we have had numerous studies upon these various devotions.[1] Since the Middle Ages they have everywhere burst into flower, and devotion to the Blessed Sacrament, to the Blessed Virgin, to St. Joseph, or to some other Saint has each had its moment of

[1] Cf. Note C.

especial popularity. A large number of Feasts which now have their place in the calendar, beside the most ancient ones, have no other origin. The Feast of the Holy Trinity, that of the Blessed Sacrament, of the Holy Rosary, of the Sacred Heart—and only yesterday the Feast of Christ the King, together with a number of others, have originated only through a popular enthusiasm and a special initiative. Each century has its own devotion, or devotions, and as we have already said, there is nothing more curious than these to be studied throughout the whole field of Christian piety.

Now during the first three centuries not one of these existed, except implicitly, if that expression be allowed. Not that any one of them is of modern invention; each having its own far-off origin, but not existing separately. Each, almost without exception, is contained in that prayer and liturgical function which is the Mass.

It would be a useful and relatively easy work to prove this. We can only do so here in a manner very summary, though, I hope, sufficient; and it would be a fresh argument to prove, better than any other, the importance of the Mass in these early centuries.

(a) *Public Prayer.* To-day, without speaking of the Rosary and morning and night prayers, we have, besides the Mass, the Divine Office and the Breviary, which has preserved numerous points of relationship with the Mass, no doubt; though it is enough to have studied its history in the most summary way to be able to state that it has usually developed, increased or diminished independently of the Mass.

In the earliest centuries official prayer was attached to the Sacrifice, in the Pre-Mass, and this, it may be said, was the germ of canonical prayer. This latter was contained in the Pre-Mass in all its varied forms:

singing of psalms, reading of the books of the Old Testament, and that of the *Acts of the Apostles*, with their Epistles, the whole crowned by the reading of the Gospel. The Pre-Mass also contains free prayers, such as the *Kyrie Eleison* and *Gloria in excelsis*, and later on, the *Credo*. Now we find all these elements in the breviary: psalmody, reading of the Bible, responsories and anthems or other prayers, all of which already had their place in the Pre-Mass.

(*b*) Centuries before a Feast of the Most Holy Trinity was instituted, this Mystery, the centre of Christianity, was celebrated in the Mass, which is above all prayer to the Father, by the Son, in the Holy Ghost. This was summed up, in the doxologies which were so numerous, before the Council of Nicea adopted the formula of the Trinitarian doxology: *Gloria Patri et Filio et Spiritui Sancto.*

Thus the final doxology of the Roman canon, which rises superior to all others by its solemnity and the force of its expressions, the latter emphasized by the gestures of the priest: *Per ipsum, et cum ipso, et in ipso est Tibi Deo Patri omnipotenti in unitate Spiritus Sancti omnis honor et gloria per omnia sæcula sæculorum. Amen.* Now this doxology is only an echo of that which closes the *anaphora* attributed with so much probability to St. Hippolytus of Rome in the first quarter of the third century:

"We praise Thee and glorify Thee, O God the Father, by Thy Son Jesus Christ, by whom be to Thee honour and glory, Father, Son and Holy Spirit, in Thy Holy Church, now and world without end. Amen."[1]

According to the formulas of the Mass the Father is specially addressed under the title: *Omnipotens,*

[1] Cf. *The Mass of the Western Rites,* p. 18, and on *Doxologies.*

παντοκράτωρ, *Domine sancte, Pater omnipotens, æterne Deus.* This is also the attribute of the Father in the Apostles' Creed, as it was destined to be in that of Nicea, which would develop the formula in these terms: *Patrem omnipotentem . . . Factorem coeli et terræ, visibilium omnium et invisibilium.*

The Son, in this *anaphora* of St. Hippolytus, is called *the Well-Beloved Son* (of God the Father) *Jesus Christ,* "whom in the latter days Thou has sent us as Saviour and Redeemer and Angel (Messenger) of Thy Will who is Thine inseparable Word, by whom Thou hast made all things, and in whom Thou art well-pleased; Thou hast sent Him from Heaven into the womb of the Virgin, where He became Flesh and manifested Himself as Thy Son, born of the Holy Ghost and of the Virgin."

In the *Gloria in excelsis Deo,* which is most probably an ante-Nicean chant, the Son is thus designated: *Domine, Fili unigenite, Jesu Christe, Domine Deus, Agnus Dei, Filius Patris, Qui sedes ad dexteram Patris,* etc.

The Holy Ghost, already mentioned in the Virginal Conception, is again recalled in this epiclesis, the archetype of all epicleses henceforth to be composed:

"We pray Thee to send down Thy Holy Spirit upon this oblation of the Holy Church, so that joining them together in one Thou mayest give to all the Saints who participate (in the Sacrifice) that they be filled with Thy Holy Spirit and strengthened in the Truth of the Faith."[1]

The Creed of Nicea-Constantinople was not introduced into the Mass until later (at the end of the sixth century in Spain, and at Rome only in the eleventh

---

[1] This question has been learnedly treated in Dom Cagin's work *Eucharistia*; see also Dict. d'arch. Chrét. et le Liturgie, v. *Epiclese*.

century). But already in the most ancient form of *anaphora* with which we are acquainted, that of Hippolytus, this prayer has a pronouncedly *theological* character; already it is a symbol of Faith.

(*c*) To-day the cycle of the Feasts of the ecclesiastical year would seem to have attained its final development, and to present itself under a definite form. There are very few days in the year which have not their own Feast and their own Saint, and sometimes several Saints on the same day. But the cycle did not reach this point without a very long evolution. Before the fourth century, there were only two Feasts in the year: Easter and Pentecost. Perhaps some other Feast might possibly be discovered, as, for example, the Baptism of Our Lord, but such may be considered exceptional cases, and they are moreover purely local.

Easter comprises a preparation of several days into which the whole of Lent is concentrated; and the fifty days which follow are a time of joy, from which all signs of penance and fasting are banished. They terminate with another Feast, that of Pentecost. Beyond these two Feasts must be counted the Sunday in each week, also a Feast and a liturgical day—that is, one on which Mass is celebrated. Wednesday and Friday of each week are called *Station Days*, that is, days of fasting, when Mass is also frequently celebrated.

The greater number of the other Feasts have arisen since the fourth century; they include Christmas, the Epiphany, the Feasts of our Lady and of Saints. Note that the greater part of these Feasts are based upon a devotion. I do not mean only those of Confessors, such as St. Martin, St. Ambrose, St. Liberius and others, for whom naturally enough a Feast was instituted through confidence in their prayers.

As for the Martyrs, we shall speak of them directly.

With regard to the other Feasts, Trinity, *Corpus Christi*, the Immaculate Conception, Sacred Heart, the Feast of Christ the King, and others, they are the result of a popular devotion finally translated into the institution of a Feast; or again, by a revelation, like that of the Blessed Sacrament or the Sacred Heart.

I repeat that not one of these Feasts existed *as* a Feast during the ante-Nicean period. But their object was not ignored. We have spoken of the Feast of the Trinity; and I have also given that of the Holy Name of Jesus as an example.

I could demonstrate exactly the same thing with regard to all the other Feasts. But it seems to me that the examples already given are sufficient to prove my thesis.

(*d*) The dead, and Martyrs. I have made an exception for the Feasts of the Martyrs. The fact is they were introduced into the calendar long before the Confessors, since the third century indeed, and perhaps before that time. These were local Feasts, sometimes confused with the *cultus* paid to the dead. The tombs of the Martyrs were preserved as precious things. The people met there on the anniversary day of their martyrdom; it was a vigil celebrated with great solemnity; but the vigil, after the chants, readings, and recitation of psalms, also necessarily ended with the Eucharistic Sacrifice.

IV

Certain customs concerning the Eucharist at this time remain to be studied, and this will permit us to see at a glance the difference between the Christians of the three first centuries and those of the twentieth.

o

To-day the Eucharist is surrounded with the profoundest veneration. No one but the priest is allowed to consecrate the bread and wine, or even to touch the Body of Christ under the Eucharistic species, or even, again, the chalice, the paten, the sacred linen. Exceptions to this rule are rare, and can usually be explained by necessity.

The Blessed Sacrament is adored in Exposition, in processions; It is kept in the Tabernacle, on the altar, with the greatest respect. Severe rules have been established on these points, which are respected by all.

And all that is very good, and may be considered in the light of a progress, beyond those other practices which were common in the first centuries. We must not, however, forget that the reason for these differences between ourselves and our ancestors is especially this:

Whatever Tertullian may say, during the first three centuries Christians were a minority in the Roman Empire, and that minority was an élite.

The Gentiles or Jews who wished to enter the Church were scarcely ever admitted within it until they were adults. The Baptism of children was not the rule at that time. The aim of the catechumenate was to select, to reject the unworthy, and to admit others only after a long preparation. Besides, the persecutions and difficulties of all kinds which at that period were the lot of all Christians, eliminated all those whom to-day we should style "arrivists" or "profiteers" —in a word, the unworthy.

From the fourth century onwards through following centuries, things changed, and went on changing. So much so, that having lost its first severity little by little, the catechumenate ended by almost completely disappearing. It became the general custom to baptise children during the days immediately following their birth; that is to say, to introduce them into the Church almost unconditionally; and the catechumenate now is summed up in the first rites of Baptism.

The minority thus became the majority, and so great a majority that it was impossible to maintain the ancient rules. Of this I will take but one example: Communion under both kinds. The true reason of Communion under one kind only, with a small host of unleavened bread, was above all the fear of accidents or profanations, and the multiplication of the number of communicants. It had become necessary to reduce, to simplify, to act far more quickly. This will easily be understood by anyone who has been present in Paris, for instance, at a Paschal Mass in certain parishes, when two or three priests give Communion without stopping during the whole Mass. It may well be asked *how* It could be given with the proper respect under both kinds?

This must always be remembered in judging and understanding the difference between those ancient days and our own times. In the first three centuries the Eucharistic synaxes were not generally very numerous. Those alone who were going to communicate were present at the Mass; neither pagans, nor heretics, nor even the penitents and catechumens were admitted. The old formulas *Sancta sanctis, foras canes, ne margaritas ante porcos*, etc., remind us of this. The *arcana* still ruled, forbidding all concerned, to betray the secret of the Mysteries to those not initiated.

It was for analogous reasons, such as the fear of Pagans or of unbelievers, that Mass was usually celebrated at night, or at earliest dawn, and that it was usually only celebrated on Sunday, or further on Wednesday and Friday, and then generally in the Catacombs, or in distant places.

(*a*) To this Mass the faithful have themselves brought the bread and wine which are to be consecrated, and they will be communicated under both kinds.

(*b*) They receive the Host in their hand, or on a veil, and communicate themselves. And much more than this: they are allowed to carry this consecrated Bread back to their homes, where they will guard it as a precious treasure and, if they are not able daily to be present at Mass, they will communicate themselves in their own houses.

(*c*) Much more than this again: when they travel they will carry, on their breast, the Eucharist, which their profound Faith leads them to consider as a sovereign protection against all dangers.

Moreover, the task of carrying this Eucharist to the sick was confided to the laity, even to women; and we may remember the case of Tarcisius.

The custom also existed of sending the Eucharist to churches afar off, if they too were in communion with that Church whence the Sacred Species was sent.[1]

(*d*) Certain facts also exist which to-day we should look upon as abuses, but which then appeared quite justified. Such, for example, was the custom of giving Communion to the dead, or even that of placing the Host on their breast and burying them together. Later on the custom spread of placing the Host beside

[1] I cannot give examples of this here, but these may be found in our chapter *De la communion sous les deux espèces*, in the Book *Eucharistia*, Encyclopédie populaire sur L'Eucharistie, Paris, 1934, p. 568 *seq*.

the other relics under the altar, in the ceremony of dedication of a church.

We are familiar with the story told by St. Gregory about St. Benedict. The fact related occurred a few centuries later, but the custom went back to the very earliest days. St. Gregory says: "A young monk who had an unrestrained affection for his family, ran away from the monastery without the blessing, but on the same day on which he arrived home, he died. This seems a very severe punishment, but what followed was worse, for on the day which followed the burial the corpse was rejected by the earth and thrown out of the grave. Again the body was buried, and again the earth rejected it. The weeping parent ran to Benedict, who, with his own hand, gave them the Body of the Lord, saying: ' Go, and place with all due respect the Body of Our Lord upon the breast of your child, and thus bury him.' It was done as he said, and this time the earth retained the body."

What surprises the Deacon Peter in all this—and also the narrator—is the merit of the Saint who enjoyed such a measure of power with Christ. But there is neither protestation nor even surprise as to Benedict's act, so little in conformity with our own customs.

In the first place the fact that St. Benedict confided the Sacred Host to the parents is not alone sufficient to prove, as has been sometimes believed, that Benedict was a priest or even a deacon. The rules for the administration of the Eucharist, to-day so strict, were then much wider. Nor are examples wanting, as I said, to prove that the Eucharist was given to the faithful, who often carried it away with them on a journey and communicated themselves. The custom of giving the Eucharist to the dead, or of placing it on the corpse, was also widely diffused. St. Gregory thus recites the fact without commenting on it.

CONCLUSION

In writing these pages I did not propose to prove a thesis, but merely to study, in a résumé necessarily very short, the history of the Eucharist, and what it was to the Christians of the first three centuries.

Nevertheless it seems to me that from this sketch we may draw a conclusion which is in agreement with a demonstration of our own theologians, of which it is a *Confirmatur*.

In the chapter on the Sacraments it is proved that the Eucharist is one of the Seven Sacraments, but that in the order of value it is the first and greatest of all Sacraments. We may indeed call it the most divine, since the other Sacraments give us Grace, while this one actually contains the Author of Grace Himself.

Moreover, the Eucharist is not only a Sacrament: it is also a Sacrifice.

On this point I may refer to one of the last works of Abbot Vonier on the Eucharist, in which he strongly insists on this very thing, and says that though the Eucharist is one of the Seven Sacraments we must not —I do not say confuse it with the rest, but we must not place it in the same rank. The Eucharist stands alone; it dominates the other Sacraments; it draws them all closely to itself.[1]

Now if I am not mistaken this is just what we have seen in the practice of the three first centuries. Of all devotions, that which holds the first place, which seems even to absorb all the others, is the Eucharist,

[1] *A Key to the Doctrine of the Eucharist*, Burns and Oates, 1925.

the Mass. It is the prayer of prayers. It is almost
the only function at which all the Christians of those
days met together. Baptism, Confirmation and Holy
Orders are so closely attached to it that they are
inconceivable without the Mass. When the dedication
of churches was constituted, the rite, in our own day
so complicated, consisted, beyond the procession of
relics, almost entirely in the celebration of the Mass.

Thus we always arrive at the same conclusion:
during the first three centuries the Eucharist is the
great devotion of Christians; resuming in itself all
the others, and forming the centre of Christian life.

The developments which we may note from the
fourth century onwards, the new rites which were
added to the ancient ones, the devotions which budded
forth like so many branches on this ancient trunk,
must not cause us to lose sight of that fundamental
truth which we have developed in this Conference.

All these developments are of a nature—I say, not
merely to increase our veneration, our admiration for
this Sacrament of Sacraments—but to develop our
devotion; and to establish the Eucharist upon its true
basis.

THE OTHER SACRAMENTS

By the Rev. B. LEEMING, S.J., M.A., S.T.D., Professor
of Dogmatic Theology at the Pontifical Gregorian
University, Rome.

OF the evidence in the Pre-Nicene Church regarding
the other Sacraments, it may be said in general that
it is ample in principle, but scanty in details: it fully
suffices to show that Christianity was from the beginning a sacramental religion, and it contains the seeds
from which sacramental doctrine naturally developed;
but it leaves indeterminate many questions regarding
practice and belief. It is clear that Confirmation,
Orders, Marriage, Penance, Extreme Unction were
sacred rites and means of grace; but their matter and
form, the conditions necessary for their validity, their
exact distinction from other rites, remain somewhat
obscure and afford ample matter for historical discussion and conjecture.

The reason for this scantiness of evidence lies
principally, I think, in the preoccupation of Christian
writers with other doctrines. The main controversies
were against Pagans, Gnostics, Arians, who denied
the fundamentals of Christianity. Then, too, sacramental doctrine naturally comes last in any theological
synthesis, after a clarifying of the doctrines on the
Church, of Redemption, of Grace. Moreover, what
is known as the *Disciplina Arcani*, the practice of a

certain secrecy or reticence with regard to the Christian mysteries, was certainly a contributing cause.

The Disciplina Arcani.

The early Church shrouded its rites in a certain mystery, partly from a sense of their sacredness, partly to avoid pagan ridicule or persecution, partly as a pedagogic method with catechumens. The extent of this *Disciplina Arcani* has, as Mgr. Battifol has pointed out, been exaggerated by certain Apologists who appealed to the *Disciplina* as a universal answer to inconvenient Protestant or rationalist inquiries; but in spite of an exaggerated use of the answer, its legitimacy cannot be questioned. It was used in the middle of the fourth century, forty years after Nicea, by St. Basil the Great, in exactly the same way as it is used to-day:

"Of the dogmas and preachings which are kept in the Church, some are derived from the written doctrine, others we have received by way of Apostolic Tradition as they were secretly transmitted to us, and these two classes are of equal value to piety. No one will dispute this, at all events no one who has had the least experience of ecclesiastical institutions. For if we were to attempt to reject the unwritten customs on the ground that they are therefore of no great importance we should unwittingly inflict a deadly wound on the Gospel, or rather we should make the matter of our preaching a name and nothing more. For example (to mention first the earliest and most common), who taught us in writing to sign with the sign of the Cross those who hope in the name of Our Lord Jesus Christ? Where have we been taught in Scripture to turn to the east when we pray? What saint was it that bequeathed to us in writing the words of invocation at the showing of the Eucharistic bread and the cup of blessing? For we are not satisfied with what the Apostle or the Evangelist recorded, but we add a preface and an epilogue which we have received from unwritten tradition, and which we consider to be of great import in celebrating the mystery.[1] We bless the baptismal water and the oil of anointing, and him likewise who is to be baptised: upon what written instruction? Is it not from tacit and secret tradition? Indeed, that very anointing with oil, by what written document is it taught? The triple immersion in Baptism, whence is it derived? And the other things done in Baptism, the renunciation of Satan and his angels, from what written record comes this? Surely from the undivulged and secret doctrine which our fathers, instructed to preserve in silence the sacredness of the mysteries, guarded in undisturbed and unquestioning reticence."[2]

Similar statements may be quoted from the Canons of Hippolytus,[3] from Athanasius,[4] from Epiphanius,[5] from Cyril of Jerusalem,[6] from John Chrysostom,[7]

[1] These words were quoted by the Eastern members of the Joint Doctrinal Commission between the Anglican and the Eastern Orthodox Churches in October, 1931, as a justification for their assertion that "Holy Scripture is completed, explained and interpreted by the Holy Tradition." (Official Report, S.P.C.K., 1932, p. 10.)

[2] De Spiritu Sancto, 66; Migne, Patres Græci, 32, col. 188–89.

[3] Can. 28 and 29; cf. Duchesne, Origines du Culte chrétien, 5th ed., pp. 531–49.

[4] Apologia contra Arianos, 11; Migne, Patres Græci, 25, 265.

[5] Hæreses, 42, 30; Migne, P.G., 41, 700.

[6] Procatechesis, 5; Migne, P.G., 33, 341–44.

[7] Hom. in 1 Cor. 50, 1; P.G., 61, col. 347; Ad Illuminandos, 1, 1, P.G., 49, 224.

giving explicit witness in the fourth century to the existence of the *Disciplina Arcani*, and pointing back to its
existence in the third and second centuries. Further
discussion of the *Disciplina*, its origins, its exact nature,
its extent, would be beyond our scope; the words of
St. Basil indicate clearly enough that it can rightly be
adduced as at least a partial cause for the scantiness
of our evidence in the first three centuries regarding
Christian rites. The reverence which certainly fostered
its introduction, worked likewise against too close a
scrutiny or too inquisitive an enquiry into the exact
nature of the Sacraments themselves.[1]

Christianity essentially Sacramental.

It was a favourite theory of the older school of
rationalists[2] to say that Christ founded a religion only
of the spirit, taught a doctrine, inculcated an attitude
of mind, turned men directly to God who is a Spirit to
be worshipped in spirit alone; and that only in later
times—in the first, in the second, in the third, or in the
fourth century—did Christianity, in imitation of pagan
religions, introduce material elements such as Sacraments, or at least begin to attach importance to them.
In fact, from the very beginning Christianity was a
religion, and hence was sacramental, that is, it was a
body of men gathered together to worship God by

[1] On the *Disciplina* a well-balanced account is to be found in
Mgr. Baudrillart's *Dictionnaire d'Histoire et de Géographie Ecclésias-
tiques*, Paris, 1924, vol. 3, col. 1497–1514, by E. Vacandard, who
differs somewhat from Mgr. Battifol in *Dictionnaire de Théologie
Catholique*, vol. 1, col. 1738–1758, Paris, 1902; Mgr. Battifol somewhat
modified his views in later editions of *Etudes d'Histoire et de Théologie
Positive*, 6th ed., 1920. Ample bibliographies are appended in these
articles.

[2] e.g., Gunkel, Harnack, Moffat, and Percy Gardner in his
earlier writings.

outward expression, and to receive gifts from God through outward visible signs. The Incarnation itself is sacramental: under the outward appearance of mere humanity exists the divine Person; the outward appearance perceived by the senses is not the whole reality, but is a means by which God comes into contact with us. The Church from the beginning was the continuation of the Incarnation: a visible body using visible means of salvation, outward visible rites, by which God comes into contact with us, by which men are incorporated into the divine.

The first command of St. Peter to believers was that they should be baptized. St. Paul explains that "the waters of baptism into which the neophytes were plunged to wash them of their sins, symbolize the death of Christ and the sepulchre wherein He was entombed. The convert emerging from the baptismal bath whence he has received new life which he ought never to lose, represents Christ coming forth from the tomb, living also a new life and henceforth immortal. The baptismal immersion therefore typifies death to sin, the death of the old man buried in the waters, as Christ in the tomb; the emersion is the birth of the new and regenerated man. The baptismal ceremony therefore is a symbol of Christ's death and resurrection, and as well, of the death to sin and of the supernatural regeneration of the Christian soul."[1]   This same

[1] Pourrat, *Theology of the Sacraments*, p. 2. Fr. Lattey holds as against de la Taille that the primary symbolism of Baptism is that of washing rather than of a death and resurrection. Each symbolism signifies the reality: washing by reference to remission of sins, death and resurrection by reference to our unity with the risen Saviour. In fact, the reality to be expressed—our mysterious participation in the divine nature—surpasses all human expression whether by word or symbol; the metaphors of the kingdom, of the vine, of the "mystical" body, of the bridegroom, each expresses something of the truth, but each is inadequate to express fully the reality which

principle of symbolism is manifest in Confirmation, where the laying on of hands, or the signing with the sign of the Cross, symbolized the blessing and the confirming in the faith and the fullness of the blessing of baptism, the gift of the Holy Spirit. The union of husband and wife in marriage was a symbol, a sign of the union between Christ and the Church; a living representation of the affection which exists between Christ and His mystical body.

Now this idea of symbolism entered into Christianity from the beginning: we have it in St. Paul, in the Apostolic Fathers, in the Apologists, and especially in the Alexandrine writers, such as Clement and Origen. At Alexandria they made much of mystic interpretations: this whole material world which we see is only a faint shadowing of the real world of spirit; under the literal sense of Scripture lies the mystic and real sense, under the material actions of Christian rites lies hid the divine activity and power making real what is signified and typified by the external action. Hence the concept of a Sacrament is that of a sign, signifying something done, the thing being both signified and done. Consequently we find the Eucharist sometimes called a type or a figure or a symbol of Christ's body; but that does not mean it is not Christ's body. The symbolism does not destroy the reality, but only manifests it.

Naturally, then, the word "mystery," μυστήριον, came to be applied to the Christian rites; the mystery

eye has not seen nor ear heard. The apparently incongruous double symbolism of baptism may perhaps be solved by St. Thomas' doctrine that the Sacraments are signs of things past, things present and things to come, that is, of the passion of Christ, of grace, and of glory. Grace remitting sin may be best expressed by the washing; but Christ's passion by the at least partial immersion. Cf. *Summa* III, Q. lxvi, a. 7, ad. 2, where Thomas holds the symbolism of death and resurrection to be essential if not primary.

certainly was not in the symbolism which was clear—
for if it were not clear it would be useless—but in the
efficacy of the symbolism. In Latin the word used
was *"sacramentum,"* upon whose origin and exact
original meaning scholars are still unable to decide.
"Sacramentum" was in Latin usage principally the
military oath by which soldiers bound themselves to
military service, secondarily it was a pledge given in
bond. In Ecclesiastical Latin it frequently corre-
sponded to the Greek word μυστήριον, and in the old
Latin translation of the Bible μυστήριον is practically
indifferently translated by *"sacramentum"* or *"mysterium"*: for instance, some versions of *Ephesians* 5, 32,
call marriage a great *"mysterium,"* others a great
"sacramentum." Whether the meaning of an oath or
pledge, or the meaning of a mystery, a hidden and
sacred thing, predominated, is not yet clear. It may
be noted in passing that the word *"sacramentum"* is
not confined to our Seven Sacraments, but is used
still in the liturgy in the sense of mystery.[1] Apart,
however, from the verbal meaning, it is clear that the
Christian rites in general were not mere prayers, but
were objective means of changing the state of soul of
the recipient.

The Efficacy of the Sacrament.

To show this, there are two striking passages from
Tertullian. In the first of these occurs an expression

---

[1] On this subject it suffices to refer to *Pour l'histoire du mot
Sacramentum*, initiated by Père de Ghellinck, S.J., 1924; and to
Dr. Joseph Huhn, *Die Bedeutung des Wortes Sacramentum bei dem
Kirchenvater Ambrosius*, Fulda, 1928. The credit for the beginning
of the study seems due to H. von Soden, who discussed the question
in 1911, in *Zeitschrift für N. T. Wissenschaft*. Pater O. Casel, in
Theologische Revue, 1925, pp. 41–47, is perhaps more interesting
than solid, as I. Hanssens indicates in *Periodica de Re Morali,
Canonica, Liturgica*, April, 1934, p. 1128.

from which derives the famous "*Credo quia impossibile.*"

A certain Quintilla had objected that it was incredible that a beggarly element like water should produce an effect upon the soul: How can material water wash the soul, and give spiritual life?

Tertullian answers: "O contemptible incredulity! Is it not characteristic of divine action to combine power with simplicity? What then? It is indeed wonderful that a washing should destroy death. Yet there is a motive for belief in the very fact that scepticism finds such a wonder unbelievable.[1] For what more benefits the works of God than that they should be beyond our wonder? We wonder, but we believe. Incredulity wonders, but does not believe; for it looks upon simple things as though they were vain and magnificent things as though they were impossible. Be it just as you think, the divine declaration has gone before, sufficient to justify simplicity and (natural) impossibility: *The foolish things of the world hath God chosen that He may confound the wise,*[2] and what is most difficult to man is easy to God."[3]

In this passage the supernatural efficacy of the material sacrament could scarcely be more strongly asserted: it is the mystery of sacramental efficacy which is called in question, and which Tertullian defends by an appeal to God's omnipotence. God's dealings with us are certainly astonishing; but He chose such ways explicitly to confound the wisdom of this world, and hence when we find something which proud intellects consider impossible of belief, and which

[1] "Atquin eo magis credendum, si quia mirandum est, idcirco non creditur." [2] 1 *Corinthians* i, 27.
[3] *De Baptismo*, n. 2, ed. d'Alès, p. 8, in *Textus et Documenta* of the Gregorian University, Series Theologica No. 10. This edition is based upon the only existing manuscript of the *De Baptismo*.

goes contrary to worldly judgements, we have an indication that God may be at work. The fact that scepticism does not believe is a reason that should make us believe. Tertullian never said "*Credo quia impossibile*"; he meant "*Credo quia sæcularibus videtur impossibile*,"[1] and he goes on to attribute the wondrous effect of Baptism to the power of the Holy Ghost who is drawn into the water by the invocation of the Blessed Trinity.

The other instance of the sacramental efficacy comes from Tertullian's dispute with the Valentinians and Marcionites upon the resurrection of the flesh. His adversaries held that flesh, being material and low, cannot participate in eternal felicity; true spiritual beings escape completely from the bonds of the flesh, and a bodily resurrection is degrading. Tertullian answers that the body, the flesh, is an essential condition of salvation, since through it the soul is made holy, especially by the Sacraments :

"No soul can in any way secure salvation, except it believe while it is in the flesh, so true is it that the flesh is the very condition upon which salvation depends. It is the flesh which renders the soul capable of service to God. The flesh indeed is washed, that the soul may be cleansed; the flesh is anointed that the soul may be consecrated; the flesh is signed with the Cross that the soul may be fortified; the flesh is shadowed with the imposition of hands that the soul may be illumined by the Holy Spirit; the flesh feeds upon the Body and Blood of Christ, that the soul likewise may be nourished upon its God. They cannot be separated in their reward, since they are united in their service."[2]

[1] There are several suggested readings of this famous passage, cf. *Gregorianum*, 1933, p. 422–33.

[2] *De Resurrectione Carnis*, cap. 8.

In this passage Tertullian refers to Baptism, Confirmation and the Eucharist: writing so confidently, and using the sacramental principle as a matter so self-evident to a Christian that it could be used as a proof of the resurrection of the body, his witness, coming at the end of the second century, is enough to establish the essential Sacramentalism of Christianity. That granted, the explicit determination of the exact number of such rites, and the general formulation into reasoned theory of unreflectory practice, becomes a secondary question, and may be left to take its course of natural development in later centuries.[1]

Two Examples of Development.

As illustrations of this gradual unfolding of sacramental doctrine, we may take the sacramental character, and some questions on the Sacrament of Penance.

The Re-Baptism Controversy and the Sacramental Character.

The Council of Trent defined that Baptism, Confirmation, Orders imprint an indelible mark upon the soul, the character, whence these Sacraments cannot be repeated. This is only the common-sense view that Baptism makes a man a Christian, Orders make him a Priest, just as Marriage makes the indissoluble bond, and that even if grace is not conferred by the Sacrament, because of the impediment of unrepented sin upon the soul, still the Sacrament is not vain but produces its effect in the character, which in turn produces grace when the impediment is removed. There are many

---

[1] It would be superfluous to multiply citations from the Fathers, which can be found in any good text-book, e.g., de Smet, *De Sacramentis in Genere;* Umberg, *De Sac. in Gen.;* or Pourrat, *Theology of the Sacraments.*

P

great theologians who hold that other Sacraments are, like the Eucharist, permanent Sacraments, precisely because of the permanent character.[1]

This doctrine, however, of the character existed in the Pre-Nicene Church only in germ. Many Fathers —Clement of Alexandria, Pastor Hermæ, the Epitaph of Abercius, Irenæus, Tertullian, Athanasius and many others—used to speak of the *sphragis*, or *seal*, or *signaculum*, impressed by these three Sacraments. However, and here lay confusion, they drew no clear distinction between the *sphragis* and grace.[2] This is a first germ. The other is that these three Sacraments were never repeated once they had been validly received. In these two germs lay the doctrine of the sacramental character; for until the time of St. Augustine the *sphragis* was never understood as the reason why these Sacraments could not be repeated. The doctrine of the indelible character was there, but in unco-ordinated elements; and this undeveloped state of the doctrine led to the famous re-Baptism controversy between St. Cyprian and the Pope, St. Stephen.

St. Cyprian, about the year 253, held that baptism conferred by heretics was invalid and must be repeated when heretics returned to the Church, or rather, as he himself insisted, should be conferred for the first time, since their baptism in heresy was invalid. The reasons for his view were theoretically very strong; he argued: "The Holy Spirit does not exist outside the Church but only in the one true Church. Hence outside the Church heretical ministrations cannot confer the Holy Spirit. It is undoubted that heretics (he always meant heretics

---

[1] Cf. Pius XI, Casti Connubii, *Acta Apostolicæ Sedis*, December 31, 1930, vol. 22, num. 12, p. 554–5.

[2] Cf. Dolger, *Sphragis, eine altchristliche Taufbezeichnung*, Paderborn, 1911.

in bad faith) cannot have the Holy Spirit with them; hence they have no grace; hence they can have no effective or valid Sacraments."

St. Stephen, on the contrary, was quite clear that baptism, even if conferred by heretics, was valid; his reasons, however, were not a direct answer to Cyprian's difficulty. He said that we must not pay attention to the worth of the minister, but to the power of the invocation of the Holy Trinity; that in any case we must follow the immemorial custom of the Church, which is not to baptize again, but only to impose hands in penance.[1] St. Cyprian, however, retorted by asking whether the invocation of the Holy Trinity was so efficacious that whosoever be baptized in the name of Christ at once receives the grace of Christ.

To this difficulty no satisfactory answer was produced, for as heretics were presumed to be in bad faith, Catholics generally could not admit that their Sacraments gave grace.[2] It was indeed true that St. Stephen was perfectly right. The immemorial custom of the Church of admitting the validity of heretical Sacraments had right reason behind it, even though this reason was not explicitly adduced. But Cyprian asked for the reason and urged that since there could be no Sacrament without grace, and since the heretics could not give

[1] Letters of St. Cyprian, Ep. 75, 9. "Nihil innovetur nisi quod traditum est, ut manus eis imponatur in pænitentiam." This is a difficult sentence to translate, and authors differ as to its exact meaning. It seems best to understand it: Let nothing new be introduced, but let the custom be preserved of laying on hands in penance. So Vincent of Lerins understood it, cf. d'Alès in his note on the text, in the appendix to his book on Cyprian, and E. W. Benson, *Cyprian, his Life and Times*, London, 1897, p. 421.

[2] The unknown author of the *De Rebaptismate* did indeed go a long way toward solving the difficulty, by his assertion that the sacrament received in heresy is profitable after return to the Church. But he never gave a cogent reason why this was so. Cf. Rauschen, *Florilegium Patristicum*, Fasc. XI, p. 59, cap. 10.

grace, it necessarily followed that they could not have true Sacraments. The Donatists took up this argument, identifying the Sacrament and grace, and the controversy raged from the year 255 until the time of St. Augustine (389–420), who solved the difficulty by a distinction which is so familiar to us that it is almost hard for us to realize the trouble there was in grasping it. St. Augustine distinguished between a valid and a fruitful Sacrament, and explained the validity by the production of the indelible character. A Sacrament may be real and valid, even though it fail of its ultimate purpose, the production of grace, because it does not fail to impress the character of Christ upon the soul; even though conferred by a heretic upon a heretic, provided it were conferred in the name of Christ, it was not devoid of effect, since it produced the character, even granted that it did not produce grace because of the bad disposition of wilful heresy. And when the heretic repents and returns to the Church, the Sacrament he has received, that is the character, begins to profit him to salvation by producing grace. This was a reversion to the older doctrine of the *sphragis* which completely solved St. Cyprian's objection.[1]

Here is an excellent example of the development of doctrine: the practice in existence; the reason for it implicitly held; the connection between the two not realized. Then a controversy arises in which heretics

[1] St. Augustine's doctrine is clear in all his works against the Donatists, e.g., *De Baptismo*, lib. 6, cap. 1, Migne, *Patres Latini*, 43, col. 197–8. Not without solid reason P. Billot pointed out that St. Augustine's argument against the Donatists involves a dispositive causality in the Sacraments; for he held clearly that the validifying effect of the Sacrament is the character, grace being an effect of the character, immediately if the recipient be in good dispositions, subsequently if the recipient be in the state of sin and subsequently repents. Cf. *De Ecclesiæ Sacramentis*. ed. 7a, p. 126.

deny the rightfulness of the practice. After long discussion, the reason for the practice is at length realized and formulated, and the practice remains unquestioned ever afterwards. The validity of heretical sacraments—granted valid matter, form and intention —has never since been theoretically questioned in the Church.

Penitential Discipline.

Another, and in some respects a very different, case of the development of sacramental doctrine is found in the Sacrament of Penance. The manner in which the Church exercised her power of the keys gives rise to complicated questions which are controverted even among Catholic scholars; and within the last five years books have appeared by Catholic scholars which help considerably in their solution. In this paper it is possible only to touch upon some central facts and to hint at the general views held.[1]

The first and fundamental question is whether the Church was always conscious of the power given her by Christ to forgive in His name all sins without exception. Historians like Harnack[2] and the Modernist Loisy[3] held that the Church up to the time of St. Callistus, between the years 213 and 222, was believed to consist exclusively of holy people and that Christians guilty of grave sins, at least of unchastity, apostasy or murder, were forever excluded from forgiveness, because the Church did not

[1] The best brief treatments are D. S. Nerney, *Adnotationes in Tractatum de Pænitentia*, Gregorian, 1933; and an article by I. Zeiger in *Gregorianum*, Vol. XIV, 3, 1933, which summarizes the views of Poschmann, Galtier, Goeller and Jungmann. My dependence upon them is almost complete.

[2] *Dogmengeschichte*, 1, 4th ed., 439.

[3] *Autour d'un petit livre*, 241.

believe she had the power to forgive such sins. Gradually, however, the Church began to believe she had universal power of remission, and in the time of Callistus, 213–22, began for the first time to forgive unchastity, in the time of the Decian persecution, 250–1, to forgive apostates, and at some later unspecified time to remit likewise sins of murder. This view is, of course, heretical, being contrary to the canon of Trent which declared that the Catholic Church from the beginning understood that it had the power of remitting sins in the Sacrament of Penance.[1]

Certain Catholic theologians, among them Petau, Sirmond, Funk, Vacandard, Battifol, Rauschen, while holding that the Church fully understood the power given her of remitting all sins, inclined nevertheless to the opinion that the Church of the first centuries, in order to uphold a moral standard against the corruptions of the age, in point of fact refused to grant absolution to certain sins. They based their opinion chiefly upon certain texts from the Shepherd of Hermas, Tertullian, Hippolytus, Origen and Cyprian. The larger number, however, of theologians and historians, among whom are found d'Alès, Galtier, K. Adam, Goeller, Poschmann, Jungmann, maintain, and not without solid reason, that the Church never in fact refused absolution to any sin, however grave. They base their opinion upon the fact that the Gospels, St. Paul, the Didache, Clement, Ignatius, Polycarp, Justin, Dionysius of Corinth and other early Fathers, all proclaimed forgiveness of sins in such universal terms that it is incredible the Church refused absolution to certain classes of sins.

It may be of interest here to observe that the much

[1] Sess. XIV, can. 3.

quoted "Edict" of the year 213 or a little later, which is attributed to Callistus, and which is often supposed to have introduced the innovation of forgiving sins of unchastity, quite probably never originated from Callistus at all, and quite probably was in no sense an innovation. Tertullian gives the "Edict"—"I hear also that there has been given forth an edict, and a most peremptory one. The '*Pontifex Maximus*,' which is the *episcopus episcoporum*, declared: 'I remit sins of unchastity and of fornication to those who have done penance.' "[1] The inference that Tertullian referred to Callistus is made partly from the titles used by Tertullian, and partly from the charge of undue laxity made against Callistus by Hippolytus. It has been shown, however, that in that age the titles *Pontifex Maximus* and *Episcopus episcoporum* were not reserved to the Roman Pontiff, and might have been used of another bishop. That it was really another bishop who was in question appears from the fact that Tertullian evidently means a bishop of a see somehow near Rome—*ad omnem ecclesiam Petri propinquam;* whereas had the Bishop of Rome been in question he would have said plainly the See or the Church of Rome—*ad Ecclesiam vel Cathedram Petri*. Moreover, Tertullian himself, before his lapse into the heresy of Montanism, was ready to forgive all sins, and after he became a Montanist, he implies that the Montanists, the "spirituals," and not the Catholics were the innovators. Nor is Hippolytus' charge against Callistus one precisely of innovation upon the more severe discipline of penance, but rather one of general laxity, which is not quite the same; and Hippolytus is a prejudiced witness in any case. Hence G. Bardy thinks that a certain Aggripinus, Bishop of

[1] *De Pudicitia*, 1; Migne, *Patres Latini*, 2, 980.

Carthage about that time, may have been the author of the famous "Edict"; Galtier gives probably better reasons for thinking it was some other predecessor of St. Cyprian in the See of Carthage.[1]

However this may be, the weight of evidence is against Callistus having introduced a new and more lax practice in regard to remission of sins of unchastity. Dionysius of Corinth seems to have commanded forgiveness explicitly of sins against chastity[2] and St. Irenæus tells the story of the wife of a deacon, who, seduced by a certain magician, returned to the Church and was exemplary in her penitence.[3] The Council of Nice, which closes our period, explicitly laid down that in the case of the dying the "ancient and regular" rule should be preserved of giving them viaticum, and no restriction whatever is placed. This canon seems decisive against the idea of a steadfast refusal of absolution to certain sins.[4]

Nor does the Church before the Decian persecution appear to have refused absolution to apostates. This persecution, most severe from 250 until Easter 251, did indeed introduce complex questions because of the large numbers of the lapsed, and because of the varying guilt of those who sacrificed, or offered incense, or who by bribery or some indirect means had procured certificates, *libelli*, of having sacrificed or offered incense. However much hesitation and discussion there may have been about the conditions upon which the lapsed might be restored, the Roman and Carthaginian Synods seem to have had no hesitation in

[1] G. Bardy, *L'Edit d'Aggripinus*, Revue des Sciences Religieuses, 1924, p. 11 *seq.*; *Dict. d'Hist. et Géogr. Ecclés.*, art. *Aggripinus*, 1, col. 1039. Galtier, *De Pœnitentia*, 2nd ed., n. 240.

[2] Eusebius, *Ecclesiastical History*, 4, 23.

[3] *Contra Hæreses*, 1, 13, 5.   [4] Denziger, n. 57.

promising the substantial fact of restoration to communion. Then, too, the lapsed themselves appear
to have looked upon the possibility of forgiveness as a
thing normally to be expected, which they could
scarcely have done had there been a traditional and
universal rule against any restoration of apostates.
Moreover, Cyprian, in his admission of the lapsed to
penance, appeals to the previous practice, and never
rebuked the undue laxity of Felicissimus on the ground
that the previous practice had forbidden any forgiveness to apostates at all. Even the rigorist Novatian
never appealed, as far as we know, to previous custom
to justify his refusal of absolution.[1]

Similar reasons avail with regard to the sin of murder.
In short, the theory of a refusal of absolution to these
three sins appears to be based solely upon a mis-
interpretation of, or at least to undue weight given
to, certain passages in the Shepherd of Hermas,
Tertullian, Hippolytus and Origen. The development
does not seem to have been a steady inclination from
severity to mildness, but rather from a previous
mildness to more severe or reactionary rigorous
severity. This tendency one might judge to have been
due to an indirect influence of Gnostic ideas, which
held that certain sins sank one irrevocably into the
bad principle of the flesh and hence were unforgivable.
It is significant that the rigorists Tertullian, Hippolytus
and Novatian all became open heretics in rebellion
against the Church.

Public and Private Penance.

Upon this question the scantiness of evidence of
which we spoke in previous pages makes itself especially

[1] Cf. Nerney, op. cit., pp. 49-54.

manifest, and leaves the distinction between public and private penance, and the precise details of each of them, matters upon which no one may justly be dogmatic. With regard to public penance, two questions are mainly in doubt, first, to what extent public penance was a mere ecclesiastical institution, and secondly, when was the absolution given, at the beginning of the period of penance, or at the end. These questions are very closely connected.

In the previous Summer School book upon the Sacraments Abbot Cabrol gave a splendid description of the process and grades of public penance. Since then, however, B. Poschmann has called attention to the question whether public penance was primarily sacramental or whether it was primarily ecclesiastical, that is, whether it involved primarily a mere canonical penalty, comparable to the suspension of a priest from the exercise of his ministry, and had in view restoration to full ecclesiastical status, or whether it principally and essentially bore a relation to the remission of the guilt before God. Poschmann inclines to the former view, emphasizing public penance as a means of ecclesiastical government and as a canonical penalty.[1] On the other hand, Galtier, in his second edition of *L'Eglise et la rémission des péchés aux premiers siècles*, 1932, adduces reasons which seem very convincing for the view that public penance was essentially sacramental and was directed primarily to forgiveness of guilt before God, that the power of the keys, of binding and of loosing, exercised in public penance, was held by the early Church to be exercised not only *in foro ecclesiastico* but *in foro Dei*.

[1] *Die abendländische Kirchenbusse im Ausgang des christlichen Altertums*. München, 1928.

Closely connected with this question is the problem whether the absolution was given at the beginning of public penance or at its conclusion. The connexion is clear; for if the absolution were given at the beginning of the penance and the sinner was thereby completely reconciled to God, then the performance of the public penance tends to reduce itself to a canonical penalty. If, on the other hand, the absolution were given at the end of public penance, perhaps after years of penance among the ranks of the penitents, then the whole process appears as sacramental and part of the public confession of sin and of satisfaction for it. I confess that the reasons adduced for either opinion seem inconclusive. Those who hold that the absolution came at the end of the public penance, say that all the descriptions of public penance present the penitent as striving laboriously toward absolution and reconciliation with God; that remission of sin is held out as the fruit of the penance; that the penitents were placed in much the same condition as the catechumens, who were still without the sanctifying grace of Baptism; that the imposition of hands at the end implied the absolution; and, finally, that remission is promised to those who *had done* penance. On the other side, we have the witness of St. Cyprian that a deacon could upon occasion remit the public penance, which supposes the absolution was not sacramental as this was reserved generally to the Bishop; then, the prayers used upon admission to penance seem to signify a remission of sin and to be in fact an absolution; finally, Communion was given to public penitents in danger of death without, apparently, previous imposition of hands in absolution, this latter being prescribed to be supplied afterwards in cases of recovery.

Private Penance.

The question of "private" penance is in no way to be confused with the question of public or private confession of specific sins, since even public penitents did not necessarily make public confession of definite sins, save perhaps in cases of grave scandal or similar cases. The question of "private" penance really asks whether the only means of obtaining remission of sin was by aggregation into the ranks of the public penitents who constituted a special class in the Church as did the catechumens; or, on the other hand, whether one who had committed a secret sin could obtain remission without so submitting himself to aggregation into the class of "penitents". The arguments for the existence of such "private" penance seem conclusive. The penance was evidently at the discretion of the Bishop, and Cyprian certainly admitted back into full communion one Trofimus, an erring priest, without submitting him to public penance.[1] Moreover, even the Montanists in the early third century seem to have admitted that sins less grave than unchastity, apostasy and murder might be remitted without public penance;[2] and, finally, even these grave sins appear to have been sometimes remitted without public penance, either in order to avoid betraying a secret which would affect others, as, for instance, in the case of virgins who were engaged to be married but had sinned with a third person,[3] or in the case of danger of death or of persecution.

One difficulty, however, to the adduced evidence for the existence of private penance has lain in the total

[1] Ep. 55, 11.   [2] Tertullian, *De Pudicitia*, cap. 18.
[3] Cyprian, Ep. 4, 4.

absence in all our records of any formulas of prayers which could be an absolution in such private administration of the Sacrament; early liturgies universally seem to presume that the formula of absolution is to be said in public over the public penitents, and there is no trace, apparently, of any formula applicable to private penance.

An ingenious and, it must be confessed, a happy, solution of this difficulty has recently been suggested by J. A. Jungmann in his history of the ritual of penance in the Latin Church.[1] He reconciles the secrecy of private penance with the universal publicity of the absolutions in this manner: the penitent, having secretly confessed to the Bishop and received the imposition of works of satisfaction, might then join the ranks of the public penitents at the time when certain prayers were said over them, in which prayers Jungmann sees the absolution. Jungmann adduces certain evidence to show that some of the faithful joined the group of penitents, even though they themselves were not of the group, while the prayers were being said. Thus private penitents could have received absolution, which would be perfectly valid, inasmuch as they had previously confessed and accepted the penance imposed. This solution certainly appears to be the only one which meets the facts; it awaits, however, further discussion and investigation.[2]

This brief indication of some of the questions regarding the Church's penitential discipline in the early Church certainly shows that our knowledge is incomplete, due to the fragmentary nature of the historical

[1] *Die lateinischen Bussriten in ihrer geschichtlichen Entwicklung,* 1932.
[2] Cf. I. Zeiger, art. cit., p. 440.

remains.   The evidence remaining, however, amply
suffices to show how the variations in the Church's
application of her power of the keys, and the gradual
development toward the practice of "confession" as
we know it in our day, are fully legitimate and leave
the substance of the Sacrament the same now as it was
then.   The exercise of the power of remission is substantial; the conditions of that exercise, determined by
the Church, are accidental.

The Syncretist Hypothesis.

These examples of development given, or indicated,
it is needful, in view of the obvious purpose of our
consideration of the Pre-Nicene Church, to refer,
however cursorily and inadequately, to what is known
as the Syncretist Hypothesis.   The general tenor of
what is known as Syncretism is that Christianity, after
the death of its Founder, was substantially influenced
by the pagan religions with which it was surrounded.
This influence is generally derived from the "Mystery"
religions which began to flourish in the Roman Empire
contemporaneously with Christianity, and is claimed
to have affected sacramental practice and belief.   It
has been vigorously and boldly asserted that the
Christian Sacraments are nothing but pagan "mysteries" a little refined; and though serious scholars of
our day have abandoned the theory in its more radical
forms, more popular writers still give the theory
currency and make a short consideration of the subject
necessary.[1]

[1] The literature is enormous.   S. Angus in *The Mystery Religions
and Christianity*, London, 1925, gives a bibliography of 35 pages.
Perhaps the best of the older treatments is that of Carl Clemen,
Primitive Christianity and its Non-Jewish Sources, translated by

Characteristics of the Pagan Mysteries.

The first three centuries of the Christian era marked the decline of the official State-Religions of Greece and Rome, a decline undoubtedly partly due to the invasion of various exoteric or mystery cults from the East. From Phrygia came the worship of Attis and Cybele; from Eleusia in Attica came the cult of Demetros and Cora; from Thrace, the Dionysic mysteries; from Egypt, the religion of Isis and Orisis; from Persia sprang the soldiers' sun-god Mithra. These cults were generally introduced into the Roman Empire by Eastern slaves, freedmen, merchants, adventurers or exiled priests, and their outlook and practices were very different from the official State religions.

First of all, in contradistinction to the older Paganism, they had no necessary connection with any nation, and their gods were not tribal deities, whose worship was a public duty; they were universal in their appeal to the individual and cared little for social distinction or for public life. "With them," says Cumont, "religion ceased to be bound to the State and became universal; it no longer subordinates the individual to the city-state, but professes above all to ensure his personal salvation in this world and likewise in the next."[1] Slaves and women were admitted,

R. G. Nesbet, Edinburgh, 1912. Among Catholic writers the best are E. Jacquier, "Mystères païens et Saint Paul," in *Dictionnaire Apologétique de la Foi Catholique*, Paris, 1916; J. Coppens, "Baptême et Mystères païens" in *Dictionnaire de la Bible*, Supplement 1928, who give ample bibliographies; and I. B. Humberg, *De Sacramentis*, Valkenberg, 1915, pp. 42–60.

[1] *Religions orientales dans le paganisme romain*, 2nd ed., Paris, 1909, p. 22.

save in Mithraism; and they constituted societies, if not "*collegia*," with cordial but not exclusive fellowship, and their regular meetings and ceremonials. In this respect they may roughly be compared to the Nonconformist chapel as distinct from the official Church of England.

Secondly, they differed from the State religions in being "salvation" religions; they promised σωτηρία to their adherents. The exact nature of the salvation promised is a little difficult to determine; Angus remarks that in them men sought deliverance "from uncertainties of social life, the upheavals of political life, from the burden of grief and sorrow, from the reign of death, the universal power of demons and the malefic astral deities, from the oppressive tyranny of fate, the caprice of *sors* or fortune, the pollution of matter, the consciousness of guilt, the wasting of disease, from the *tædium vitæ*, and from all the ills that made human life a hell."[1] Doubtless some of the priests of these religions were quite willing to promise salvation in as comprehensive terms as was desired, though in Mithraism the salvation seems to have been from dishonour and from eternal death in the next life. However this may be, it is clear that they shifted the emphasis from worship and adoration, to some attainment of salvation through communication with the god.[2] Their gods were gods who had suffered and died and so attained immortality

[1] *The Mystery Religions and Christianity*, p. 226. This book, though full of references and shrewd remarks, is most unsatisfactory and unreliable, in that it uncritically juxtaposes evidence from different sources and from different places and ages and adduces the result as a fair comparison. It is typical in this respect of much popular writing upon comparative religion.

[2] Cf. U. Fracassini, *Il Misticismo Greco e il Christianesimo*, 1922, p. 310 *seq*.

or supernal power; union with them was somehow salvation.

Another characteristic was their use of symbolic or dramatic ceremonies to induce emotion and to promise salvation. They had elaborate initiations, comparable to reception into a modern secret society; sacred rites at which only initiates were present; sacred dramas in which the myth of the god or goddess was re-enacted, and in which the "*mystæ*" or initiates attained communication with the deity. Hence their name of "mysteries," since, as Clement of Alexandria said about the year 200, everything was symbolic and mysterious, veiled "in ænigmas, signs, symbols, allegories, tokens, metaphors, so that only the initiate could understand." Apuleius, a pagan writer towards the end of the second century, thus describes the ceremony of initiation into the mysteries of Isis:

"You may anxiously enquire, careful reader, what then was done and what said. I would say if I might; you should hear it if it were lawful. But a curse would fall on ears and eyes from such curiosity. Yet will I not hold you in suspense, you perhaps eager with religious desire. Listen, then, and believe, for it is the truth. I came to the confines of Death; I trod the threshold of Proserpina; after having been carried through all the elements, I returned to earth. At midnight I saw the sun shining with its bright splendour; I came to the presence of the gods below and the gods above, where I worshipped face to face. Lo! I have told you, but though you hear things you cannot understand them."[1]

This citation is characteristic of much that remains to us of the "mystery" religions; they *were* mysteries

[1] *Metamorphoses*, XI, 23, ed. Helm, Leipzig, 1913.

Ω

and their secrets were well kept. Nevertheless, we know that the essence of most of the central ceremonies was based upon a re-enactment in some form of the death of nature in autumn and its resurrection in the spring, or of the phenomena of life, generation and birth. Often the believer mystically died and was reborn, through participation in the ceremonies or mysteries. The Eleusinian mysteries dramatized the legend of Demeter and Persephone; the latter, while gathering flowers, is snatched by Hades to the realms below. Her mother, Demeter, seeks her vainly, until Zeus intervenes and decrees that Persephone shall spend the summer on earth and the winter with Hades. The symbolism is clear: Persephone is personified Nature, and her descent and resurrection symbolizes the decline of the forces of nature in the autumn and their rise in the spring. The same idea is represented in Mithraism, the slain bull representing in mysterious terms that from death springs fertility. The symbolism varied much in its dramatic representation, sometimes being inexpressibly coarse and inducing frenzy, sometimes being comparatively pure and elevated.

Resemblances to Christianity.

There is, it is clear, an underlying resemblance to Christianity in these religions which is lacking in the official State religions; there is need of salvation, a saviour god who dies and rises again, there are sacred rites which produce communion with the god and so life with him after death. These superficial resemblances are carried further in alleged similarities to each of our Seven Sacraments; Tertullian tells us that the religion of Isis and of Mithra used a *"lavacrum"* in their initiations, and the Eleusinian devotees were baptized to win regeneration and impunity from their crimes.[1] Something similar to Confirmation is found in Mithraism in certain impositions of hands, or " signings,"[2] and Firmicus Maternus, writing about 350, tells us that in certain unspecified Mysteries the priest anointed the heads of the initiates, saying, "Take courage, initiate of the saving god, let there be to us salvation from grief":—Θαρρεῖτε, μύσται τοῦ θεοῦ σεσωμένου, ἔσται γὰρ ἡμῖν ἐκ πόνων σωτηρία.[3]

The same Firmicus Maternus relates that in the Mysteries of Attis certain food and drink gave mystic powers, and evidently regards it as a profane imitation of the Eucharist,[4] as did St. Justin, about 152, when describing the Mithraic bread and chalice of water consumed with an accompanying sacred formula.[5] Cumont thinks that wine was afterwards substituted in the Mithraic liturgy.[6] Sacred meals, in which the god participated, were common enough in many religions.[7] As regards Orders, priests in a hierarchy were of course common to all these religions, though the ceremonies of appointment or ordination remain unknown; there were, too, in these religions various

---

[1] *De Baptismo*, 5, ed. d'Alès, p. 10. Cf. Apuleius, *Metamorphoses*, 11, 21: "Numen deæ solet eligere et sua providentia quodam modo *renatos* ad novæ reponere rursus salutis curricula." P. Blotzer, *Stimmen aus Maria Laach*, 1907, pp. 72, 186, admits that these pagan baptisms contained the idea of a mystic death and resurrection, of an expiation and renovation.

[2] Cf. Tertullian, *De Præscriptione Hæreticorum*, ed. Rauschen, *Florilegium*, 4, 55. Coppens, however, thinks that Mithraism never used a laying on of the hand in its initiations (*L'Imposition des Mains et des Rites connexes*, Paris, 1925, pp. 361-2).

[3] *De Errore Profanarum Religionum*, c. 22, *M.P.L.* 12, col. 1032.

[4] *Ibid.*, M. 12, col. 1022.

[5] 1 *Apology*, ed. Rauschen, *Florilegium*, 2, p. 70.

[6] *Die Mysterien des Mithra*, 3rd ed., Leipzig, 1927, p. 146.

[7] Cf. Umberg, op. cit., p. 45.

expiations and sacrifices for sin, sometimes accompanied by abstinence and occasionally by more or less severe mutilation.[1]

Besides these similarities to the Sacraments, emphasis is often placed upon the similarity of language used in the Mysteries to some of the Christian language; for instance, μυστήριον, or sacrament,[2] σωτηρία, salvation, κάθαρσις, purification, πίστις, faith, χάρις, grace, πνεῦμα, spirit, ψυχή, soul, νοῦς, mind, γνῶσις, perfect knowledge, σοφία, wisdom, δόξα, glory, πλήρωμα, fullness. Each of these words with their derivations, and others also, has occasioned a whole literature of erudite speculation, often tending to show that with language, ideas filtered into Christianity from Paganism.[3] Appeal is likewise made to the well-known fact of religious syncretism: that is of the compenetration of one pagan religion by another, so that names of the deities, myths, feasts, formulas, prayers and ideas passed from one to another to form a bewildering kaleidoscope: Helios becomes Mithra or Seraphis; Dionysius, Baal; Isis becomes the God-Mother, and Hera, and Venus, and Demeter, and Io and Tyche. This tendency became further complicated by the injection of various philosophical notions, derived from Platonism, Stoicism, Pythagoreanism, in an attempt to form a universal theosophy. Christianity, we are told, was a superior form of religious synthesis, whose elements all existed before and were gathered together in the early centuries, and hence it is essentially the same as these man-made religions.

[1] Umberg, op. cit., p. 45.

[2] Cf. the excellent note on the word by J. Armitage Robinson in his *Epistle to the Ephesians*, London, 1928, pp. 233–41.

[3] Cf. the brief but excellent study by E. Jaquier in *Dictionnaire Apologétique*, Vol. III, col. 982–98.

The Dogmatic Answer to the Hypothesis.

As the theory is supposed to be based upon facts, it might seem wiser to discuss the facts at once. Nevertheless, Catholics are so often accused of having a preconceived set of dogmas into which they are forced to try to fit the facts, that it may be well to set down at once what dogmatic positions are or might be affected by this theory or by variations of it, and to indicate why a Catholic student of religious history can approach this subject with a fearless and unprejudiced mind.

The main dogma in question is the institution by Christ of the Seven Sacraments.[1] This means that our Saviour Himself selected certain signs and gave them the power to produce grace under due conditions. This is the basis of our whole sacramental system and the ultimate fact about the Sacraments. But what does this institution by Christ mean? First of all, it does not mean that Our Lord chose new material things, hitherto unused in religious rites; on the contrary, we know that in the case of Baptism and of Marriage He left the material part of the rite substantially as it was, but added a new significance and power to produce grace. The material elements of the other Sacraments, too, were not new inventions; impositions of hands and anointings, in blessing, in strengthening, in healing, were very common and frequently bore a religious significance. In consequence, since Our Lord sweetly adapted His institutions to human nature, similarities between our rites and the rites of other religions are almost to be expected and are in no wise surprising.

Secondly, the institution by Our Lord does not

---

[1] Council of Trent, Sess. VII, can. 1.

necessarily mean that He Himself fixed immutably the
exact matter and form—the exact materials, actions
and words—in each Sacrament, though He did do
so in Baptism and the Eucharist. Indeed, in the
opinion of many theologians, "in some cases He left
the actual determination of the matter and form of
the Sacraments to His Apostles, or to the Church,
contenting Himself with a general indication that a
suitable sign—to be specified by them—should be
chosen, which by His will should produce grace for a
certain purpose. They think this view acceptable
since it enables them more easily to explain how the
matter and form of certain Sacraments (Holy Orders,
for example) has varied at different periods in the
Western Church, and to explain the divergencies still to-
day existing between East and West in the administration
of some of the Sacraments."[1] Upon this view, even
the material part of the sacramental sign itself, save in
Baptism and the Eucharist which were settled by
Christ Himself, is subject to the authority of the
Church, which might, for instance, substitute an
anointing for an imposition of hands in Confirmation,
or the touching of the sacred vessels, for an imposition
of hands, in Orders. All that must remain unchanged
is the "substance" of the Sacrament, as Trent declared;
and the "substance" is by many theologians understood to mean whatever Christ settled, which may be
in some Sacraments the meaning of the rite and its
embodiment in any material sign which the Church
thinks satisfactory.[2]

[1] Dr. George D. Smith, in *Six Sacraments*, Cambridge Summer
School Papers, 1929, p. 42.
[2] Upon this subject likewise there is a large literature. J.
Coppens declares: "En effet, les études de Harent, de Baets, Schmid,
Mangenot, de Guibert, Galtier, Cavallera, Lennerz, d'Alès ont

Thirdly, as regards accidental ceremonies, we have the declaration of the Council of Trent that: "The Church has always possessed the power, in her dispensation of the Sacraments, ever keeping their substance intact, to establish or to change, in view of variation of circumstances, time and place, whatever she should judge expedient in the interest of the faithful and of the reverence due the Sacraments."[1] Thus the power of the Church is fairly wide, and extends obviously to questions of language, formulas, prayers, vestments, gestures, ceremonies, music, lights, blessings and such incidentals which help to bring home to the faithful the meaning of the Sacraments and so increase devotion. We may readily admit, likewise, that feasts, processions, devotion to saints, and sacramentals were instituted by the Church with some regard to previous customs of its converts, accepting, for instance, the existence and date of a pagan feast, but changing its object and meaning.[2] The purely ecclesiastical discipline of the Church, as regards sacramental questions as in others, was certainly influenced by Roman law; and sacramental doctrine in its development found in Roman language, and in the meaning often underlying language, a convenient means of expression, just as in other doctrines Greek philosophical expres-

---

prouvé d'une facon définitive que le Concile de Trente n'a pas voulu rapporter à la volonté du Christ la détermination spécifique de la matière et de la forme sacramentelles." *Imposition des Mains et les Rites Connexes*, Paris, 1925, p. 404, where ample references may be found.

[1] Sess. XXI, cap. 2. "Præterea declarat, hanc potestatem perpetuo in Ecclesia fuisse, ut in sacramentorum dispensatione, salva illorum substantia, ea statueret vel mutaret, quæ suscipientium utilitati seu ipsorum sacramentorum venerationi, pro rerum, temporum et locorum varietate, magis expedire iudicaret." Denz. 931.

[2] Canon Marshall pertinently called attention to this point at the end of my lecture.

sions aided clarity and definition. Had the Church found its beginnings in China, let us say, and not in a Greco-Roman world, many accidentals of its rites, organization, art, language and whole outward appearance would have borne an entirely different aspect.[1]

Thus a Catholic historian of dogma can begin entirely without prejudice, and is *a priori* not unwilling to admit an influence upon Christianity from other, even Pagan, religions.

The Question of Fact.

Granted, then, in theory that Christianity might have been influenced in accidentals by these pagan religions, we may ask if the facts prove it was so. Confident assertions that they do have been made in bewildering variety by scholars of undoubted learning, but questionable judgement: Gunkel and Zimmern derived Christianity from Babylonian religions, Dietrich, Pfleiderer from Mithraism, Bousset from the Greek, Issliet from Egypt, Koch, Reinach from Parsism. The date, likewise, and the manner of the asserted infiltration of ideas and rites are most disconcertingly various; some assert a direct influence upon Christ Himself, some upon Paul, others upon John, others late in the second century, still others, like Brillioth, "in the period after Constantine."[2]

Such attempts to establish direct influence upon Christianity from the pagan "Mysteries" are now generally admitted to be hopeless. Our knowledge of the Mysteries is too scanty, for one thing. "We have extant," says Dr. Angus, "but few literary works

[1] Tromp, *De Revelatione*, pp. 316–17.
[2] *Eucharistic Faith and Practice*, London, 1930, p. 64.

dealing with the Mysteries, many scattered references, verses of poetry, fragments of hymns and prayers, mutilated inscriptions, damaged papyri, cult emblems, bas-reliefs, frescoes, painted vases, ruined chapels and temples. These are the varied and imperfect material out of which we have to attempt a reconstruction. Our difficulties are much heightened by the insecurity of chronological sequence, and the uncertainty as to the particular usages or beliefs of a cult at a particular period. During the centuries from Alexander the Great until Constantine these Mysteries have undergone marvellous remodelling to adapt them, as they were constantly adapted, to the needs of the day. Further, when literary notices, inscriptions, and monuments begin to increase in volume, the Mysteries have each and all been affected by religious syncretism in doctrine and cult, and so, by borrowing and mutual interaction, have approximated to each other so as to be in many respects indistinguishable."[1]

Differences between Sacraments and "Mysteries."

Even our scanty knowledge of the Mysteries is enough to show the abyss which separates their whole setting, significance and essence. The first and most striking difference between the Mysteries and Christianity is that the former were based upon myth, the latter upon fact. Mithra, Cybele, Isis and the others faded back into the dim impenetrable mists of legend and folklore; Mithra never lived and never slew the mystic bull. Christ was an historical person, who lived at a definite date and instituted rites to

[1] S. Angus, *The Mystery Religions and Christianity*, London, 1925, p. 40.

which, as He was divine, He gave supernatural power. Tatian could say to the Greeks:

"We do not utter idle tales in declaring that God was born in the form of a man. I challenge you, our detractors, to contrast your legends with our narratives . . . your legends are but idle tales. . . . O Greeks, believe me now, and do not attempt to resolve your myths or gods into allegory." Here at once Christian Sacraments rise to a different plane: they were means instituted by a real Person, who was divine, who was able by His power over the forces of nature, over life and death, to produce spiritual effects by His own supernatural action in material rites.

The second striking difference is the relation of the Christian Sacraments to the moral life of the recipient. The Christian Sacraments were all directed against sin; the "salvation" they gave was remission of sin and the power to lead a holy life, according to Christ's commands. From the very beginning Baptism was for the remission of sins; and the host of Christian witnesses with one voice connect the Sacraments with remission of sins and a life worthy of a Christian. Indeed this truth was exaggerated by some Christians, who thereby became heretics: the Encratists, and Tertullian, and even Cyprian who believed Sacraments must necessarily be administered only by those whose doctrine was correct. In this Christianity stands at the opposite poles from the Pagans, as R. Reitzenstein, a Rationalist, well says:

"That the salvation—$\sigma\omega\tau\eta\rho\iota\alpha$—should not only be an expulsion of passions and vices, a freedom from death, and the security of eternal life with God, but that it should be primarily a forgiveness of sin; this seems to me new in the Christian religion. The terrible seriousness with which sin and forgiveness were preached was, as far as I can see, unknown to Hellenism. That judgement of the dead, from which γνῶσις freed, or that suffering in Hades, from which the initiations of the Mysteries released, even the zeal for attaining 'purity,' can in no way seriously be compared with the Christian restoration of the conviction of sin and satisfaction, a conviction which had been evolved in the Jewish religion and which was the efficacious and sublime basis of the prophetic preaching. Then, when the primitive Church conjoined the death of Jesus with that profound sense of sin and with the belief that the most grievous sins could be forgiven, in this, and in this pre-eminently, the doctrine of Christian salvation had a force and a power, peculiar only to itself, capable of conquering the world."[1]

This difference is borne out by all our knowledge of the pagan Mysteries; and it marks in general the essentially superior—and essentially different in kind —idea and ethos of Christianity. In this the Sacraments were an essential, and they themselves thereby become incomparable to the vague emotion-producing rites of the Mysteries.[2]

There were other differences too obvious to insist upon. The Mysteries never freed themselves from their origins of nature-worship, and many of their processions and ceremonies were inexpressibly crude and savage. They linked themselves with astrology, magic, sorcery, necromancy. The incident at Ephesus

---

[1] Poimandres, *Studien zur griechisch-ägyptischen und frühchrist. Literatur*, 1904, p. 180.

[2] The Mysteries did indeed produce some beautiful prayers, and doubtless in some cases led to moral improvement; but we speak of their general doctrine and general effect.

when those who followed curious arts brought out their
books and burnt them before all, shows the stand of
Christianity; St. Paul and the Apologists are full of
warnings against worship of demons.   Cumont remarks: "Christianity alone set its face against astrology."[1]   The Mysteries, too, never had anything
approaching a coherent doctrine; they made no appeal
to the intellect of man, and though it may be true
that various writers, like Julian the Apostate, attempted
to engraft philosophy—Stoicism, neo-Platonism, Pythagoreanism—upon the Mysteries, the attempt was a
failure, and the Mysteries remain as they ever were,
totally lacking in any attempt at a coherent theology.
In contradistinction, Christianity from the beginning
not only held a clear doctrine and justified it before the
bar of reason, but as early as the second century began
speculation upon its Sacraments to distinguish them
from magic and to explain their efficacy.[2]

Perhaps the most striking and most important difference lay in the exclusiveness of Christianity.   Brillioth
well remarks: "The normal relation of the mystery-
cults to one another was one of tolerance.   Especially
in the later period, the accumulation of mystic initiations was the common practice; it was prudent to
acquire as many guarantees of salvation as possible.
Philosophy saw in the various rites only different ways
of approach to the same Deity.   But it was on the
ground of intolerance, from first to last, that Christianity
fought and won.   It was unthinkable to partake of the
Lord's table and the table of the devils."[3]

In addition to this, the general weight of historical

[1] *Astrology and Religion among the Greeks and Romans*, London,
1912, p. 167.
[2] v.g. Tertullian, *De Baptismo*.
[3] *Eucharistic Faith and Practice*, pp. 53–4.

evidence shows that Christianity found its origins and general line of development in the ritual and ceremonies of the Jewish synagogue. Dr. F. Gavin, in his penetrating study of the Jewish antecedents of the Christian Sacraments, thus concludes: "The elaborate sacramental system, with its intricate liturgical and its ramifying theological developments, which has distinguished Catholic Christendom, derives from Judaism, if within Judaism be included the Person who is called Jesus of Nazareth. Long nourished in Judaism, Christianity began its independent life, to go through the centuries bearing always in its most intimate religious observances the certain marks of its beginnings. Two factors explain sacramentalism—Judaism and Jesus." St. Paul, a Jew by education,[1] before his conversion intent only upon the traditions of his fathers, zealous for the law (*Acts* xxii, 3), after his conversion is almost incessant in his reiterated statements that he preaches only Christ and the Gospel he received from Christ. He denounces those who would "pervert the gospel of Christ. But though we, or an angel from heaven, preach a gospel to you besides that which we have preached to you let him be anathema."[2] The whole of the letter to the Colossians is an exhortation against pagan influences, against a "religion of angels" and of "the elements of this world,"[3] and for Paul "the things which the heathen sacrifice, they sacrifice to devils. And I would not that you should be partakers with devils."[4] To imagine Paul permitting

[1] Cf. the excellent study by A. E. Garvie, *The Gentile Influences on Paul, Expositor*, 8th series, Vol. 2, p. 471.

[2] *Galatians* i, 7–8.

[3] *Colossians* ii, 18–20; cf. Lightfoot's excellent comments upon the whole letter.

[4] I *Corinthians* x, 20.

the introduction into Christianity of ceremonies or ideas borrowed from the Mystery cults is simply fantastic.

The attitude of all the Christian fathers towards the pagan worship is the same as that of St. Paul; they look upon it as heathen and contemptible, and their language concerning it is vigorous to excess. They, too, knew of the parallels in the Mysteries to the Christian rites; but their explanation is that the Mysteries borrowed from Christianity. The syncretist hypothesis has been well said "to be one of the freaks of historical scholarship and a symptom of a childish ailment which is not uncommon in young sciences. To-day this theory appears only in the popular expositions whose mission seems to be to grant a further lease of life to the less fortunate hypothesis of real scholars."[1]

[1] Brillioth, op. cit., p. 49.

THE DOCTRINE OF THE HOLY TRINITY IN THE PRE-NICENE CHURCH

By the Rev. AELFRIC MANSON, O.P., M.A.

THIS paper is a study not of the doctrine of the Holy Trinity but of its history. At the same time the very fact that we can speak of the history of the dogma necessitates certain preliminary remarks on the characteristics of its revelation as of revelation in general. The mystery of the Trinity, like the other mysteries of our religion, was not revealed to mankind suddenly in a treatise or a formula. Centuries of providential preparation preceded its revelation. This is not the place to analyse the contribution of Judaism to this progressive work: we can only note in passing its doctrine of the one only God, the essential presupposition of the doctrine of the Trinity, and the development of the ideas of the Wisdom, the Word and the Spirit of Yahveh. Similarly we can only mention the Hellenic philosophical conception of the Logos and the Pneuma which played their part in the formulation of the doctrine. An exhaustive study of the early doctrine of the Trinity would nevertheless demand patient research into these and many other concepts. In this way only could we enter fully into the minds of the early Christian writers—whether orthodox or heretical—share their viewpoint and fully understand the meaning and associations of their language and formulæ. For our present purpose, however, we must be confined to a survey which inevitably involves a simplification of what is in reality exceedingly rich and complicated.

But if our simplified survey is not to be a positive distortion we must reiterate and stress that even the final revelation of the Mystery of the Trinity by Jesus Christ was not made by the setting forth of a dogmatic formula or a theological treatise. We have no record that He ever said, in so many words, that in God there is one ουσια and three Hypostases: that these Hypostases are distinguished solely by relationships. He formulated no Credo and wrote no treatise *De Trinitate*. Yet we hold that the Creed of Nicea is the formulation of what He revealed.

Jesus Christ reaffirmed what the Chosen People had always held as the central truth of their distinctive faith: "Hear, O Israel: the Lord thy God is *one* God." He also revealed, gradually and progressively, Himself. He was the Son of God; He was Himself divine; Kyrios, the Lord. He asserted both a oneness with God and a distinction between Himself and His Father. He spoke also of Another, the Holy Ghost, a gift which is divine and yet neither the Father nor Himself. At the end of His earthly life He bade His disciples regenerate the world in the one name of the Father, the Son and the Holy Ghost. The whole content of the revelation of the Trinity in the New Testament from Christ's first words about His Father and Himself to its final statement in the inspired writings of St. John cannot now be discussed. It may be summed up in the affirmation that there is one God who is God the Father, God the Son, and God the Holy Ghost, and that the Father, Son and Holy Spirit are really distinct. In that affirmation, indeed, the entire dogma is contained. In the New Testament the revelation of the *reality* of the Three (Persons) *is as formal as possible*. It is impossible to deny that Christ, while maintaining the divine unity and absolute simplicity—the Jewish tradition—at the same time distinguished in God the Father, the Son and the Holy Ghost. This is certain; but it is also certain the *conceptual elaboration* of this teaching was rudimentary: we do not find the notions of Person, Nature, Unity and Trinity, nor any philosophical discourses on the *relations* between the Persons. This elaboration was the work of the future: *Spiritus docebit vos omnia quæcumque dixero vobis . . . et introducet in omnem veritatem.* The entire history of Christian thought during the first three centuries that followed Our Lord's death is only a long effort of the human mind to formulate according to its own laws, on the plane of speculative truth the Gospel data transmitted by tradition. It is, perhaps, necessary to remark that this process was not the humanizing and debasement of something originally transcendent and divine. Revelation, by its very nature, is the gift, the social gift of certain knowledge about the utterly mysterious being of God, expressed in human, and therefore inadequate terms. To be real to us it must be in our language: to be in our language it must be miserably inadequate to the supreme Reality it expresses. Nevertheless its expression remains of incomparable value: and the work of theology is to make these human terms precise and consistent, to see their relationship, to state the revealed dogmas in a harmonized totality. Thus while the majesty of God is not diminished, the benefits of His immense donation are established in the intellectual life of men.

R

Accordingly in this history we must distinguish two aspects. There is first of all the *living tradition*, the common faith of the Church, which was plentiful and rich, but from the intellectual viewpoint lacking in precision, and then the strictly intellectual efforts which led up to the decisions of Nicea in 325, and to those of the Council of Constantinople in 380, which in this matter are inseparable from those of Nicea.

That the Church of the first three centuries constantly and everywhere taught and believed, in some fashion, the Trinity is indisputable, and is not, so far as I am aware, seriously disputed at the present time. On this point the witness of such liturgical fragments or of references to liturgical rites as have come down to us is conclusive. This liturgical witness is of the first importance and has too often been neglected by non-Catholic historians of dogma. Its importance is due to the fact that in handling liturgical documents we can be sure, to an extent that is impossible with the writings of individual Fathers, that we are dealing with the common faith and teaching of the Church and not with the private views or the personal reflections of a particular Christian or group of Christians. Liturgical prayer expresses the faith of all believers, lettered or unlettered, and in the unanimous consent of such liturgical fragments we can be confident that the common belief of the Christian Church is revealed to us.

It is true that the liturgical remnants which have come down to us from this period are scanty. But they reveal, beyond all question, not only that the Trinity was believed in, but that this belief was central and fundamental, the basis of the Christians' belief, the acceptance of which was the first condition of admission

into the Christian Church. Baptism was constantly
and universally administered in the name of the Father,
the Son and the Holy Ghost. The most ancient witness
to this (I exclude, of course, the witness of the New
Testament) is that of the *Didache*, written probably
in Palestine at the end of the first or beginning of the
second century. "Baptize," it orders, "in the name
of the Father and of the Son and of the Holy Ghost."
Whatever date we assign to its composition, it certainly
represents a very primitive stage of the development
of the Church. The same practice is reaffirmed later
by Justin, Irenæus, Tertullian, Origen; representing
Syria, Rome, Palestine, Gaul, Asia Minor, Africa,
Egypt.

The threefold formula was enforced, even at the time
of the *Didache*, by threefold immersion. The neophyte
at a primitive baptism could make no mistake that the
Trinity was the object *par excellence* of his new
faith, the source and the end of his new life.

This truth was yet further impressed upon him by
the interrogations which were made and the profession
of faith which was demanded of him previous to or
concomitantly with his baptism. These interrogations
and profession of faith appear to have been universal,
although the manner of making them seems to have
differed in different times and localities. The general
practice regarding interrogations appears to have
consisted in the demanding of the neophyte before
each respective immersion: "Dost though believe in
the Father . . . in Jesus Christ . . . in the Holy
Spirit?" to each of which the neophyte replied, "I
believe." Several "Acts of the Martyrs" of the third
century, Denis of Alexandria, Firmilian, St. Cyprian,
Hippolytus, Tertullian bear witness to this practice.

In addition to these interrogations, made in the act of baptizing, a profession of faith was universally required of the candidate before his baptism. In these professions of faith we have, undoubtedly, the origin of the Apostles' Creed. The sources suggest that there were two types of these baptismal symbols—one a three-articled confession of faith in the three divine Persons; the other a Christological confession rehearsing the principal events of the Saviour's life. At an early date, possibly as early as the time of St. Justin, these two symbols became fused into one, the Christological symbol being attached to the second article of the Trinitarian, as we have it to-day in the Apostles' and Nicene creeds. Not until a later date was a uniformity imposed upon these symbols, but their general characteristics seem to have been the same; and profession of faith in Father, Son and Holy Ghost was undoubtedly a *sine qua non* of admission into the Church everywhere. Tertullian truly says of this profession or rule of faith that it had been handed down from the beginning and is anterior to all heresies (*Adv. Prax.*, 2), that it is the distinctive mystery of the Christian faith whereby it is distinguished from Judaism. "What need would there be of the Gospel," he asks, "if thenceforward the Father, the Son and the Spirit are not both believed in as Three and as making one only God?" (*Ibid.*, 31.)

That this faith in Father, Son and Holy Ghost was central for the ante-Nicene Christian is fully borne out by liturgical fragments and references other than those of Baptism. Describing the celebration of the Eucharist in the middle of the second century St. Justin says: "There is then brought to him who presides among the brethren bread and a cup of wine

mixed with water, and he taking them gives praise
and glory to the Father of the universe, through the
name of the Son and the Holy Ghost." (1 *Apol.*, 65.)
Again St. Justin tells us: "For all things wherewith we
are supplied we bless the maker of all through His
Son Jesus Christ and through the Holy Ghost."
(*Ibid.*, 67.)

Such is the customary form of Christian doxologies.
Sometimes, as in this instance, glory and blessing is
rendered to the Father and Creator through the Son
and the Holy Ghost; less often, though more signifi-
cantly, alike to Father, Son and Holy Ghost, as in
the formula of Hippolytus: "Glory be to Thee, to
Father, Son and Holy Ghost, in the Holy Church,
now and ever and in all ages." (*Traditio Apostolica.*)
Sometimes, as in the Acts of St. Polycarp, both forms
are combined, the Son appearing both as the mediator
and object of the doxology: "I praise Thee, I bless
Thee, I glorify Thee, through the eternal and heavenly
High-Priest Jesus Christ thy beloved Son, through
whom and with whom and the Holy Spirit be glory
both now and ever and for ages to come." (*Mart.
Poly.*, 14.)

No less significant, as an indication of the ante-
Nicene faith in the Trinity, are the prayers, hymns and
doxologies addressed directly to the Second Person.
They prove beyond doubt that He was recognized as
divine, as an object of worship. The importance of
these hymns and doxologies to Christ was stressed by
Origen when arguing against adoptionism. "We sing
hymns to the Most High alone and to His only Begotten
who is the Word and God." (*Contra Celsum*, VIII, 67.)

Unquestionably, then, the ante-Nicene Christian
believed in the Father, the Son and the Holy Ghost,

and this belief he held to be the central and distinctive mystery of the Christian faith. But we must now turn to a more delicate and controverted question. *What* precisely did he believe about this Father, Son and Holy Ghost? How did he conceive their mutual relationships? Did he acknowledge the faith which was later authoritatively formulated in terms of three Persons and one Nature? Did he believe in the eternal pre-existence of the Son and the Holy Ghost? Did he believe in the eternal generation of the Word and the eternal procession of the Holy Ghost? Or did he believe in three Gods, or alternatively in one Divine Person at once Father, Son and Holy Ghost? Did he believe that Father, Son and Holy Ghost were Divine in the same sense and God on an equal footing; or did he not suppose rather that the Son and the Holy Ghost were Divine emanations, subordinate and inferior to the Father?

In order to answer these questions we must turn to the second and more considerable set of sources—to the writings of individual Christian pastors and thinkers, to the works of strictly intellectual reflection. At first, undoubtedly, the doctrine of Father, Son and Holy Ghost did not present itself to the average Christian as a problem, but simply as the central truth of his faith. It was enough for him to record and assert that faith. The fact that he did so, even before the problem of reconciling the divinity of Son and Holy Ghost with the unity of God is of great importance. It shows that the doctrine of the Trinity preceded all controversial preoccupations and consequently was not an invention to meet controversial exigencies. In this connexion the First Epistle of St. Clement of Rome is very important. It is not a doctrinal exposition, it opposes no heresies, it has no dogmatic axe to grind, its doctrinal references are purely incidental. Yet it asserts at once the unity of God (it is inspired throughout by the Old Testament) and the divinity of Father, Son and Holy Ghost. "Have we not," he asks the Corinthians, "one God, and one Christ, and one Spirit of Grace who is poured out upon us?" (46.) Still more significant is the celebrated christianised adaptation of the Jewish form of oath. "As God liveth," said the Jews. Clement says: "As God liveth, and as the Lord Jesus Christ and the Holy Spirit live, who is the faith and hope of the elect."

St. Clement wrote in the year 95 or 96. Some fifteen years later we have the letters of St. Ignatius of Antioch. No more than Clement is Ignatius concerned to write a dogmatic treatise; his letters are purely personal and occasional. But between Clement and Ignatius heresies had grown and, more important still, the Fourth Gospel had been written. Ignatius is saturated with the teaching of St. John.

The theology of Ignatius has been the subject of considerable discussion and controversy. That Ignatius believed firmly in the Godhead of Christ is indisputable. So strong indeed is his Johannine emphasis on the unity of the Father and the Son that he has been charged with ignoring their distinction and of being guilty of Modalistic tendencies. The charge seems nevertheless to be unjust. He asserts frequently the procession of the Father from the Son, and His pre-existence with the Father before the Incarnation. It is not so clear that he recognized His eternal pre-existence before the creation. Shortness of time forbids our discussing this intricate question. It must suffice us to note that Ignatius affirms the unity of

God and is, to use his own words, "fully persuaded that there is one God, who manifested Himself through Jesus Christ His Son, who is His Word that proceeded from silence." The Father, the Son and the Holy Ghost are all concerned in our salvation. (*Magnesians* 8, 13; *Eph.* 9.)

If Ignatius's allusions to the generation and filiation of the Son seem inadequate and even, judged by the creed of Nicea, inaccurate, it must be remembered that his Epistles are but letters and are nowhere directly concerned with the problems raised by the Mystery of the Trinity. The heresies with which he was confronted did not touch directly upon it, but solely with the reality of the Incarnation.

Nevertheless it was not long before the Christian's belief in Father, Son and Holy Ghost was to present him with problems, with challenges from heretics, Jews and Pagans. How could it be said that he worshipped one only God when he asserted that Jesus Christ was God, when he paid Him divine honours as well as to the Father? Not only Jewish and Pagan controversialists delighted in twitting the Christian Apologists with this difficulty, but the rank and file of Christians were apt to meet with the problem in the tribunals. In the Acts of Pionius and his Companions martyred at Smyrna in the middle of the third century, we read that three Christians, Pionius, Sabinus and Asclepiades, were charged before the magistrate Polemon. Polemon asks Pionius: "What God dost thou worship?" Pionius replies: "The God Almighty who made the heavens and the earth . . . whom we have known by His Word, Christ." "Whom dost *thou* worship?" Polemon asks Sabinus. "The God Almighty who made the heavens and the earth . . . whom we have known by His Word, Jesus Christ." Polemon then turns to Asclepiades: "Whom dost *thou* adore?" Asclepiades replies: "Christ Jesus." Polemon asks: "Is this then some other God?" Asclepiades replies at once: "No; it is the same as these others have spoken of."

But long before this problem had presented itself in the form of challenges from controversialists. The first recorded instance is that of Trypho the Jewish opponent of St. Justin Martyr, the most important and typical of the group of Christian thinkers in the latter half of the second century who set out to expound the new religion and overcome its pagan and Jewish adversaries. Trypho was an educated and liberal Jew, free from the vulgar pagan prejudices against Christianity, but who, being a convinced monotheist, found an insuperable difficulty in the Christian worship of a crucified man. In the *Dialogue with Trypho* Justin defends the divinity of Christ and in order to conserve the unity of the God-head states the doctrine in the famous terms of *the Word* and of *generation*. The starting-point of this conception is, of course, the prologue of St. John's Gospel about the Word, the Logos, made flesh. For St. Justin the Logos is God and is pre-existent to all creatures. He is not made nor created but generated. This generation makes Him really distinct from the Father and yet not separate from Him. He issues from the Father but like light from another light: the Father suffers no diminution. In this teaching we find the beginnings of a theology which supplied the Greek Fathers with a satisfactory terminology, and which in its spiritual conception of the interior intellectual word generated by the mind, established an analogy which has afforded the truest approach for the human intellect in its attempt to seize something of the mystery of the Trinity. It is true that the doctrine of the Holy Spirit is little developed by the Apologists, but He is definitely recognized as distinct and eternal together with the Word and the Father, and in Theophilus of Antioch we meet for the first time with the expression that the Three constitute a Trinity (τριάς). Naturally in this first attempt we are not surprised to find a certain imprecision: the language of Justin, for example, sometimes suggests that the engendered Word is inferior to the Father, but it seems more probable that this subordination is simply a subordination of origin, the fact that the Word comes *from* the Father; it does not imply that the Word is not of the same divine nature as the Father. Again, St. Justin does not always observe the absolute difference between the Greek doctrine of the Logos, the seminal word or light of reason that is in every man, and the Christian concept. But this inaccuracy is due to his anxiety to lead his pagan auditors to the absolute truth by way of the truths they already possessed. In this particular instance the effort was not laudable: but it does not mar the credit of his and the Apologists' achievement. For us the terminology is incomplete; if, however, we pause and reflect on the immensity of the intellectual problem implied in the two assertions: there is one God, and, this man Christ is God, we shall find only admiration for the men who paved the way for the expression of this mystery in terms that can be inserted in a catechism.

There is one other theologian of the second century of great importance: St. Irenæus, Bishop of Lyons. Unlike the Apologists he is not a speculative thinker, but he is an impressive witness of the most ancient traditions, that of Asia, where his master St. Polycarp had handed on to him the teaching of St. John, and that of Rome, where he gathered the teaching of the Apostolic See. His unequivocal affirmation of the Trinity is, therefore, of considerable interest as attesting the authenticity and antiquity of the Church's official teaching of this doctrine.

One common way by which doctrine develops is by the necessity which heresy provokes of stating its contents more clearly. Theologians have to explain themselves, and what was implicit becomes explicit. During the third century heresy was a principal occasion of certain developments in the doctrine of the Trinity. This heresy has the general name of Monarchianism: it flourished in Rome 180–250 and for a while later in the East. As is evident from its name it stood for an assertion of the divine monarchy. Its origins were orthodox. It was a reaction against certain Gnostic tendencies of the time which inculcated the idea that there were several or at least two principles at the source of all things. To assert the divine monarchy was, therefore, to reaffirm monotheism, to say that there is only one first principle. Unfortunately Monarchianism did not remain at this point. Attention was turned not only to the question of what was the first principle in the universe, but to what within the Godhead itself was the first principle. We should say now that the Father is the one source of Godhead and that Son and Spirit are derived from Him, the Son by being "begotten," the Spirit by "proceeding." At this stage, however, these terms were not formulated, and the question was difficult to solve. In the attempt to solve it two main positions were taken up.

Some in order to conserve the unity of God gave up the divinity of Christ; they considered Him as a man who was visited by a divine power (δύναμις) by which in the end He was adopted into the Godhead. These are termed Dynamic or Adoptionist Monarchians and in the West were represented by two men called Theodotus, the one a tanner and the other a banker, and by Artemon, who seems to have passed the heresy on to the East, where it was taken up by Paul of Samosata, the Bishop of Antioch. Its tendency was in harmony with the Antiochene school whose realist exegesis, in contrast with that of Alexandria, was always in danger of neglecting the divinity of Christ. The other school of heretics, the Modalist Monarchians, had a greater fortune in the West. The Modalists retained the divinity of the Son, but in order to conserve the unity of the Godhead they gave up His personality. Christ's Person was for them simply a mode of the Father's existence. Their leaders were Praxeas, Noëtus and Sabellius. They received the name of Patripassians because in identifying the Son with the Father they attributed the sufferings of the Son to the Father. In reaction to this heresy we find the leaders of two great schools of theology: Tertullian, the first name of renown among the African thinkers whose race was to die out only with Augustine, and Clement and Origen the principal masters of Alexandria.

With Tertullian the Latin language comes into theology. This man, a pagan lawyer converted to the Christian religion, who, nevertheless, died in heresy, passionate, hard and a rigorist, was in no sense a speculative thinker. He had indeed contempt for philosophy of any kind, but he was a master of language and hammered out with legal precision a theological vocabulary which has remained a permanent contribution to Western thought. From this viewpoint his *Adversus Praxeam* is one of the most influential theological books ever written. In it also we find an excellent exposition of his doctrine of the Trinity. Tertullian is a Monarchian in the true sense and he insists on the unity of the Godhead. But within this unity there is a certain "economy" by which this unity is communicated to a trinity, a communication which does not divide but only distributes the unity. He calls the new terms thus obtained, spiritual substances, forms, species and above all *persons*. He is writing against the Modalist heresy which confounded the persons, and he therefore insists vigorously that they are numerically distinct. At the same time he never forgets their unity, and he defines the kind of unity it is. They cannot be called "*unus*" because that would imply that they are one in number: but they must be called "*unum*" because there is between them an absolute unity of *substance*. Thus he has brought out the fundamental notion of *consubstantiality*, and he wrote the great formula "three persons, one substance," "*tres personæ, una substantia*", which was to be the watchword of Latin theology. The West had secured a terminology which safeguarded the traditional faith. If the question was asked "How can you speak of a one and only God, and yet name a Father, a Son and a Holy Spirit?" the answer was that the three persons are of one and the same substance—substance designating the infinite being of the divinity whence the life of the Three Persons springs.

In the brilliant international city of Alexandria, the centre of Hellenic culture, the home of neo-Platonism, the intellectual atmosphere contributed to produce a

type of theology very different from that of the West.
The Christian school had ideals similar to those of the
Apologists, though its sympathy with and understanding of Greek thought was more profound.
Clement, its first distinguished figure, directed the
school from 190–202. He combined deep piety with a
great love of philosophy, and his ambition was to
create a theology that should be the true gnosis, the
ultimate wisdom. His work is interesting in many
ways, but we must confine ourselves to his teaching
on the Trinity. He expresses his idea of God after
the manner of the Platonists—an utterly transcendent
being, above all creation and above all thought. In
this being he posits three really distinct terms, the
second of which is the eternally generated Logos, the
Son who is in the Father as the Father is in the Son.
Clement has been accused of both Modalism and
Subordinationism: it seems probable that he fell into
neither, but his extreme interest in the nature of the
relations between the Word and the Father led him at
times into curious expressions which need not be
interpreted harshly. He has been overshadowed by
the vast genius of his disciple and successsor Origen.
He was a man of immense erudition and, although
not a philosopher in the creative sense, his was the
first really synthetic mind that Christianity produced.
With him, again, we have to select from the multifarious
aspects of his doctrine that alone which bears on the
dogma of the Trinity. His idea of God, like Clement's,
bears the marks of the Platonist absolute: and within
this absolute there are three hypostases or persons,
the Father, the Son, and the Holy Spirit. The Son
or the Word is God, distinct from and yet consubstantial with the Father and eternally engendered by

Him. This generation, therefore, was not an event, but is an eternal process, and the Son is God essentially; He is of one substance with the Father: the word with so dramatic a future, ὁμοούσιος, is found in Origen. The notion of *procession* which is probably his most important contribution to the dogma of the Trinity, is found again in his teaching on the Holy Spirit. He enquires into the mode of procession of the Holy Spirit and decides that since all things have been produced through the Word the Holy Spirit was the first and most worthy of all creatures to be produced by the Father through Christ, although He is not strictly engendered by the Son since in the Trinity is only one Filiation. Origen's influence was tremendous and his enemies correspondingly numerous. Among other things he has been accused of subordinating the Son to the Father and the Holy Spirit to the Son. There is no doubt that several passages in his writings, taken alone, would justify this accusation, but apart from the fact that before Nicea there was much imprecision in terminology, in so extensive a writer it is not unnatural that exaggerations and inaccuracies are sometimes to be found. Before concluding the notice of the Modalist heresy it may be well to observe the attitude of the Popes towards it, especially since it has been declared that certain of them actually favoured it. Pope Zephyrinus (202-18) apparently did not at once discover the dangerous trend of Sabellius' teaching: it was pointed out to him by the Roman priest Hippolytus—upon whose *Philosophoumena* the accusations are based—but since he thought Hippolytus' own theology was quite as dangerous, and his archdeacon Callistus agreed that the danger was not urgent, he refrained from a condemnation, and in 218 he died. Hippolytus hoped to succeed him, but it was Callistus who was elected. Whereupon Hippolytus retired into schism, saying that life was impossible with an heretical pope. It is quite certain, however, that the Pope very soon condemned Sabellius, and the heresy quickly disappeared from Rome and the West.

In Cyrene, where perhaps Sabellius had fled after his condemnation, we find a new form of Modalism between 250 and 260. The word "person" (prosôpon) is applied to the Father, the Son and the Holy Spirit, but only in its etymological sense of a theatrical mask: the Persons of the Trinity are simply three successive and passing manifestations, the three successive masks under which the one divine substance presented itself: the three were identical and the Son could be called consubstantial with the Father. The bishop Denis of Alexandria, a disciple of Origen, expressed his disapproval of this doctrine in a series of letters to the Bishops of Cyrene. But in defending the real distinction between the divine persons he was said to have over-emphasized them and to have tended to subordinationism. At any rate he was denounced to Rome and received a letter from the Pope St. Denis asking for an explanation and including a long and very important statement of the doctrine of the Trinity. The Pope blamed those who by a too absolute distinction of the Persons came almost to speak of three Gods, and rebuked especially the use of the word poiema (a creation)—a word used by Origen—for the Son. This would have been avoided, he said, if the doctrine that the Son is consubstantial (homoousios) with the Father had been firmly adhered to. Denis replied respectfully and suggested he had been more or less misrepresented; only with regard to the word

"homoousios" he urged that since it had been used by
the Sabellians in an heretical sense he could not
approve of it, although he agreed with the doctrine
underlying it in the Pope's letter. This letter was well
received; and from this time Rome adopted the con-
substantialist formula officially; and with Rome was
Alexandria.

Nevertheless it was in Alexandria that the last great
heresy before Nicea arose. In this city Arius was
born in 256. He became a priest and began to
promulgate a doctrine of his own under the pretext
that his bishop was Sabellian. He asserted that the
Son was so distinct from the Father as to be inferior
in substance. Further, the Son was not eternal, but
only the first creature of the Father. Any other teaching than this he declared to be Sabellian. Very quickly
the Church realized the gravity of his teaching. This
was a heresy that annihilated the very life of Christianity and reduced it to an arid theism with a Christ
who whatever else he might be could not be a Redeemer. Historians have dismissed the affair as a
quarrel about words: but all quarrels are about words
unless they are merely brawls. The only point to
decide is whether the words represent things; and the
more important the things the more vital are the
words. This necessarily superficial survey will not
have entirely failed if it has suggested that the long
effort to get the right words during the first centuries
of the history of the Church was not an academic
and sterile game pursued by persons remote from the
real interests and life of the world. That effort was
made because if the wrong words had prevailed something infinitely precious would have been lost to
mankind. If we believe that Christianity has the

s

power to invigorate humanity we must remember that it comes to man under human conditions. Its saving power is reached and incorporated into man by physical, visible, audible, intelligible means: by words and signs. Once destroy those means and the bridges between ourselves and the supernatural world are broken. Keep the deposit of faith—not because it is a kind of museum specimen, but because it is a principle of life. And it must be kept *alive*, and to live is to grow. The deposit of faith grows not objectively—there is no new revelation—but in its increasing explicitation in the minds of men. Theological language, then, the right words for the right thing, is an essential part of Christian life. It was this life that the wrong words of Arius would have destroyed.

Arius was condemned at a synod of Alexandria by about a hundred Egyptian bishops. But he was ingenious: he could explain himself : he had friends at court. So other synods upheld him. At this time Constantine the Great was Emperor. The Church had come out of the persecutions into peace, into triumph. She was the only thing alive in a dying empire. Constantine saw in her a principle of order, a kind of spiritual police force for princes. He was therefore duly annoyed at all this fuss in Alexandria, which among other things was the granary of the Empire. He sent Hosius, Bishop of Cordova, to stop it. Hosius could not. He saw the situation was much too menacing. He told the Emperor that a council should be convoked, not a merely local and provincial council, but a council of the whole Church. The idea appealed to Constantine, who had a sense of the spectacular, and also liked to think of himself as a divinely appointed mediator.

He thereupon invited all the bishops to come to the little town of Nicea in the summer of 325. From two hundred to two hundred and fifty accepted: those from Egypt, from the civil diocese of the East, and from Anatolia were in the majority: others came from the Balkans, one from France, one from Africa, one from Persia, and from Rome came two legates from Sylvester the Pope. It was a great assembly and Constantine behaved with impressive magnificence. The discussion was furious and heated. Arius had many friends, nevertheless they did not prevail, and the Council summed up the work of centuries in the words of its creed: "One God Almighty—one Lord Jesus Christ Son of God only begotten of the Father, God of God, Light of Light, begotten not made, *consubstantial with the Father.*" The last expression represents the contribution of Western theology.

We have followed the doctrine of the Trinity a little way: we have seen how some of its principal terms came to be fixed and formulated. But Nicea is not the end: consubstantiality was secure, but there were many other terms yet to be established before a synthesis could be formed, before Augustine could write his *De Trinitate.* Above all, the divinity of the Holy Spirit had to be pronounced authoritatively, and in 380 at Constantinople this was done. Even then much work remained; but the bases were settled. Controversy over the fundamentals was finished. Theologians had the chief points from which to start. It has been our intention just to glance at the process by which those points, those right words, were gained. The history of dogma, like all history, is useful only in so far as it contributes to a richer life for us in the present: it is not a mere *recherche du temps perdu:* it shows us the function of mind in Christian life, the function of mind in forming the Christianity that is our possession, and it indicates the supreme importance for Christians in every age if they would receive the full gift of their religion, to see that they have the right understanding, the right concepts, the right words, so that they can move freely in the new world of revelation and see it clearly to the horizon and obey its precepts with a rational obedience.

PRE-NICENE CHRISTOLOGY[1]

By Fr. ALPHONSUS BONNAR, O.F.M., D.D.

THE Catholic teaching concerning Jesus Christ is that in Him there are *two natures*, that of God and that of man, each complete, perfect and distinct, and that these two natures are united *in one only Person*, that of the Word, the Second Person of the Blessed Trinity. This doctrine was obscured particularly by the Arian heresy, which comes at the end of our period, and by some earlier minor heresies which eventually culminated in Arianism. Arianism was formally a heresy against the doctrine of the Trinity, but materially it was a Christological heresy. Let me explain this. That there are three Persons in God and that Christ, true God as well as man, is the Second Person of this Divine Trinity was difficult to reconcile with the fundamental idea of monotheism which Christianity had inherited from the Jewish revelation. Hence the tendency, among those who would give a reasoned explanation of Christian doctrine, to make the Second Person of the Blessed Trinity, the Word or Son, less

[1] The Soteriology of the Pre-Nicene Church I have only touched upon incidentally for two reasons. The first is that full treatment of the subject would have carried the paper beyond all reasonable limits of length. The other is that it is in Christology proper that the Council of Nicæa is a definite landmark in the definition and development of doctrine. In the preparation of this paper I have derived considerable help from the unpublished lectures of Fr. Ulricus Hüntemann, O.F.M.

than the Father. This tendency reached its full development in Arianism. Our scope in the present paper is to show that the Catholic Christological doctrine can clearly be shown to be the teaching of the early Church. I say "of the early Church" and not simply "of the early Fathers of the Church," because, although we shall draw for the most part upon the works of these early Christian writers, the early Fathers are the early Church speaking to us. Indeed I shall introduce two of the early Fathers, St. Ignatius and St. Irenæus, who are in an especial way the personification of the Church in their time and also are as trustworthy witnesses as could be imagined of the divine tradition handed down from Christ and the Apostles.[1]

From the preceding paragraph it can be seen that Catholic Christological teaching contains these points : (i) that Christ is, by nature, God; (ii) that He is, by nature, man; (iii) that He is the Second Person of the Blessed Trinity, the Son of God, the Word; and (iv) that the true nature of God and the true nature of man in Him are, though distinct, a unity through the union (but not admixture) of both natures in the Divine Person of the Word: this union is called the Hypostatic (=Personal) Union. It follows from these four points that in Christ there is no human person, though there is a real, full and perfect human nature, comprising a human body with all its co-natural

---

[1] The Fathers, writing of the Logos or Word, distinguish between the indwelling (ἐνδιάθετος) and the uttered (προφορικός) Word. The uttering of the Word by the Father is not meant as the eternal generation of the Word but as the creation of all things by Him. "All things were made by Him (the Word)" (*John* i, 3). Of course there is no real distinction in the Word Itself. The expressions used by some of the Fathers might easily be interpreted in an unorthodox sense if this distinction were not kept in mind.

faculties and a real human soul with intellect and free-will. It would be heresy to deny any of these points.

In showing that these things were the teaching of the early Church regarding Jesus Christ, I am confronted with two difficulties which I must overcome as best I may. The first is that many of the passages to be quoted enunciate, perhaps in a very few words, not just one of the points which I have enumerated but several or even all of them. Then there is the difficulty of avoiding a dreary sameness in my exposition, especially if an explanation of the passages is attempted, since there is necessarily a sameness in the quotations to be made. This difficulty is, I am afraid, inherent in the subject and quite insurmountable.

We will first take a few short quotations from St. Ignatius of Antioch,[1] which declare unequivocally the Godhead of Christ, His true full human nature and the close union of both natures.

> "There is one physician, of flesh and of spirit, begotten and unbegotten, God existing in flesh, in [His] death [our] true life, from Mary and from God, subject before to suffering and now impassible, Jesus Christ Our Lord." (*Ephes*. vii, 2.)

In this passage Christ is explicitly called God. He is God made man—"God existing in flesh." The phrase "in flesh" is that of St. John in chapter i of his Gospel. Both in the Gospel and in this passage from

---

[1] St. Ignatius suffered martyrdom at Rome in the year 108. It was while going to Rome to his death that he wrote the letters from which our extracts are taken. The letters are in no wise controversial and, as he takes for granted that his Christian belief is the same as that of all the churches to which he writes, his evidence on points of doctrine is testimony also to the belief of these churches.

St. Ignatius it is clear from the context that "flesh" means "human nature." To confine ourselves to St. Ignatius we see that Christ was "begotten" of Mary and was "subject to suffering." These phrases denote a true and full human nature. Only human nature, soul as well as body, can suffer, for the flesh cannot by itself suffer if there be no human soul. The doctrine of the Atonement is also quite clear in that from Christ's death comes our true life, i.e. not our bodily life but our spiritual re-birth.

The same points are contained just as explicitly in another part of the same letter.

"Our God Jesus Christ was by Mary carried in the womb, according to God's dispensation from the seed indeed of David but by the Holy Ghost; who was born and baptized, that by His passion He might sanctify the waters." (*Ephes.* xviii, 2.)

The personal unity of Christ in two natures is definitely asserted by St. Ignatius when he says:

"You all come together each one by grace, in one faith, and in *one Jesus Christ*, who being according to the flesh of the line of David is the son of man and the Son of God." (*Ephes.* xx, 2.)

The true human nature of Christ, together with the points already illustrated, appears in the following:

"I praise Jesus Christ, God, who has made you so wise: for I have observed you to be perfect in an immovable faith as being fastened body and soul by nails to the cross of the Lord Jesus Christ and rooted in charity by the blood of Christ, believing with a full and steadfast faith in Our Lord who truly rose from the line of David according to the flesh, the Son of God by the will and power of God, truly born of a virgin, baptized by John . . . truly transfixed by nails in the flesh for us under Pontius Pilate and Herod the Tetrarch." (*Smyrn.* i, 1-2.)

In the passages quoted, as in passages to be taken from St. Irenæus and others, a conclusive argument for the Godhead of Christ could be formed from the application to Him of the title "Lord." This, however, would involve us in too long a consideration of the term as applied to Him in the writings of the New Testament. Let it suffice to note here that the Fathers of the Church in calling Christ "Lord" are simply following the teaching of the Apostles, and like the latter definitely understand the word "Lord" as the equivalent of "Yahveh," the ineffable name of God in the Old Testament.

St. Irenæus[1] is no less explicit in declaring the Christological teaching of the Church. In the following passage he gives what amounts to a paraphrase of what we know as the Apostles' Creed. I quote the relevant parts:

"The Church planted throughout the whole world, even to the ends of the earth, received both from the Apostles and from their disciples that faith which is in One God, the Father Almighty, . . . and in one Jesus Christ, the Son of God, become incarnate for our salvation; . . . and the birth from a virgin, and passion and resurrection from the dead; and the ascent into heaven in the flesh of the

[1] St. Irenæus was born in Asia Minor *c.* 120–30: he died at Lyons *c.* 202. The peculiar value of St. Irenæus' witness is explained in detail in *St. Paul and his Teaching*, Edinburgh, 1930, pp. 44–45, footnote. A strong scriptural patristic argument for the divinity of Christ will be found in the same place.

beloved Jesus Christ, Our Lord, that every knee
. . . be bowed to Christ Jesus, Our Lord, and God
and Saviour, and King." (*Adv. hær.*, L. 1, c. 10, § 1.)

Here the enumeration of the incarnation, the birth,
passion and resurrection of Christ show St. Irenæus's
belief in the true humanity of Our Lord. He also
says that He is "the Son of God" and "God." His
insistence on the belief of the Church in "one Jesus
Christ" implies the union of Christ's two natures in
the Person of the Word. This is made even clearer
in the following passage, in which he denounces
the error of those who would deny this unity in
Christ:

"If one indeed suffered and the other remained
impassible; and if one was born and the other
descended upon Him who was born and later left
Him; then they are not one but two. . . . Be not
mistaken; one and the same is Christ Jesus, the Son
of God, who reconciled us to God by His passion,
and rose from the dead, who is at the right hand of
the Father and perfect in all things. . . . He is
indeed the Saviour, He is the Word of God, He is
the Only-begotten of the Father, Christ Jesus our
Lord." (*Adv. hær.*, L. 3, c. 16, § 9.)

The co-eternity, and therefore consubstantiality, of the
Son, the Word of God, who became man, is laid down
in another passage.

"The Father of Our Lord Jesus Christ through
His Word, His Son, by Him is revealed and manifested to all to whom He is revealed. . . . The Son
always coexisting with the Father, of old and from
the beginning reveals the Father . . . to all to

whom God wishes to reveal." (*Adv. hær.*, L. 2, c. 30, § 9.)

In a very beautiful passage Clement of Alexandria[1] sums up the Catholic teaching very clearly and very definitely. Clement was a priest at Athens before 200 A.D.

"This Word, Christ, was not only of old the cause of our being (for It was in God[2]) but also of our well-being; and latterly the same Word appeared unto men, and in Itself was both, God and man, giving to us all good things." (*Protrepticus*, c. 1, n. 7, 1.)

This passage is very striking in declaring Christ, the Word of God, to be the source of our supernatural life: He is the cause of "our well-being" as well as of our "being" and He gives us "all good things." It would be difficult to imagine a clearer or more explicit expression of the Hypostatic Union than that which Clement here gives us. He says that the Word (i.e. the Second *Person* of the Blessed Trinity) was in Itself both God and man: the same Person terminates both natures, the divine and the human.

We come now to a writer, Tertullian, who is one of the most extraordinary figures in the whole of the history of the Church. He was born in the year 180 and educated at Carthage. He died about the year 240. He was a Catholic roughly from 195 till 205, when he lapsed into one of the narrowest of fanatical sects, Montanism. His writings are a rich mine of information regarding the teaching of the Church. Even when he lapsed into Montanism his writings show us the great unity of Church doctrine to which

---

[1] Clement was born about 170.   [2] Cf. *John* i, 1.

he had become opposed. We will quote only from two works, written when he was a Catholic. In many parts of his writings he gives us the *Regula fidei* which is, with occasional amplifications, our Apostles' Creed. I will quote one of these passages.

"The Rule of Faith is . . . that by which we believe that there is one only God nor any other besides the Creator of the world; who produced all things out of nothing by His Word which came into being before all things; this Word, called His Son, was from time to time seen by the patriarchs, heard in the prophets, and at last from the Spirit of God the Father and His power came down to the Virgin Mary, became flesh in her womb, and born of her Jesus Christ . . . was fastened to the Cross and rose the third day. . . ." (*De præscript.*, 13.)

The unity of God is insisted upon (against the Gnostics) but we see the Word as really distinct from the Father in the Godhead. The Word is not created but "came into being before all things." This Word of God which is not a created thing "came down to the Virgin Mary, became flesh in her womb, and [was] born of her Jesus Christ." This implies the union of the divine and human natures of Our Lord in the Person of the Word. The real and consubstantial Godhead of the Word is enunciated with amazing accuracy by Tertullian elsewhere when he says:

"We have learnt that this [the Word] was uttered by God and begotten in the utterance and therefore by reason of the unity of the substance [i.e. the nature of God] is called the Son of God and God. . . . And so what came out from God is God and the Son of God and both are one." (*Apologeticus*, 21.)

In the same passage of the *Apologeticus* he goes on to say that the Word of God, true God, became man.

> "Hence this ray of God (as was always preached in the past), come down to a virgin and become flesh in her womb, is born, a man united [*mixtus*] to God." (*Apologeticus*, 21.)

Some slight difficulty may be experienced over the use of the word *mixtus* in this passage, used to express the union of the two natures, divine and human, in Christ. It certainly expresses very definitely the union of both in the Person of the Word. But does it not go too far and imply a union so close that the human nature of Christ is lost in the divine? This would be the error which was later known as Monophysitism. I do not think this meaning can be read into Tertullian, firstly, because, as we have seen, he says that Christ was truly God and is at pains to show that He was also truly man by enumerating the various human qualities, phases and vicissitudes of His earthly life. All we can say against the use of the word *mixtus* is that, if it had been used during or after the Monophysite dispute and Tertullian had known of that dispute, it would then have been an expression of, at least, suspect orthodoxy: before the dispute (and this was long before it) its only reasonable interpretation is that to be found in the other clear passages of Tertullian and his contemporaries.

From Origen[1] I will give only one passage because in this one quotation we find as explicit and detailed a declaration of Catholic teaching as could be desired:

> "He who came was born of the Father before any

Origen was born in Egypt *c*. 186 and died at Tyre *c*. 255

creature. He had ministered to the Father in the creation of all things (for all things were made by Him) and in the latter times emptying Himself He became man, took flesh though He was God and, having become man, remained what He had been, God. He took a body like to ours, differing only in that He was born of a virgin and the Holy Ghost. And this Jesus Christ was born and suffered in very deed and not by mere appearance, truly dying the common death; and He truly rose from the dead; and after His resurrection He mixed with His disciples and then was taken up." (Περὶ ἀρχῶν, L. 1, Praef., 4.)

This profession of faith of Origen's shows us the equality of the Son with the Father in the eternal generation "before any creature." We see the true full human nature in that He "became man, took flesh": He "took a body like to ours . . . was born and suffered in very deed and not by mere appearance." The union of the two natures in the Person of the Eternal Son, the natures remaining distinct, is clearly laid down in that it was He, the Eternal Son of God, who "became man . . . and, having become man, remained what He had been, God."

In a work written c. 180, St. Theophilus of Antioch, who was born near the Euphrates, gives us some idea of his Christological teaching. Unfortunately the work, as it has come down to us, is fragmentary. He says:

"Since then the Word is God and begotten of God, He, the Father of all, sends it at His will into places where, when It has come, It is seen and heard,

and, sent by the Father, is found in that place."
(*Ad Autolycum*, L. 2, n. 22.)

Taken by itself this passage seems rather cryptic but,
especially since the writer also quotes St. John, "The
Word was God," it evidently means that Christ was
sent by the Father into the world and is truly God.
Since, as I have said, the writer quotes the first chapter
of St. John's Gospel he evidently knew its doctrine
of the Incarnation of the Word and accepted that
doctrine.

St. Justin[1] speaks of

"Jesus Christ, crucified under Pontius Pilate, who,
we are taught, is the Son of the true God: Him we
shall show that we adore not without reason in the
second place, and the prophetic Spirit in the third.
Indeed, for this they accuse us of madness, saying
that after God, immutable and eternal and the
Father of all, we give the second place to a crucified
man: but they are ignorant of the mystery of this
matter." (*Apologia*, 1, 13.)

St. Justin tells us that Jesus Christ who was crucified
is the Son of the true God and, we may say, therefore
God. He brings out the true human nature of Christ
in saying that we are accused of adoring a crucified
man. But difficulty might be experienced, had we
only this passage of St. Justin, when he says that we
adore the Son in the *second* place and the Holy Ghost
in the *third*. This might seem to imply an inferiority
to the Father in the Son and the Holy Ghost. Though
St. Justin says that the whole thing is a mystery, he
removes all doubt as to his orthodoxy when, after

[1] St. Justin was born in Samaria and he died in Rome *c.* 165.

declaring that, before the Incarnation, Christ was the Word, he goes on to say :

"And, since the Word is the first-born of God, He is also God." (*Apologia*, 1, 63.)

Hence Christ is true God and the Second Person of the Blessed Trinity (and therefore also the Third) is adored as true God equally as the Father. The Incarnation of the Word, by the taking of human nature, is explicitly laid down by St. Justin as an historic fact.

"Now, within the time of your own empire, as we have said, of a virgin was He made man according to the will of the Father for the salvation of those who believe in Him and He underwent being despised and suffering that by dying and rising again He might conquer death." (*Apologia*, 1, 63.)

The Hypostatic Union of the divine and human natures in Christ is implied in the statement that Christ was the eternally begotten Word *and* was born and suffered.

The writers quoted so far have all been Christians. We should scarcely expect Pagans even to be able to tell us anything about the doctrines of Christianity, especially in that time. Nevertheless one very ancient and precious piece of evidence has reached us from a pagan source on just this point of the divinity of Christ. Under the Emperor Trajan (98–117 A.D.). Pliny the Younger was Governor of Bithynia. In this capacity he wrote to the Emperor, probably in the year 112, asking for instructions regarding the Christians. I must resist the temptation to quote the vivid description he gives of the troubles which beset the large

Christian community in Bithynia. Some Christians who recanted "have honoured thy image and the images of the gods and they have cursed Christ." These apostate Christians

"declared that this was the sum of their fault or error: that they were accustomed to come together on a fixed day before daybreak and recite a hymn to Christ as to [?a] god . . ."

It is clear from this letter that the Christians paid religious honour to Christ: we can go further and say that in explaining this to the Governor they said that they honoured Christ as God. In Pliny's mind this would not necessarily mean that they honoured Him as the one true and only God. But Christians, like Jews, certainly held that there was only one true God, supreme and infinite. Hence we must conclude that this assertion made to Pliny means that they worshipped Christ as God: in other words that they believed Christ to be God. This evidence is particularly weighty as coming to us from a pagan authority who is at pains simply to state the case accurately as he found it on examination. Moreover, this evidence was collected not from learned writers but humble workaday Christians in an outlying province of the Empire. It is therefore of great value.

The evidence we have brought forward to show the belief of Christians in the Godhead and humanity of Christ and in the Hypostatic Union has been purposely taken from every part of the Church from the Euphrates across Asia Minor, Egypt and Proconsular Africa to Rome and the South of France. We have seen the voice of the Church to be unanimous in proclaiming the Christological doctrines which we hold

T

to-day. "Jesus Christ, yesterday and to-day: and the same for ever." (*Heb*. xiii, 8.) Even the heresies, which we shall enumerate presently, only served to bring out the teaching of the Church more clearly as they caused the Fathers to enunciate more forcibly the orthodox position.

From the very beginning of Christianity some Jewish Christians, wishing to cling to the Jewish law as well as accept the Christian revelation, were unwilling to admit the divinity of Christ as it detracted from the supremacy of Moses, their lawgiver. These were called Ebionites. A more serious theological difficulty, as we have already noted, confronted Christians. The doctrine of the Trinity was in apparent conflict with Monotheism and the doctrine of the divinity of Christ brought the difficulty home more forcibly still. We are not in this paper directly concerned with the doctrine of the Trinity but only with that doctrine in so far as it affects the dogma of the divinity of Christ. A certain number of heretics wished to reconcile Trinitarian doctrine with Monotheism by saying that the Trinity of Persons in God was only an accidental distinction of different external manifestations. Since these heretics admitted the Godhead of Christ, they held that, as there was only one Person, the Father, in God, Christ was that Person. These heretics went by the name of Patripassians for obvious reasons. They were condemned by a synod in Asia Minor towards the end of the second century. Other heretics, best called by the descriptive name of Dynamic Antitrinitarians, taught that Christ was not God by nature: according to them Christ was illuminated by an impersonal divine logos which conferred a divine power ($\delta\acute{v}\nu\alpha\mu\iota\varsigma$) upon Him. The logos or word of God was, in the teaching of these heretics, impersonal because they held that there was no distinction of Persons in God but that the word and the spirit in God were merely faculties much as in man, implying no real distinction.   Various supporters of these opinions were condemned at different times and places.   One was excommunicated by Pope Victor at the end of the second century.

It will readily be seen that the Gnostic heresy[1] could not attribute real divinity to Christ.   For them God was too sublimely remote from everything to have even caused creation.   The æons or divine powers which, in Gnostic doctrine, were thrown out from God certainly did not possess the divine nature.

The Council of Nicæa marks the end of an epoch and is a turning-point in the history of the Church. In many ways the year 325 marks the beginning of a new period in the life of the Church but the necessity for this first Œcumenical Council—which God's Providence now made possible—was urgent from the point of Christological doctrine.   The Arian heresy had arisen and the solemn pronouncement of Nicæa was the definite declaration of war on Arianism by the Church.

[1] A brief exposition of Gnosticism will be found in my paper on "Sin" in the Cambridge Summer School volume on *The Atonement*.

APPENDIX

Segreteria di Stato
di Sua Santità.

DAL VATICANO,
February 25, 1935.

YOUR LORDSHIP,

In conformity with Your Lordship's request of
February 5, I have presented to the Holy Father the
letter and prospectus in which are set forth the purpose
and programme of the Cambridge Summer School of
Catholic Studies, as also the volumes containing the
conferences given since 1924.

His Holiness charges me to express to you His grateful
appreciation for thus completing His collection of the
Lectures of the Cambridge Summer School. He desires
Your Lordship to know of His deep interest in the School
and in the courses on Church and State projected for this
summer. Convinced that such discussions of Catholic
Doctrine and related subjects, opportune to the times in
which we live, are essential to the development of an
enlightened coterie of Catholic leaders for the purpose of
well-directed Catholic Action, His Holiness felicitates Your

Lordship upon the accomplishments of this scholarly initiative in the past, and assures you of His prayerful hope that this year's course of lectures may be more than ever successful in the number of students enrolled and in its effect upon Catholic life in England.

Very willingly, then, the Holy Father imparts His Apostolic Benediction to the promoters, lecturers and students of the Cambridge Summer School of Catholic Studies and renews at the same time His blessing upon this well-deserving enterprise.

With my own cordial good wishes and prayers for the continued success of your labours for the diffusion of Christian culture, I am, My Lord,

Devotedly yours in Christ,

(signed) E. CARD. PACELLI.

His Lordship

The Right Rev. Laurence Youens,

Bishop of Northampton.

The Mayflower Press, Plymouth. William Brendon & Son, Ltd.